History and
the Dialectic of Violence

EXPLORATIONS IN
INTERPRETATIVE SOCIOLOGY

GENERAL EDITORS

PHILIP RIEFF

Benjamin Franklin Professor of Sociology
University of Pennsylvania

BRYAN R. WILSON

Reader in Sociology, University of Oxford
Fellow of All Souls College

ALSO IN THIS SERIES

MAX WEBER AND SOCIOLOGY TODAY
Edited by Otto Stammer
Translated by Kathleen Morris

THE SOCIAL FRAMEWORKS OF KNOWLEDGE
Georges Gurvitch
Translated by Margaret A. Thompson and
Kenneth A. Thompson

LUCIEN LÉVY-BRUHL
Jean Cazeneuve
Translated by Peter Rivière

FROM SYMBOLISM TO STRUCTURALISM
Lévi-Strauss in a Literary Tradition
James A. Boon

THE AGE OF BUREAUCRACY
Perspectives on the Political
Sociology of Max Weber
Wolfgang J. Mommsen

IDEOLOGY AND THE IDEOLOGISTS
Lewis S. Feuer

Raymond Aron

History and the Dialectic of Violence

An Analysis of
Sartre's *Critique de la Raison Dialectique*

TRANSLATED BY BARRY COOPER

HARPER & ROW, PUBLISHERS
NEW YORK, EVANSTON, SAN FRANCISCO

Contents

	Translator's Note	vii
	Preface to the English Edition	ix
	Preface	xvii
I	On *Critique*	1
II	The Practico-Inert; or, the Hell of Daily Life	25
III	The Rock of Sisyphus; or, from the Bastille to the Kremlin	54
IV	Practice-Oriented Ensembles; or, Between Marxism–Leninism and Leftism	87
V	The Golden Age of Historical Consciousness	119
VI	From Freedom to Violence	159
VII	Concluding Remarks	200
	Appendix	
	Note A	217
	Note B	219
	Note C	221
	Note D	221
	Note E	224
	Note F	226
	Note G	227
	Note H	228
	Note I	231
	Note J	232
	Note K	234
	Note L	239
	Note M	240

Translator's Note

Both Sartre and Aron use a number of different terms with highly specific meanings and distinct connotations that, superficially, may seem to refer to the same or the same kind of phenomena (*e.g.* group and grouping, collective and collectivity). I have tried to retain these distinctions in English, even though it meant, at times, altering the available translations of the works of Sartre and Lévi-Strauss which are cited in the text. I have added a few notes, identified as 'Tr. note', where I thought clarification of certain, chiefly philosophical, terms was required, or where unfamiliar allusions needed some brief elaboration.

B.C.

Preface to the English Edition

I have been told that this extraordinarily French book ought to be presented to an English-speaking public. After considerable hesitation I allowed myself to be persuaded and, in the next few pages, shall try to explain what is involved in this dialogue between two men who were friends in their youth, who were separated by their quarrels and united by their interests. But I fully realize that just as a book must be introduced and, so to speak, justified, its author is normally poorly qualified to undertake the task: how would he rid himself of all the peculiarities that, objectified in his writings, appear incomprehensible or at least very odd to individuals who speak another language?

To overcome this sort of problem, let us first take a brief overview of French philosophy as taught in universities during the last half-century. During the early twenties, when Sartre and I were students at the École Normale Supérieure, neo-Kantianism still dominated the Sorbonne. Léon Brunschvicg had guided it in the direction of a reflection upon the evolution of science. To summarize in a single phrase the titles of his three great books, the progress of consciousness may not be isolated from innovations in mathematical thought or experimental physics.[1] Today Léon Brunschvicg, for whom I have the greatest respect, seems to me to have been the last representative of one style of philosophy or one moment of French thought, a style and a moment whose origins go back to the last quarter of the nineteenth century, to the era when the Third Republic tried to

---

[1] *Les étapes de la pensée mathématique* (1912), *L'expérience humaine et la causalité physique* (1922), and *Les Progrès de la Conscience dans la Philosophie Occidentale* (1927).

re-establish the universities, which had been eclipsed since the French Revolution.

If the generation to which Sartre and I both belonged looked, or seemed to look, to Germany for our inspiration, we simply repeated the step taken by the generation before us. The watchword of the late nineteenth century, the 'return to Kant', did not require one to spend time in German universities although, among French sociologists, Durkheim, Bouglé and I all undertook the pilgrimage across the Rhine. Durkheim made his report in some articles, Bouglé and I wrote short books.[2]

In its final phase, French neo-Kantianism came close to a kind of positivism through the interpretation it gave to Kant's *Critique of Pure Reason*. Léon Brunschvicg resolved the four antinomies of Kant in the same way, by eliminating those questions to which consciousness could not reply. He had already taught us the formula that, from the pen of Sir Karl Popper, presently enjoys universal recognition: a proposition must be falsifiable in order to be scientific. Propositions that refer to the transcendent do not meet this criterion. Idealism (the construction of the real by the mind), a radical immanentism, would allow the maintenance of an apparent continuity with the philosophical tradition all the while it was in fact reducing philosophy to reflection upon science and to the repudiation of metaphysics.

Henri Bergson, however, did not belong to the French posterity of the German philosophers. As he was closer to the Anglo-American world, he defined himself neither with respect to Kant nor to Hegel. But, so far as I can recall, we read him even then as if he belonged to the classics and the dead. As Professor of Philosophy at the Collège de France he attracted his own crowds; as Nobel laureate in 1927 he reached during his lifetime the height of his renown. After World War I he retained disciples and admirers but no longer influenced philosophical instruction in lycées or universities. As for Alain,[3] whose person-

---

[2] C. Bouglé, *Les Sciences Sociales en Allemagne: Les Methodes Actuelles* (Paris: Alcan, 1896); R. Aron, *German Sociology*, Tr. M. & T. Bottomore (London: Heinemann, 1957).

[3] To give him his real name, Emile Chartier; he was a friend of Elie Halévy and taught senior or sixth-form philosophy in the Lycée Henri IV. The most famous of his pupils was André Maurois.

ality impressed us and whose prestige, on the fringe of the Sorbonne, inspired a fanatical minority, his own philosophical thought consisted in a curious syncretism of major doctrines, all re-interpreted *sub specie aeternitatis* in such a way that the fragments of each of them constituted a single and same truth when put together.

In those remote times one seldom found a footnote to a French work in any German book of philosophy. I remember one of my teachers showing me with indignation a German book and saying to me, with his finger poised above the index, 'the only Frenchman cited is Dr. Coué'. I should add that at that time we students (and was it different with our teachers?) knew next to nothing of phenomenology: neither Hegel nor Marx found a place in the philosophy we were taught.

In 1930 I left Paris for Germany because I felt a need to free myself from the narrowly national education I had received. I did not wish, like some of my friends, to devote myself to the history of philosophy, the ultimate refuge of professors who no longer believed that, in our era, philosophy retained a function. I was easily convinced that reflections upon science by those who were not committed to it were generally inferior to the reflections of scientists themselves. I wanted to find a way out and did so by reading Husserl and the phenomenologists on the one hand and Dilthey, Scheler, and Max Weber on the other. Together they suggested the problematic that has fascinated me all my life: the specific features of consciousness of man by man or of human history by an historically situated subject, the relation between knowledge and action and, in the end, between philosophy and politics.

Upon my return from Berlin, as Simone de Beauvoir has said in her memoirs, I introduced Jean-Paul Sartre to the existence of Husserl and to other aspects of phenomenology. Sartre felt none of my uncertainty. In a certain way, in 1932, he had developed a number of the themes of his *Weltanschauung*; he wanted to publish some of his ideas in philosophy and some in fiction. He overflowed with energy and abstract imagination; he stoked up abandoned philosophical systems only to get rid of them next day in order to invent new ones. What he lacked, he said to me one day, was a method; he found it in Husserl rather than in Heidegger even though one may doubt that the Sartrean style conforms to its Husserlian inspiration.

Does Sartre owe to his German masters what is essential to his thought or what is secondary, a part of his vocabulary and his method, or the hard kernel of his thought? I would go beyond the limits of this short preface if I were to give an adequate reply to such a question. Besides, the distinction between what is essential or secondary, what is substance or form on this occasion would lead to ambiguities. What remains true is that Sartre, who in my view is the most Germanic of French philosophers, owes his experience and his vision of the world only to himself. The part that he drew from the Husserlian theory of consciousness, his conception of freedom, the metaphysical pride of the ego never a captive of anything or anyone, not even its own past, existential psychoanalysis, bad faith—all these ideas belong to him as his own, just as does that oscillation between *Dichtung und Wahrheit*, between the philosopher who writes for the theatre and the playwright and novelist who philosophizes.

So far as I know, Jean-Paul Sartre never attended the lectures of Alexandre Kojève at the École pratique des Hautes Etudes that so profoundly influenced Maurice Merleau-Ponty or Jacques Lacan. Today I am tempted to see a 'new start' for French philosophy in the thirties. Perhaps it should be called the *Return to Hegel* in opposition to the *Return to Kant* of Léon Brunschvicg's generation, but I doubt whether either Sartre or Merleau-Ponty devoted enough time to reading Hegel for one to be able justifiably to speak of a return to Hegel in the same sense as the return to Kant. They received a part of the Hegelian heritage that was available and dispersed by the German thinkers of our era. Above all, Marxism found its way into university studies in philosophy and became an integral part of the philosophical tradition that lycée teachers uphold and spread throughout France.

The Hegel of Alexandre Kojève was already a Marxist, but it was the Hegel of the *Phenomenology* rather than of the *Encyclopaedia*. However great the distance from the *Phenomenology* of Hegel to that of Husserl may have been, it was still crossable. Thus, before even Georg Lukacs, the author of *History and Class*

Consciousness, was known and translated in France, the immediate teachers of the contemporaries of the Hungarian Marxist, Dilthey, and Max Weber, had become references for French philosophers. The connection between the theory of understanding (*Verstehen*) in the form given to it by Wilhelm Dilthey, Max Weber, or Karl Jaspers, and Marxism was initiated during the thirties. I think I see one of the results in Sartre's *Critique de la Raison dialectique*.

There were never any political disagreements between Sartre and me of a kind that would compromise our friendship until the united front of the Resistance fell apart in 1946–47. Of course, intellectual closeness, those limitless discussions about the world and the future so encouraged by student life, would have to give way to more intermittent relations. In any event his meeting Simone de Beauvoir necessarily altered the nature of the ties among those who at the École Normale were called his '*petits camarades*'. In 1938 Sartre was less 'anti-Munich' than I was because he had reservations about dealing with other men's lives. Once again what was involved was only a matter of nuance or difference of opinion, without much passion on either side.

The politico-philosophic quarrels—between Sartre and Camus, between Sartre and Merleau-Ponty, between pro- and anti-Communists—filled the years from 1945 to 1956, the date of Khrushchev's famous address to the Twentieth Party Congress. Simone de Beauvoir has evoked those days in her novel *The Mandarins*, after having taken pen in hand to criticize Merleau-Ponty's *Aventures de la dialectique*.

This era of French thought belongs to the past, even if certain of the protagonists in those battles are still alive. It is not up to me to judge either merits or defects. It is enough to recall certain features. For the first time, Marx appeared to French philosophy teachers as one of the heroes of human thought. For the first time, Marxism escaped from the positivism and materialism of the Second International. Interpreted by way of Hegel, Marxism lent itself to a reconciliation with existentialism and, at the same time, with historicism, in a specific sense of the term, namely the conception of the movement of humanity, by way of societies and civilizations, up to its self-fulfilment.

The *Critique de la Raison dialectique* marks the ultimate end of Sartrean reflection upon the relationship between Marxism and existentialism. Having chosen, after the liberation, in 1944, the camp of the Revolution in a country where it was incarnate or seemed to be incarnate in the Communist Party armed with Marxist–Leninist ideology, for fifteen years he elaborated variations on the theme: how to be, how not be, a communist? Under what conditions can existentialism be Marxist without at the same time ceasing to be faithful to itself? Whereas *Being and Nothingness* only marginally dealt with the problem of historical consciousness, which I treated directly in my two theses, the *Critique* does consider questions that I have not ceased to ponder and upon which the Gifford lectures, delivered in Aberdeen, led me once more to meditate. Just as the *Critique de la Raison dialectique* marks a final effort by Sartre to place himself within the main stream of Marxist thought without betraying his own thought, so too this book puts an end to the dialogue[4] that I have undertaken with various forms of Parisian Marxism in order to define my own position and justify the reasons for my allergy not to Marx but to these several Marxisms.

Was I right or wrong to prolong this dialogue and to suggest my own positions by way of the indirect route of a critique of Sartre? It is not for me to say. I may be allowed only to mention one of the reproaches that has come my way from the pens of British critics, as it has come from French ones; the Sartrean jargon—for-itself, in-itself, practico-inert, practice-oriented ensemble, active passivity, passive activity, seriality, alterity—may well irritate some readers. I readily admit it, but most philosophers have used and do use a jargon. The jargon of sociologists does not avoid the censure of lovers of beautiful language. What matters, in the final analysis, is the experience hidden beneath jargon or the questioning expressed in it. Provided he overcomes the distaste that this vocabulary may perhaps inspire, the reader will gain access, it seems to me, if not to the essential answers, at least to the essential questions.

I well know that a good number of my English colleagues and friends, habituated to the manner of reasoning and writing of

---

[4] *The Opium of the Intellectuals*, tr. T. Kilmartin (London: Secker & Warburg, 1957); *D'Une Sainte Famille à l'autre* (Paris: Gallimard, 1969).

Sir Karl Popper or Ernest Gellner, will not overcome their dislike and will ask why I have written in a style that, for a long while, has not been mine—if it ever was. There again, let us look with the eyes of a sociologist or an anthropologist upon the tribes of philosophers in Great Britain, in Germany or in France. The discipline that more than any other aims at universality seems today devoted to ethnocentrism, at least in the sense that a specific way of writing philosophy appears characteristic of a specific culture or a specific national community. Consequently, the propensity of philosophical schools to ignore and reject each other is easily explained; the more an intellectual activity pretends to be above or outside social differences, the more each school judges itself authorized to excommunicate the others.

The accidents of life led me to receive my training within the context of neo-Kantianism, to move beyond neo-Kantianism thanks to the German hermeneutic and historicist tradition, and today to read especially Anglo-American analysts for my intellectual health. I derive a kind of pleasure—must one say perverse pleasure?—in moving from one mode of thought to another and from one vocabulary to another. I hope, in the book that follows, to recover, beyond the multiplicity of languages and ways of reasoning and writing, the common and constant data of analysis bearing upon knowledge of the human past.

I should like to end with a somewhat personal remark. There is a chance this book will be interpreted as a balance-sheet between two youthful friends who, through the events and passions of the age, have become opposed to one another. Let me say that in the evening of my life the memory of our freindship remains to me more alive than our polemics. It may happen that when the opportunity arises a new polemic will be stirred up. I doubt it—and besides, what does it matter? We have never separated philosophy and politics. But Sartre, from his existential choice, does not separate the condemnation of society as it is from his revolutionary will, be it Marxist–Leninist or Leftist. Not that he feels assured that the post-revolutionary society will be worth more than what we have today; the opposition which leads to revolution seems to him the only thing compatible with morality within a class-society.

I think quite differently, but I accept him as he is—even while opposing him indefinitely with reasons he will never be ready to listen to.

Raymond Aron

Preface

The circumstances that brought me to write this book, which I had neither conceived nor planned beforehand, are such as may interest the reader. Having been invited by the University of Aberdeen twelve years ago to give the Gifford Lectures in 1962 and 1965, I chose the theme of *Historical Consciousness in Thought and Action*. I set myself two objectives: first, to resume my examination of the problems of historical consciousness by contrasting the method and results of Anglo-American analytic philosophy with the philosophical approach of the German neo-Kantians and phenomenologists that had inspired my *Introduction to the Philosophy of History*. Second, I wished to write the book that I had announced on the last page of the *Introduction*,[1] dealing with *action in history*.

Study of Sartre's *Critique de la Raison dialectique*[2] appeared to be a necessary preparation for these lectures and for the book that would come out of them. The *Critique*, in fact, constitutes a kind of *summa*, since it deals with the whole problematic that I had but partly considered in the *Introduction*. It elaborates a theory of *understanding* in the sense, following Dilthey and Weber, that I had taken the term. It deals with the limits of the *understandable* or the *intelligible*, as Jaspers had done for psychology and Weber had done for the study of social and historical reality. It endeavours to elaborate a typology of

[1] *Introduction to the Philosophy of History: An essay on the Limits of Historical Objectivity*, tr., G. J. Irwin (London: Weidenfeld and Nicolson, 1961), p. 347, n. 69, [Tr. note].
[2] *Critique de la Raison dialectique:* (Précédé de *Question de Méthode*), Tome I, *Théorie des Ensembles pratiques* (Paris: Gallimard, 1960).

practice-oriented ensembles, or in other words, a typology of the different modalities of reciprocal relations between the individual and collectives, of the different modes of integration of collectives into consciousnesses and, inversely, of consciousnesses into collectives. And finally, but without providing the sustaining argument, which is left to a second volume, the *Critique* takes as an ultimate goal the intelligibility of a *single* History, which tends towards the foundation of Truth, or the possibility of Truth, from a totalizing of the becoming of man. All the while Sartre follows the road that had led neo-Kantians and phenomenologists to a contrary conclusion: the more that understanding the past expresses the historicity of the historian, the more it is identified with the perception of a combination of circumstances by the actor, and the less it avoids perspectivism. It seems to justify the otherwise trite formula that each generation and each epoch re-writes history. Because the future is not yet present, and because each generation and each epoch gives itself a different past because of the future towards which it is oriented, it is the future that determines the present.

The first reading of the *Critique* bothered me. I found the disproportion between the length and difficulty of the book and its valid ideas exasperating. Then I felt a kind of guilty conscience for having so severely judged such an enterprise without forcing myself to understand it. I read the *Critique* again, pen in hand; I worked over the text as one works over the text of a classic philosopher; I ended up by taking an interest and almost finding some pleasure in this conceptual game, interspersed as it was with descriptions that were often arbitrary or gratuitous, sometimes dazzling, and almost never neutral.

Between the first and second series of Gifford Lectures, I devoted an entire year's course to the interpretation of the *Critique*. The class, among whom were a number of candidates for the *Ecole Normale Supérieure*, drew some profit from the course, I was told, and more easily assimilated the material of this certainly difficult work. I refused, however, to allow the stenographic record of the course to be published, convinced from experience that I would not succeed in properly editing the book for which the course was only a rough draft. At various times during the following years I put together certain lectures, while continuing to reflect on the theme of the Gifford Lectures, which by then had been given, but had not been edited for publication.

Finally, I decided to finish my critique of the *Critique* and to publish the result as the first volume of the Gifford Lectures: the confrontation of the analytical philosophy of history and the phenomenology of historical consciousness will follow in a second volume, and a theory of historical action or of politics in history will end the series, if there is enough time left to me. Precisely because the *Critique* contains a theory of understanding and of historical action—understanding inseparable from action since action, a projection towards the future, structures the situation from which it breaks loose by negating it—the exposition of this generalizing synthesis, accompanied by remarks and objections, will allow me, in conclusion, to isolate the questions that I shall seek to answer in the following volumes.

The *Critique* has not, at least not directly, had the same repercussion or the same influence as *Being and Nothingness*.[3] It has discouraged a number of readers, even among Sartre's admirers. It was the object of a savage attack on the part of Claude Lévi-Strauss to which Sartre replied, a few years later, by a political denunciation of structuralism rather than by a counter-argument. It remains a sort of baroque monument, overwhelming and almost monstrous, comparable perhaps to Pareto's *Traité de Sociologie Générale*,[4] in spite of its entirely contrary inspiration: the expression of a rich, complex, and contradictory personality, the work repulses some, seduces others, and perhaps fascinates every reader. It has either been totally accepted or totally rejected rather than methodically discussed. Perhaps logically or existentially a thought that wishes to totalize everything, that objects to the ordinary procedures of analysis, to separating things into their constituent parts, to

[3] *Being and Nothingness. An Essay on Phenomenological Ontology*, tr. H. E. Barnes, with an introduction by M. Warnock (London: Methuen, 1958) [Tr. note].

[4] Vilfredo Pareto, *The Mind and Society*, ed. A. Livingston, tr. A. Bongiorno and A. Livingston [4 Vols.] (London: Jonathan Cape, 1935) [Tr. note].

deduction and reconstruction, calls for a plain reaction: I agree or do not agree to play the dialectical game,[5] or rather to remain within the dialectical domain originally given to lived experience.

Personally, I do not think it must be this way: even if, as I believe, human reality, existence, is revealed only to a kind of knowledge that is unable to be integrally assimilated into the knowledge of physical or physico-chemical sciences, consciousness of the lived becomes knowledge at all only by an objectification of itself and by procedures of investigation and verification (or confirmation) that do not essentially differ from the procedures of all knowledge that can be made universal.

Besides, over the years, the *Critique* has little by little escaped from quarantine and brief citation. In English, two summaries of the book have appeared.[6] The relation between *Being and Nothingness* and the *Critique* has been the subject of polemics: some affirm the radical discontinuity between the theses on freedom in the first book and those contained in the second one;[7] others, on the contrary, affirm the continuity and compatibility among them all. Numerous articles have been devoted to a *cause célèbre*, the debate between Jean-Paul Sartre and Claude Lévi-Strauss.[8]

In 1968, events gave a political weight to the *Critique* that, for the most part, readers had failed to detect when it first appeared. During the early sixties in France, attention was still fixed on the tortuous relations between Sartre and the Communist Party, relations whose superstructure was represented by the dialogue of existentialism and Marxism–Leninism. The revolutionary or pseudo-revolutionary apocalypse,

[5] Cf. James F. Sheridan, *Sartre: The Radical Conversion* (Athens, Ohio: Ohio University Press, 1969), pp. 154–6.

[6] R. D. Laing, D. G. Cooper, *Reason and Violence: A Decade of Sartre's Philosophy* (London: Tavistock, 1964); Wilfred Desan, *The Marxism of Jean-Paul Sartre* (Garden City: Doubleday, 1966).

[7] *See*, for example, Mary Warnock, *The Philosophy of Sartre* (London: Hutchinson University Library, 1965); Walter Odajnyk, *Marxism and Existentialism* (Garden City: Doubleday, 1965).

[8] *See*, for example, Laurence Rosen, 'Language, History, and the Logic of Inquiry in Lévi-Strauss and Sartre,' *History and Theory*, X:3 (1971), pp. 269–94,

the lyrical illusion of the May days, encouraged another interpretation. Epistémon, a professor of psychology at Nanterre,
who was touched (but not saved) by its grace, wrote a book,
These Ideas that Have Shaken France.[9] Among these ideas the
opposition of *series* and *group*, the description of the group-in-
fusion, the phenomenology of the movements of the crowd and
the fall of the Bastille held some prominence. The individual
escapes from his solitude by taking part in a collective action
in which all the participants are agents because all of them
together, and each separately, spontaneously seek a single,
identical object. It does not matter that, in order to be contained, the initial outburst is first organized, or that, to succeed,
the action then becomes an institution: it is the initial outburst,
the community in action, the rebellion against the dispersal
of individuals and the weight of collectives that signify the
beginning of humanity.

Sartre's Marxism, coming just after the war, arrived too
late: by what sort of aberration did he insist upon confusing
'socialism that was coming in from the cold', revolution from
above, and the accession to power by the party thanks to the
presence of the Red Army, with revolutionary humanism or
the realization of man by the revolution? On the other hand,
the theory of the group-in-fusion and the fighting crowd pre-
viewed the spontaneity of leftist movements during the sixties.

American sociologists, inspired by the spirit of the day, discovered in the *Critique* a Gospel of human emancipation, the
new theory that sociology required in order to fulfil its self-
appointed task of thinking through this emancipation and
helping to bring it about. 'The human future is not, fundamentally, to be an extrapolation of the past; indeed, man is
defined by Sartre as a flight *out of the present* into the future. For
the very activity that is knowing, we are reminded, changes
that which would be known. This is, perhaps, the essential in-
sight of existentialism: that man retains the capacity to "invent his own law". The "totalization" of any one instance is
capable of trascendence through the interaction of knower and

---

[9] Epistémon, *Ces Idées qui ont ébranlé la France* (Paris: Fayard, 1969) [Tr.
note].

known in the next. The fundamental logic of sociology becomes, in this light, the grammar of emancipation.'[10]

After twenty years of philosophic and political dialogue with the Communist Party and Marxist–Leninist orthodoxy, of which the *Critique* marks but a moment, though perhaps its conclusion, Sartre, through favourable circumstances, has become the herald (and the hero?) of revolutionaries confronting the bureaucratic conservatism of Moscow as well as the imperialism of Washington. Is this a misunderstanding, or just the opposite? Does not the unnatural alliance between a philosophy of freedom and Stalin (or his successors) finally fall apart the day when history (historical reality) offers the philosopher, in the form of the new left, the incarnation of which he had dreamed in vain, freedom-in-act and freedom in action?

Sartre the philosopher does not consider these political repercussions of the *Critique*, even as a function of his philosophy, to be external or foreign to his work. All understanding is action because the situation as such exists only for a consciousness and by the projection of consciousness towards the future. Not to affirm the primacy of the unconditional freedom of man is, in his view, to commit not only an intellectual error but is evidence of a moral fault. Not to choose man is to choose the anti-man. To refuse the dialectic is to affirm the anti-dialectic. In other words, philosophical choice is identified with political choice, or at least is inseparable from it. Both express an existential choice, the determination of oneself by oneself, or a certain choice of being by consciousness. In this way Sartre's inclination to condemn morally and to inflict injuries upon those who take political positions different from his own can be explained.[11]

Of course, Sartre the philosopher probably puts a higher value upon demonstration, bringing to light the understandability and intelligibility of every human reality as such. In other words, he gives more weight to the critical experience, an experience that allows for the reconstruction of the dialectic,

[10] Robert W. Friedrichs, *A Sociology of Sociology* (New York: Free Press, 1970), p. 280.

[11] For example, his phrase: 'anti-communists are dogs'.

which goes from individual *praxis* to the practico-inert, from the constituting dialectic of individual *praxis* to the constituted dialectic of institutionalized ensembles, a dialectic without which the externalization of the internal or the internalization of the external would always suppress the intelligibility of historico-social reality. There is no doubt that he takes the (still abstract) dialectical movement that *shows* the intelligibility of human reality and that reaches the threshold of History to be a major achievement in the theoretical realm. Marxism would be the Truth of this dialectical movement, and by itself would be the announcement of the Truth. By not separating this theoretical accomplishment of Sartre from his political intentions, I remain true to the intentions of a thought that has never separated understanding and action or philosophy and politics.

Neither *Nausea* [12] nor *Being and Nothingness*, it is true, suggest an interpretation of the becoming of man through time and they seem not to be oriented in this direction. The fundamental structures of existence, freedom, and the choice by each individual for himself, are rather part of the Kierkegaardian than the Marxian posterity of Hegel. *Being and Nothingness* gave notice of an ethics (of which, it would appear, many hundreds of manuscript pages exist) that has never been completed. From this fragment, the *Critique* emerged. Among other meanings and objects of the *Critique*, however, one meaning is to establish precisely the impossibility of an ethics before the Revolution, and perhaps, should the Revolution in the end prove impossible, even to show the impossibility of any genuine ethics. (The *Critique* allows the foundation of ethics; it *shows* what ethics must be.)

Having turned to politics after he had achieved literary fame, Sartre has never consented to present his judgements within and upon on-going history as one set of opinions among others, susceptible to error, lacking in information, or as containing any incompatibilities between equally valued objectives or between objectives and the means necessary to attain them. He has always tied his political positions to his philos-

---

[12] Tr. L. Alexander (London: Hamish Hamilton, 1962). First translated as *The Diary of Antoine Roquentin* (London: John Lehmann, 1949) [Tr. note].

ophy or, if you prefer, he has always given his political positions a philosophical interpretation.

The *Critique* therefore lends itself to numerous interpretations.
Concerning the thought of Sartre, the book has a two-fold
interest. It is of speculative interest first of all: the theory of
practice-oriented ensembles elaborates the status of collectives
from within a philosophy that, at the level of ontology, knows
only individual consciousnesses, the *for-itself* or *praxis*. Second,
it is of practical or political interest: how can *praxis*, caught
within the practico-inert, alienated and yet not being determined, ever surmount alienation? How can one create a
society wherein *praxis* would affirm its freedom other than by a
revolutionary project, that is, other than by fighting and
violence?

The *Critique* is also interesting with respect to Marxism or,
more generally, to all philosophy of history that claims to
totalize the human past with a view to a collective salvation.
Has Sartre succeeded, and by what steps, in showing not only
the intelligibility *of* history, but the possibility of a *single* History
that is intelligible *and* true? Has he reconciled the ontology of
a consciousness condemned to be free with the ontics of a consciousness caught within the practico-inert or alienated in
series or in institutions? Can one conceive of an historical
totalization that retains the singularity of lived experience?
Can understanding, the foundation of a militant Marxism, end
up in a totalization of universal history without letting lived
experience—the sufferings and the hopes, the sacrifices and
the exploits of men—disappear in the totalization? That is to
say, having the very things disappear that, according to
Sartre, historical understanding aims at saving!

The interpretation sketched in the following three chapters
ignores the relations between the *Critique* and *Being and Nothingness* (which I analyse briefly in the last chapter), because these
relations demand longer and more intricate analyses. From
time to time my account abandons the Sartrean vocabulary;
this has the at least apparent advantage of greater clarity but
it also runs the risk of falsifying the meaning of the text (insofar
as it endeavours to be rigorously theoretical). Of the different
possible ways to interpret the *Critique*, I have kept in mind two

in particular: the transfiguration of Marxism into a *Marxism of understanding*[13] in order to elaborate the status of collectives and the relations of individual consciousnesses with collectives, and, secondly, the movement, whether possible or not, from this Marxism of understanding to action in history and to the intelligibility of a *single* History, understood as the advent of Truth.

This first interpretation will serve as an introduction to my second volume, dealing with the phenomenology of history and analytical philosophy; the second approach will serve as an introduction to action within history, but without a *single* interpretation *of* History. Both together, therefore, introduce *Historical Consciousness in Thought and Action*.

Joucas, August, 1972

---

[13] An explanation of what is meant by *marxism compréhensif* or, to use an equivalent German expression, *verstehender Marxisimus*, can be found below, pp. 5 ff. [Tr. note].

I

On Critique

The three words of the title, *Critique, Reason,* and *Dialectic* issue from a long tradition, and do not readily lend themselves to a univocal definition. It is perhaps necessary to read the entire book before grasping at the same time their exact and their total signification. An account of their sense requires less a choice of a restricted meaning than a start to find a meaning: it seems to me appropriate to begin with the term *Critique* which, we must add, requires at least the provisional elucidations of the two others, *Reason* and *Dialectic.*

Sartre himself wrote in the preface that 'logically', *The Problem of Method* should follow the *Critique of Dialectical Reason* because the latter 'intends to constitute the critical foundations' of the first. But, he added, he feared that 'this mountain of pages would appear only to bring forth a mouse'. Only a superficial reader could have been the victim of such a mistake. The 'methodological considerations' of *The Problem Method*[1] proceed from the *Critique* or are based upon it. It contains but a small part of the theses and themes of the *Critique.*

To simplify, one could say that the first, an *ouvrage de circonstances,* is developed at the level of *methodology* while the second goes back to the critical foundations and, as we shall see, to the ontological foundations as well. But *The Problem of Method* gives

---

[1] In order to avoid repeating the complete title or simply to use initials, I decided to refer to *La Critique de la Raison dialectique* as *Critique* [R.A.]. *Question de méthode* has been translated by Hazel E. Barnes under the title *The Problem of Method* (London: Methuen, 1963); the North American edition was entitled *Search for a Method* (New York: Knopf, 1963). Page references are given in the text [Tr. note].

us both *more* and *less* than the methodology whose foundations
are constituted by the *Critique*: *more* because Sartre devoted
most of his efforts towards the refutation of a degenerate and
fossilized Marxism that had become 'voluntarist idealism';
less because he did not elaborate the methodology of the anthropological sciences rigorously or in detail.

Nothing prevents the use of *The Problem of Method* to clarify
the *Critique* insofar as the polemical text destined for a Marxist
public[2] reads more easily and dispels some difficulties. It remains
true that the *Critique* is self-sufficient and that, by contrast,
The Problem of Method does not even suggest the goal and the
full extent of the Sartrean enterprise, an enterprise of Kantian
inspiration that would accomplish for *Dialectical Reason* what
Kant's *Critique of Pure Reason* was to have accomplished for
Analytical Reason. But as nobody in the tribe of philosophers,
before Sartre's book appeared, knew what distinguished Dialectical Reason from Analytical Reason, nor how such a distinction between two Reasons was justified or even if it could be,
the *Critique* (or pursuit of the foundations) must also pursue
Dialectical Reason itself. It is a matter of showing at the same
time the reality, the limits, and the validity of Dialectical Reason
whose methodology, outlined in *The Problem of Method*, appears to be the consequence and the illustration.

*   *   *

Sartre himself presents his critical enterprise as being above
all destined to lay the basis for historical materialism: 'I have
said and I repeat that the only valid interpretation of human
History was historical materialism. It is not a question, therefore, of repeating here what others have said thousands of times;
it is not my subject anyhow. But, if a summary of that introduction is wanted, it could be said that historical materialism is its
own proof in the milieu of dialectical rationality but that it does
not form the basis of that rationality; above all it is proof of
itself if it restores History to its development as constituted

[2] A preliminary version of *The Problem of Method* appeared under the title,
'Marksizm in Egzystencjalizm,' in the Polish review, *Twórczość*, XIII, 4
(April, 1957), pp. 33–79 [Tr. note].

Reason. Marxism is History itself becoming conscious of itself; if it is valid, it is because of its material contents, which are unquestioned and unquestionable' (p. 134).

A text of this order raises numerous questions: why is historical materialism proof of its own validity? (By an unexpected return to a kind of Spinozism?) Of what does historical materialism consist so that its evidence is imposed of and by itself? Is it reduced to the vague or empty formulae such as 'man makes his own history but on the basis of given material conditions'? Of what do the 'material contents' of historical materialism consist if they must never be questioned? Are they the contradictions of capitalism, the class struggle, and the means of production? Although as we shall see below,[3] the book does not give a categorical answer to these questions, the absence of reply does not prevent us from understanding the Sartrean enterprise itself. It is enough to allow the distinction between Marxism as a *concrete or substantial interpretation of History* and the *forms or schemata*[4] *of intelligibility*, internal to Marxism, or, in other words, *the necessary conditions for Marxism to be able to be true.*

From this same distinction, the critical[5] questions cease to depend upon a Marxist framework even though Sartre formulates them in Marxist terms. These questions are essentially theoretical: 'under what conditions is consciousness of a *single history*[6] possible? What are the limits beyond which the conditions that would give birth to it became *necessary*? What is dialectical rationality, what are its limits and its basis?' (p. 135).

The first question, if I understand it correctly, concerns not the consciousness of just any kind of history, not the consciousness of a fragment of the human past, but of a *single* History or, in other words, of the unity of History. (The unity of *known* History implies the unity of *real* History, thanks to the dialectical relation between doing and knowing.) The second and

[3] See below, Chapter V, pp. 119 ff.

[4] The term 'schema' is used in a precise, Kantian sense. See Kant's *Critique of Pure Reason*, A 137 ff, B 176 ff; A 674, B 702 [Tr. note].

[5] The term 'critical' is also used throughout in its Kantian sense [Tr. note].

[6] For the remainder of the book, history has to be written History. Capitalization is intended to indicate Sartre's meaning of the totalized whole of the human adventure.

third questions imply each other even though the reverse order would have been more logical. All the same, the question of the *unity* of History must follow the questions of dialectic (or freedom) and necessity. The order followed by Sartre in this text depends upon its reference to Marxism.

If we were to begin with Sartrism or the Sartrean philosophy of freedom, the formulation of the critical problem would become clearer and more satisfactory. We must emphasize as strongly as possible—though we shall have occasion to repeat it— that the source of all reflection is and can only be the free and transparent *praxis* of the individual. 'As the living logic of action the dialectic is discovered in the course of *praxis* and, as a necessary moment of it, . . . it becomes a theoretical and practical method when action in the course of development gives itself its own illumination. During this action, the individual discovers the dialectic as transparent rationality that he completes, and as absolute necessity that escapes him, which is to say, quite simply, that others complete' (p. 133).[7] Freedom, the *praxis* of each individual, thus runs into necessity, which creates the freedom of the other for it. The 'reciprocity of constraints and autonomy' translates this dialectic, rooted in a radical nominalism: evidence and transparency are first of all and before everything else given to individual *praxis* as a moment of its own development. Necessity emerges with the encounter with the Other.[8] The third moment corresponds to the question asked in the first: is knowledge of a *single* History possible? In fact, if I begin from dialectical and totalizing individual *praxis*, the human world is dissolved into an indefinite plurality of dialectics or singular totalizations, even though the truth of Marxism demands as a condition of possibility 'the totalization of concrete totalizations effected by a multiplicity of totalizing singularities' (p. 132).

By reversing the order of the three questions noted above, the critical enterprise may someday appear as tied to Marxism more by biographical or political accident than by nature. Let

---

[7] In fact, completed action or past action eventually becomes necessary in the double sense that it can no longer be other than what it has been and that it becomes the inert or material condition for new *praxis*.

[8] Materiality arouses it in another.

us forget for a moment Sartre's allegiance to Marxism and look back at the thought of *Being and Nothingness*. Let us substitute the term for-itself for *praxis*. Man, or rather, consciousness *is* freedom. Commentators have often judged paradoxical Sartre's allegiance not to Marxism–Leninism but to Marxism or a certain Hegelianized or existentialist Marxism. The *Critique* tends to resolve the paradox by treating a problem that Sartre dealt with even when he was not interested in Marxism and the Revolution, namely: what is the nature of the knowlege that we can obtain of the human world, of the world interwoven with innumerable actions and free consciousness (let us call them *praxeis* from now on)? In what does the knowledge of freedom (or the for-itself) differ from the knowledge of things, or the in-itself?

Sartre is scarcely troubled by epistemology and perhaps would never have examined the methodology of the social sciences nor written of a prolegomena to every future anthropology had circumstances not forced him into a dialogue with Marxism–Leninism. As we will show in Chapter VI, *Being and Nothingness* already contained in the bud many of the analyses of the *Critique*. The serpentine relations of the in-itself, the for-itself, and the for-another called for a specific mode of interpretation and knowledge. He found this mode, at the methodological level, in *understanding*, and referred explicitly to 'what the German psychiatrists and historians called "understanding",'[9] as being indispensable for grasping the meaning of human behaviour. He adds: 'What is involved here is neither a particular gift nor a special faculty of intuition: this knowledge is simply the dialectical movement that explicates the act by its final signification in terms of its starting conditions.' Anglo-Saxon philosophical analysts speak of teleological explanation or teleological explication. The conjunction between historical materialism and the 'understanding' of the German psychiatrists and historians gives rise to what I propose to call a *Marxism of understanding*, a *verstehender Marxismus*.

The origin of this Marxism of understanding is readily explained by a biographical note. As a student at the Ecole Normale supérieure, Sartre, along with Nizan, revised a

[9] *The Problem of Method*, p. 153; *i.e. Verstehen.*

translation of Jaspers' *General Psychopathology*.[10] As for the others,
he was not ignorant of Dilthey, Max Weber, or Simmel whom
he probably had neither read nor studied but those major ideas
he knew through the intermediaries of my university thesis and
my small book on *German Sociology*.[11]

After the fashion of the German historians and psychiatrists,
Jaspers, Dilthey, and Max Weber, Sartre affirms the originality
of the social sciences, history, sociology, ethnology *etc*. Like them,
he bases this originality on the nature of their object, namely,
man. The behaviour of men is not to be explained as one explains the behaviour of ants or the movement of electrons.
The sociology of ants, but not the sociology of men, neglects
the radical alterity of the in-itself and the for-itself, and the
freedom of the for-itself, which is always conditioned but never
determined by the situation (besides, it is defined by its project,
and hence by the freedom of the for-itself); it ignores the totalizing character of *praxis*, of active or acting consciousness.

Dilthey and Weber would have accepted the definition that
Sartre gives to understanding in the text we have just cited.[12]
'Terminal signification' is equivalent to goal, and initial conditions constitute the situation. Rather than retain a means–
end relation,[13] characteristic of goal-directed rational (*Zweck-
rational*) action, he employs a formulation that may be given a
wider application: the concept of a *project* of consciousness towards a future to be accomplished, a project that *understands
itself* in terms of the starting conditions but does not allow them
to determine its end. The strategy of a military leader as well
as the conduct of a neurotic bring such understanding to light.

Max Weber would have called neither the project of consciousness nor the awareness we have of it dialectic. But, with this

[10] Jaspers himself did not know about it, as I learned from him in the
only conversation I have had with him, in Basel in 1960 [R.A.]; Cf. Jaspers,
Psychopathologie générale, Tr., A. Kastler, J. Mendousse (Paris: Alcan, 1928),
p. iii, and the comments by M. Contat and M. Rybalka, *Les Ecrits de Sartre*
(Paris: Gallimard, 1970), entry 28/4, p. 50 [Tr. note].

[11] This thesis was entitled *La philosophie critique de l'histoire. Essai sur une
théorie de l'histoire dans l'Allemagne contemporaine* (Paris: Vrin, 1969, 4th ed.)
[R.A.]; *German Sociology*, Tr., M. and T. Bottomore, (London: Heinemann,
1957) [Tr. note].

[12] *The Problem of Method*, p. 153. See above, fn. 9 [Tr. note].

[13] Sartre analyses this relation in *Being and Nothingness*, pp. 199–200.

terminological reservation, he would not have seen any major opposition between his own theory of understanding and that of Sartre, *as it is outlined in the text cited.* As an epistemologist of historico-social knowledge, Sartre belongs to the tradition of philosophers who, for the most part, were Germans emerging from the tradition of idealism but anxious, around the turn of the century, to lay a foundation for the social sciences (*Geisteswissenschaften*), to reconcile strict knowledge, on the one hand, with hermeneutic knowledge or knowledge obtained from the immanent significations of human reality, on the other. Sartre's Marxism, having become a Marxism of *understanding*, is based upon human existence: 'Man, for himself and for others, is a signifying being since one can never understand the least of his gestures without going beyond the pure present and explicating it by means of the future. He is, as well, a creator of signs to the extent that, always ahead of himself, he employs certain objects in order to designate other absent or future objects; but, both operations are reduced to a pure and simple surpassing: to surpass present conditions towards a subsequent change, and to surpass the present object towards an absence are one and the same. Man constructs signs because in his very reality he is signifying; and he is signifying because he is he dialectical overcoming of everything that is simply given; what we call freedom is the irreducibility of the cultural order to the natural order.'[14]

The progressive–regressive method, the coming and going between conditions and project, presents no radical originality concerning the method of understanding, which has been used spontaneously by historians and ethnographers when either were forced to deal directly with lived experiences or to reconstruct them. Behaviour, a work, or only a decision gives up its signification or significations by reference both to the situation wherein the actor is found, and to the project by which the actor himself defines his situation and moves beyond it. The project transforms the situation that conditions it.

The Sartrean method does contain one original contribution, the accent put upon the *project*. Sociologists who ignore or misunderstand the humanity, that is to say the *projective being*, of

[14] *The Problem of Method,* p. 152.

the men in the societies they study will fall beneath the blows of the Sartrean critique. Not that man is essentially defined by historicity, since he exists in societies without history, but that he is defined 'by the permanent possibility of living *historically* through the breakdowns that sometimes throw even societies of repetition into confusion'.[15] In other words, he is defined by the permanent possibility of historicity, which history itself reveals *a posteriori*.

Sartrean consciousness encompasses the goal-directed rationality (*Zweckrationalität*) of Weber at the same time as the lived experience of Dilthey. It presents us with the totalizing or encompassing characteristics of Dilthey's concept along with Weber's notion of an orientation towards something beyond the given. Having become *praxis* and *action* (labour) by Marxist naturalization, Sartrean consciousness remains the transcendent ec-static project, at each moment outside itself, nothingness with respect to the in-itself. The *Critique* has the epistemological result or conclusion of a Marxist-existentialist theory of understanding and of the social sciences. But it is situated at a transcendent or even ontological level. For a sociologist or an epistemologist such as Max Weber, it matters less to affirm the understandability of actions or of human works than to establish the precise conditions of truth or the conditions of verification of historical or sociological judgements. Now, the critical experience of Sartre does not deal with this problematic. Everything takes place as if his goal was to lay the foundations for the intelligibility of the *whole* of history, and of *the least fragment of this totality*. The critical experience does not *demonstrate or prove*, it *reveals*; it does not argue, it describes phenomenologically. It is an experience at the same time as it is critique because it has become conscious of the History lived by each and by all. From the *project* or *praxis* (the acting for-itself) the critique follows, by a phenomenological description, the process of objectification of the subjective, and the internalization of objectivities; it brings to light the irreducibility of history (*i.e.* of historical reality) to the intentions of actors, all the while maintaining the *de jure*, if not the *de facto* intelligibility of the whole of history, which is ontologically reducible to *praxeis*, which, in turn, have

[15] *The Problem of Method*, p. 167 fn. 1.

been deflected and alienated, both from each other and from their common work. They are *praxeis* that have become prisoners of each other and prisoners of their own work.

At one moment, Sartre seems to allude to the distinction between two kinds of sciences in order to reject it radically. In fact, it is a terminological question. At the beginning of the *Critique*, in the chapter entitled 'Critique of Critical Experience', he introduces the term *intellection* and he compares it with and distinguishes it from *understanding*, which is defined in *The Problem of Method*. He writes: 'As a matter of fact, it is customary to oppose intellection (reserved for the proceedings of analytical Reason) to understanding (which is found only in the social sciences). This distinction, common as it may be, makes no sense. There is no *intelligibility* in the sciences of Nature: when *praxis* imposes its seal upon an area of the externality of inertia, it produces and discovers necessity as the impossibility of facts being other than they are . . . then Reason *makes itself* into a system of inertia in order to recover factual succession externally, to produce and at the same time to discover necessity as their sole *external* unity. Necessity as external succession (instants are *external* to each other and it is impossible that they should succeed each other in a different order) is only the mind producing and discovering its own limit, that is to say, producing and discovering the *impossibility of thinking in externality*.' [16]

This text seems to reject the distinction between the natural and social sciences and to transfer this distinction to a transcendental or ontological level. The vocabulary employed implies that *intelligibility* must be incompatible with *necessity*; in other words that a mathematical demonstration or a logical reckoning contains no intelligibility. This is certainly a strange vocabulary since demonstration and logical reckoning lead to conclusions that nothing can rationally refute, but which Sartre dubs unintelligible. The explanation seems to me as follows: intellection (and understanding is a kind of intellection) is bound to the project of consciousness, to the thinking thought. Thought disappears along with the necessity that hinders it in the same way that thought implies freedom, an active

[16] *Critique*, pp. 160–1; *See* Appendix, Note A.

totalization and not a passive submission to a necessity inscribed in a succession of instants or mutually external propositions—in short, in things.

To be sure, *praxis* operates within the natural sciences when it organizes materials, establishes variables, or puts together a series of related propositions. But it operates only in order to be negated or to discover its own limits, to know the limits of its free project. If one speaks of understanding a mathematical demonstration or an experimental proof, it is because understanding, in this case, represents the very procedure of thought and its orientation while it makes 'an irreducible innovation in the order of Knowledge and its practical applications' (p. 149) appear. In this case, the novelty consists in the substitution of proven knowledge for a vague hypothesis.

Dialectical Reason finds the model of intelligibility, 'which perfectly distinguishes the new from the old', in individual *praxis*; intelligibility 'attends the transparent and practical production of the new in the light of *totalization* and on the basis of previously defined factors' (p. 159 fn. 1). This intrinsic intelligibility is not to be found outside the human realm or, at least, having clearly been given to consciousness, it can at best be presented as an hypothesis where nature is concerned. Sartre devotes a few pages (pp. 124 *et seq.*) to Engels' dialectic of nature and his three laws: the law of the transformation of quantity into quality and vice versa, the law of the interpretation of opposites, and the law of the negation of the negation. To the extent that the dialectic reveals the self-consciousness of individual *praxis*, we possess the immediate certainty that human action, at least individual action, exhibits a dialectical nature. Experience alone could tell us if this same characteristic affects certain natural phenomena. It is necessary again to add that a dialectic of nature, which Sartre considers hypothetical, would become impossible if the totalization and transcendence of the project appeared inseparable from the for-itself at the ontological level.

How, in fact, must the opposition between externality and internalization and between the analytical relations of externality and the synthetic relations of internality be interpreted? Sartre employs a number of different formulae that do not al-

ways suggest the same idea or the same image. Sometimes the
dominant influence is directed towards the opposition of extended things (*res extensa*) and thought: there subsists in the
obscure underground of Sartrean philosophy a Cartesianism
that he himself admits when he compares the freedom of the
Cartesian God, unlimited even by truth, with the freedom of
the for-itself that is unable, in the final analysis, to avoid its
destiny of being responsible for itself. At other times, the Kantian
distinction between analytical and synthetic judgements crops
up. Intrinsic intellection exists only in and by the movement of
consciousness: analytical judgements, essentially a chain of
identities, constitute a mechanical skeleton that consciousness
submits to even if it has constituted it itself. On the other hand,
dialectical Reason must be defined as 'the absolute intelligibility of an irreducible innovation *insofar* as it is an irreducible
innovation. It is the opposite of the positivist and analytical
effort, which tries to clarify new facts by tracing them back to
old ones. . . . The demands of intelligibility, under these circumstances, can appear paradoxical. The new seems, *insofar
as it is new*, to escape the intellect: the new *quality* is accepted as
a brute appearance or, better, it is assumed that its irreducibility is provisional and that analysis will subsequently discover the prior elements in it' (p. 147).

These expressions suffice to show that innovation, the creation of *praxis*, differs radically from synthetic judgements and
that the critical foundations of dialectical Reason have nothing
in common with the critical effort needed to demonstrate the
possibility of *a priori* synthetic judgements. 'The practical agent
is transparent to himself as a unifying unity of himself and his
environment' (p. 150). This intelligibility is linked to quality,
innovation, and particularity. Human thought as *praxis* 'is
fundamentally characterized as the awareness of innovation,
as the perpetual reorganization of the given by way of acts
illuminated by their goal'[17] (p. 150). What Sartre calls synthetic, in contrast to analytic, is the totalization by consciousness, the pro-ject towards the future, the reorganization of an

---

[17] In these early pages, Sartre indicates that his propositions are not yet
proven. In fact they will never be proven other than by the appeal to experience that consciousness-*praxis* gives to itself.

ensemble by means of an intended goal. This movement of active or reorganizing transcendence is merged with the experience that *praxis* has of itself. *Praxis* subsequently recognizes[18] analytical relations, the coercive exterior, and the structure of machines, the result of organizing activity that is both practical and synthetic. But the analysis of necessary external relations or of external necessity will not account for the synthetic movement, that is, for the *particular* adventure of a consciousness or of humanity; both are fundamentally homogeneous (p. 143).

The methodological distinction of the German psychiatrists and historians thus becomes that of analytical Reason and dialectical Reason, of necessity and evidence, and of externality and internality. The two characteristics of *understanding*— the harmonization of the elements and the whole, which is more or less irreducible to the sum or the combination of the elements, and the permanent reorganization of totalizations with respect to the future—remain those of *intellection*. And intellection covers no less an area than the concept of understanding. Now, understanding presupposes reference to an individual *praxis*, and to the *intentionality* of an agent, a person, or a group. On the other hand, intellection and not understanding rediscovers the dialectic, in the absence of individual *praxis*, in the form of 'actions without agents, productions without producers, totalizations without totalizers, counter-finalities[19] and infernal circularities' (p. 161).

There again, what is involved is a problem implied by Dilthey's theory of understanding as well as that of Max Weber. The teleological explication of individual behaviour imposes itself, so to speak. What can we call the act that I am now performing, leaning over a table, surrounded by books, multiplying scribbles in blue ink upon white paper, without saying that I am writing? And if my wife asks me what I am doing, I will answer that I am writing the first chapter of a book on the political thought of Sartre. The very content of my action is determined only by its finality.[20] In this sense, the definition

[18] Evidently what is involved is in the reflexive and not the chronological order.

[19] Cf. Kant, *Critique of Judgement*, II, para. 21 (82) [Tr. note].

[20] Cf. *loc. cit.* [Tr. note].

of human action is teleological. On such an understanding, the methodologist wonders how *to know* the finality that others have in mind, and the epistemologist wonders if and within what limits socio-historical reality is understood in the way that written, textual reality is understood.

Critique in its Sartrean sense here takes a precise distance compared with Kantian critique. The starting point is not the *synthetic a priori judgement* but the synthesizing and unifying activity of consciousness in the sense that *Being and Nothingness* defined it. The goal is not to demonstrate the conditions under which this synthesizing activity is possible: the Kantian demonstration (interpreted by Sartre) rests upon a judgement of fact (and hence is unintelligible), while for Sartre, experience has taken place (p. 136). It is a fact that establishes the foundations of synthetic *a priori* judgements to the extent that, without them, experience would be impossible. Individual, transparent *praxis*, the model of intelligibility, thus needs no foundation. It calls forth a regressive procedure to discover the *necessity* that, in appearance, contradicts the immediate structure of organizing *praxis* and free totalization; it brings to light the *intelligibility* of what is not understandable, in other words, the presence of the intelligible schemata of understanding in human ensembles that cannot be derived from the intentionality of an agent; finally, it calls forth the possible totalization of the whole of human History or the unity of human History that, having as its origin the *praxis* of organic beings, is presented as being dispersed in an indefinite multiplicity of particular totalizations.

* * *

Defined this way, the Sartrean critique suggests, it seems to me, not so much the Kantian critique as the project of Dilthey, a critique of historical Reason. Like Dilthey, Sartre strives to bring concepts, the necessary *universals* for the intellection of the historical world, into existence. Like Dilthey, he wishes to safeguard the particularity of each existence and of each era; he does not wish to reduce the new to the known, or to explain the concrete by the abstract. Like Dilthey, he dreams of going from biography to universal History, which together are both totalization and unique adventure. Even in the second part of his life, Dilthey never moved beyond the project; he was too much the historian, too much the positivist, and not enough of a philosopher to get past the stage of outlines or intuitions. Sartre, on the other hand, ignores enough of history–reality to imagine the totalization of it. Philosopher and novelist, he succeeds in writing the biography of one existence, Flaubert, and he conceives the practico-inert universals with the aid of which, history, as it has developed, remains in principle integrally intelligible (but not understandable).

Rather, let us say, to use other, less weighty expressions, that critique tends to show the *intelligibility* of all history even though only historical fragments lend themselves to understanding, or, in other words, only historical fragments can be clarified by the intentionality of agents. If men were to know the history they make, the distinction between intellection and understanding would disappear. But they do not know the history they make, and, even though Marxism might give them the chance to know it, they have necessarily ignored it. If *praxis* becomes self-conscious and attains complete lucidity and transparency with respect to its project, action accomplished in the midst of things and under the gaze of others no longer retains the evidence of its signification. 'The intelligibility of *praxis* will eventually conflict with the *result* of this *praxis*, which is both what was projected and *always something else*. The result, *qua something else*, (that is, tied to the whole by externality *as well*) will appear as being *unable to be* different than what is' (p. 159 fn. 1). Necessary freedom (*praxis* cannot not be free) freely encounters necessity: external diversity communicates to the project a part of the necessity that constitutes it as externality. The evidence of the project and the necessity of the result, the dialectical reconciliation of totalizing freedom and its inevitable dispersion, establish or must establish the basis for the intelligibility of History, the necessary work of free men. By this procedure, the critique of historical Reason, or the genesis of the intelligibility of human reality on the basis of, but moving beyond, the understanding of *praxeis*, answers the demands of what I have called a *Marxism of understanding*.

The Marxism of both the Second and the Third International

has officially been interpreted within the framework of a positivist or materialist, and, in any case, an objectivist philosophy.
The laws of history appeared as the necessary tendencies of
large-scale movements. These laws or alleged laws operated
over the heads of actors; they were dialectical only because the
observer glimpsed, or thought he glimpsed in them, the connections of their moments, in particular the moment of contradiction, negation, and negation of negation, which structured the
logic of human action. In *praxis* man discovers the dialectic:
to denude it of human attributes and to project it into nature
is to end up stripping it of its rationality and its intelligibility. Having become a law of things by an arbitrary decree,
it becomes blind, unintelligible necessity.

Sartre, to be sure, having categorically set forth a dialectical
nominalism—individual *praxis* is and remains the model and
origin of all *praxis*—does not painlessly succeed in restoring the
large-scale dialectic to the aggregate movement of History.
The critical experience has as its object precisely the restoration of the intelligibility of individual *praxis* in collectives at the
same time as the restoration of a large-scale dialectic or a totalizing unification of scattered totalizations. When Sartre presents
his enterprise as destined to establish the foundation of Marxism (or the possibility of the Truth of the Marxist interpretation,
which he takes to be self-evident), he neglects to add explicitly
that he is searching for these foundations on the basis of his own
philosophy or his own ontology, that of the for-itself, the
project, and freedom. And so the paradoxes multiply: Sartre
bases the necessity of aggregate history upon the freedom of
individual agents; dialectic appears with individual action,
not with dialogue; it totalizes diversity in the light of a goal
yet to come; it is free by essence (or having as its essence the
property of not having one) and submits, *qua* dialectic, to no
law, whether natural or ideal.

Does the Sartrean critique, this stranger to Marxism–
Leninism, retain any kinship with the critique of Marx himself? We know that Marx used the term *critique* during his
career as an intellectual and a revolutionary. During the early
1840s, just before and after his marriage, he announced works
that would successively have criticized religion, politics, and art

itself. *Capital* has the sub-title *Critique of Political Economy*. A famous formula of the *Introduction to the Critique of Hegel's Philosophy of Right* reveals the double end he had in view for it: the arm of criticism is to be replaced with the criticism of arms.[21] Critique *unmasks* reality by discovering it to be inadequate to its concept; action remains just as necessary, in order to carry out the decree of thought and to reconcile being with reason. On the question of Marxist solidarity of understanding and action, of history that accomplishes itself, Sartre can say that he remains true to Marx's intention.

Over the years, however, Marx just as often conceived of critique in other ways. To give a summary, which, I am aware, is inevitably crude, three moments or three interpretations can be distinguished: the critique of Hegelian vocabulary, most often of Feuerbachian inspiration, the historical critique that tends to explain the working of history by the classes expressed in it or by the relations of production that determine or condition them, and finally, the critique of political economy. And the critique of political economy is the unmasking of the duplicity of the picture that bourgeois economics gives to capitalism and, at the same time, it shows the ideological truth of this picture, namely, that it is a typical perception of those who seek to profit from the capitalist world.

Althusser[22] tries to establish an *epistemological rift* between the Hegelio–Feuerbachian critique and the science or theory of history that would constitute Marx's decisive contribution. In fact, however, a reading of the *Grundrisse*,[23] where the themes and concepts of the *Economic and Philosophical Manuscripts of 1848*[24] are found, is sufficient to prove that the rift never appeared in Marx's mind to be radical. The Hegelian notion of alienation (*Entäusserung* or *Entfremdung*) serves both as the instrument of the

[21] Karl Marx, 'Toward a Critique of Hegel's Philosophy of Right: Introduction,' in *Early Texts*, tr. and ed., D. McLellan (Oxford: Basil Blackwell, 1971), pp. 122–123 *et seq.* [Tr. note].

[22] Cf. on this point my *D'une sainte famille à l'autre* (Paris: Gallimard, 1969).

[23] *Grundrisse: Foundations of the Critique of Political Economy (Rough Draft)*, Tr. with a foreword by M. Nicolaus (Harmondsworth: Penguin, 1973) [Tr. note].

[24] In McLellan, ed. and tr., *Early Texts*, pp. 130–83 [Tr. note].

critique of religion and of the commodity fetish. Man projects his essence, which he cannot accomplish here below, into the beyond, into a transcendent fiction. In a way that is at least analogous, he becomes the prisoner of commodities, of the market and its laws; he loses his consciousness of himself as ultimate and essential reality; he ceases to communicate directly with his fellow-men; relations of production are placed between him and his fellow-men. Commodities become things in themselves when in fact they are nothing but crystallized labour. The theme of the return to the concrete man once he has been purged of his religious or economic alienation serves as a clue to the puzzle of Marx's humanism, and gives us *one* of the interpretations or currents of Marx's thought.

The other tendency is manifest in the historical and economic critique: the concepts of infrastructure and superstructure, in spite of their ambiguities, at least allow us to ask questions. Since men make their history but do no know the history they make, it must be examined from the other side of lived experience, beyond systems of thought or beliefs, so as to expose the basis of the social system. The imputation of a doctrine, whether religious, juridical, or philosophical, to a class or to a certain kind of relation of production represents one modality of Marxist critique.

Lastly, this kind of Marxist critique attained its final and most complete form in *Capital*, since this book unmasks bourgeois political economy, the scientifically perverse self-consciousness of the capitalist regime. Here the diverse modalities of critique are reconciled: 1. the Feuerbachian critique of commodity fetishism; 2. the historical critique that exposes the infrastructure, the forces and relations of production, by distinguishing it from the appearances within which men, including the men of science, the conscious or unconscious spokesmen for the dominant class, live; 3. the critique of political economy that establishes the truth of a science of the capitalist mode of production, an historical science at the same time as an economic science, a science that accounts for both the capitalist reality and the partial interpretation of it given by the classical economists.

Of these three critiques, Sartre holds on to the first one above all. Without any kind of critical analysis, Sartre has accepted the truth of Marx's *Capital*, as evident. Thus, he has no need to repeat the third kind of critique. He does not reject in principle the second kind of critique, critique by imputation—Valéry is simply a petit-bourgeois—but he does denounce Zhdanovian[25] absurdities. Finally, to the extent that the *Critique*, as a transcendental analysis of the possibility of a *single* History and of *knowledge of a single History*, also allows for a Marxist critique of human illusions, with a view to returning to authentic intersubjectivity, it belongs to the Hegelian descendants of Marx of whom Lukács is justly considered to be the most distinguished representative.

It remains true that at the transcendental level Sartre does not proceed to man but to *praxis*. The evidence and translucence of *praxis* constitutes the first datum of the critique that combines the *methodological* primacy or reflection with the *anthropological* principle according to which the concrete person is defined by materiality. *Praxis* is presented from itself and to itself in its evidence and temporal totalization. It demands neither foundation nor proof. *Praxis* is an ontological realm that presents a dialectical structure intelligible by its evidence to the actor and by its necessity to the observer, who is but the actor after his act. Thus, *qua* transcendental critique, Sartre tries to show that the whole of History remains reducible to *praxeis*. He dissolves the alleged reality in-itself of the historico-social world, and, *qua* Marxist critique, he follows the movement of consciousness that objectifies itself, alienates itself, loses itself, and, having never been stripped of its freedom, tears itself away from worked-upon matter in order to assert itself in rebellion.

This duality of critique characterizes the attempt itself, Sartrean Marxism or Sartre in quest of a reconciliation between the absolute of the for-itself and the unsurpassable Truth of Marxism. How can a philosophy of individual freedom be reconciled with a Marxist interpretation of history? How can history, in principle reducible to individual consciousness, at the same time admit of an aggregate meaning that is blended with the

---

[25] Vladimir Viktorovitch Zhdanov is a Soviet literary critic who was particularly admired by Stalin [Tr. note].

Truth of man and becoming? The Hegelian odyssey of consciousness was to answer these questions, to supply the equivalent to a Kantian transcendental deduction. It was to show the
necessity of alienation, th limits of intellection, and the conditions for the totalization of a single History.

The status of this critique is a problem. Is it situated at a pre-
determined moment of history? Does it presuppose, as does the
Kantian critique, a science assured of its truth but not of its
foundations? Or does it presuppose the existence of a certain
social order, in the sense that *Capital* pre-supposes capitalism,
that, obviously, could not be criticized by the philosopher before it was brought into being? Logically, the Sartrean critique
implies the priority of historical materialism since it seeks to
discern the schema of intelligibility in it. In turn, historical
materialism implies the philosophies of Hegel and Marx. But to
take Sartre's word for it, the *Critique* involves a good deal more
than that: The *Critique* 'cannot appear at all *prior* to the *errors
and abuses* that have obscured the very notion of dialectical
rationality and produced a new divorce between *praxis* and
knowledge that clarifies it. In effect, the *Critique* assumes its
etymological sense and gives rise to a real need to separate the
true from the false, to limit the scope of totalizing activities in
order to restore their validity to them. In other words, the
critical experience cannot take place *in our history* before Stalinist idealism had hardened epistemological practice at the same
time as epistemological method. It can only take place as the
intellectual expression of the *restoration of order* that characterizes the post-Stalinist period within this "one world" that
is ours' (p. 141).

The author of the *Critique* upholds the historicist idea, an
idea, we might add, that is rather trite today, that the historian
or sociologist is also a member of a group (*Question of Method*,
p. 51), or a time (*Ibid.*, p. 141), and so is part of history itself.
The *Critique*, which was impossible before de-Stalinization,
becomes possible for anybody today. 'In anybody's life (but
more or less explicitly according to the circumstances) totalization accomplishes the divorce of blind and unprincipled *praxis*
from sclerotic thought, or, in other words, the obscuring of the
dialectic, which is a moment of totalizing activity and of the

world. By this contradiction, which makes one's life uncomfort-
able and sometimes tears it apart, *praxis* prescribes as a remedy
to each person, as his individual future, the calling into question
of this intellectual tools; this act represents, in fact, a new, more
detailed, more integrated, and richer moment of the human
adventure' (pp. 141–2).

It may be asked if this contradiction, which is said to be
characteristic of the Stalinist or post-Stalinist situation, does not
result from the human condition itself. In any case, setting aside
some of the analyses (such as that of the cult of personality of the
dictatorship of the proletariat), the first volume of the *Critique*,
'the dialectical experience that, in its regressive moment, can
only give us the static conditions of possibility of a totalization,
that is to say, of a history' (p. 155), appears, *in principle*, to be
possible at any moment in historical time, since it brings to light a
static and, so to speak, an eternal dialectic, that of a consciousness that loses and rediscovers itself, that becomes caught and
escapes, that objectifies its interior and internalizes its objectification.

On the other hand, what matters philosophically is that the
critical experience, a reflective experience, presents the same
structure as the experience it reflects. Critique is dialectical as
the existence or consciousness that it criticizes is dialectical.
'Dialectic, as the living logic of action, cannot appear to a con-
templative reason: it is discovered during *praxis* as a necessary
moment of it' (p. 133). Critique understood as discriminatory
reflection unfolds in the same ontological realm as the action
(or active consciousness) from which it emanates and from which
it detaches itself. Knowledge is dialectical because so is reality;
lived experience, knowledge of this lived experience, and
critical consciousness of knowledge are but three moments of
the same adventure, the adventure of temporalization or of
human history.

*   *   *

In the event that the reader may have judged this exposition
to be rather obscure, we shall attempt to give a second account of
Sartre's thought in other words.

Let us return to the methodological or reflective starting point, *praxis*, which amounts to a Sartrean for-itself that has been injected with a slight dose of Marxism. This individual and *self-transparent praxis* is constituted by the inseparable conjunction of a negation and a project, a negation of a datum that it *totalizes* by negating it, and a *project* of a future on the basis of which the negation is understood. All three terms, *totalization, temporalization,* and *innovation* define *praxis*, which is *individual* at the same time as it is *dialectical*. Thus, it would seem that for the first time in the history of philosophy, Sartre takes as a model for dialectic not the dialogue but the individual or even solitary consciousness.[26] The dialectic of individual consciousness is put into operation from the time that it finds, in the presence of *another*, the materiality sufficient to constitute this other.

Just as individual *praxis* presents all the characteristics of the dialectic and, at least in principle, is self-transparent, so too does understanding or knowledge of the dialectic (or the attaining of consciousness of the dialectic by itself), take advantage of the same evidence, which, once in a while, Sartre dubs apodicity. This intelligible knowledge grasps innovation together with the internal ties of totalization by which each consciousness is projected towards the future. Since individual *praxis* is the model of the dialectic, of intelligibility, and of evidence, it is not surprising to learn that, in the last analysis, 'the forum of our critical experience is nothing other than the fundamental identity' of a single life and human history' (p. 156). Certainly the Hegelian Sage, living at the end of (real) History thinks through the total system of Knowledge. But he could not think that system through before other men, during the course of centuries, had conceived the numerous theoretical and practical possibilities of Man and Philosophy.

On the other hand, *praxis* or acting consciousness has no need at all for past history in order to attain its perfection. As absolute freedom, it is perfect from the beginning. It is up to the critic to explain alienation and the inert necessity of history. Since individual *praxis* provides the model for the dialectic on the basis of which knowledge is defined as understanding,

[26] Solitary, but in a situation in the world.

immediately and logically the next question to arise is: what of intellection? How is it opposed to analytical knowledge? Sartre uses the opposition between internal ties and external relations. Internal ties are the grasping of the elements of a situation by consciousness; external relations, which eventually are necessary relations, are the determination of an effect by a cause. Internality is the result of the synthetic activity of consciousness; externality is the result of the relapse of this act or of the objective crystallization of what was once easily grasped.

Sartre's *Critique* attributes the transparency and evidence of the for-itself to *praxis*, and of the ontological realm, where a dialectic-in-action is set forth, to knowledge, which is itself *praxis* also. Henceforth, the ensemble of society and culture, as well as their future, is situated between 'the epistemological starting point', 'the apodictic certainty (of) self as consciousness *of* such and such an object' (p. 142), and universal History. Now, by a new decree, Sartre decided it is necessary to choose between everything and nothing. This ensemble must be wholly intelligible or not at all intelligible.[27] 'Precisely what must be decided at once is whether the dialectical experience is possible or not' (p. 144). Otherwise we will fall into eclecticism. 'We must, at the limit (but it is impossible), suppose that we know everything' (p. 145).

In short, Sartre wishes to establish, on the one hand, that there is no limit to intellection in the ontological realm where the social sciences carry out investigations and, on the other, that all History must be understandable to the extent that it approximates the adventure of a consciousness. In order to reconcile these two propositions, he declares that the totalization of and by individual consciousness does not by nature differ from the totalization of and by human history. 'If the Unity of History exists, the one who experiences it must take hold of his own life in the dialectical movement of Unification as a Whole and as a Part, as the link between the Parts and the Whole,

---

[27] 'If History is a totalization that is temporalized, culture is itself the temporalized and temporalizing totalization, despite the "disparity" that characterizes *my* knowledge and perhaps knowledge in general, in the *objective culture* of the era' (p. 144).

and as the connection between the different Parts; he must see to it that he overlooks his single life for the sake of History by the simple and practical negation of the negation that determines it' (p. 143).[28] In order to overlook one's single life for the sake of universal History, it is necessary to be given, hypothetically, total knowledge.

As for the Truth of History that Sartre is trying to establish (p. 142), either it is formal, in which case it is confused with the critical experience that confirms the intelligibility of all History, or it is substantial and, in that case, will only appear in the second volume that 'will try to establish that there is a *single* human history with a *single* truth and a *single* intelligibility' (p. 156). Lacking the second volume, we know only the formal truth, the intelligibility of the human universe, which is totalization and temporalization.

We shall close this chapter by elucidating the distinction between totality and totalization. 'Totalization has the same status as totality: it pursues a synthetic labour throughout multiplicity that makes each part a manifestation of the ensemble and that binds the ensemble to itself by the mediation of the parts. But it is an *actual* act that cannot be stopped without the multiplicity returning to its original status' (p. 138). Even though Sartre does not rigorously and in detail analyse the notion of totalization, the idea is clear enough: totalization ends in totality when it is stopped; as totality, it is different than the parts or their sum. It becomes their synthesis, and is present and effective in each. 'The whole (as totalizing act) becomes the connection among the parts' (p. 139, note 1). 'The intelligibility of dialectical Reason is nothing other than the very movement of totalization' (p. 139).

This last formula immediately raises a question. Why speak of Reason here at all? In Sartrean philosophy, the intelligibility of the dialectic is not, in fact, separated from the movement of totalization. All the concepts, *praxis*, *totalization*, *temporalization*, and *dialectic*, are interchangeable since they refer to complementary aspects, indissociable from active consciousness itself, since intelligibility results from the ontological structure of the particular realm considered, namely that of

[28] What word does the pronoun 'it' refer to? Probably to 'single life'.

consciousness or of man understood as consciousness and action. But why Reason? There are two possible answers. Either universal History ends in the advent of Truth, in which case dialectical Reason takes us back to Hegel's *Vernunft*, or dialectical knowledge is essentially opposed to the analytical consciousness of the natural and social sciences, which are unaware of the dialectic. In this case, dialectical Reason is equivalent to a mode of consciousness, namely that which in *The Problem of Method* Sartre dubbed understanding, and which now expands into intellection.

Each of these two interpretations (and both conform to Sartre's thought) presents difficulties. The first because only the second volume would justify it and because the first seems to make it impossible; the second because, as a mode of knowledge, intellection, even supposing that it differs effectively from analytical knowledge (in the way that understanding in Dilthey's or Weber's sense differs from explanation), is not, as such, dependent either upon a Reason or even a rationality. All *praxis*, as totalization over time, is intelligible. The historian reproduces in his own consciousness the totalizing *praxis* of the Mountain or the Gironde, of Robespierre or Danton, and apprehends the intelligibility of it. But how is he assured of the truth of *his* intellection as compared with the intellection of another historian? Even if he consents to reproduce the *praxis* of an historical actor in his own totalizing *praxis* as an historian, this reproduction, assuming it to be faithful, is not, *eo nomine*, rational or the expression of a Reason. Neither dialectic nor the intelligibility of dialectic deserves to be dubbed *rational* unless *all praxis* is rational as well as *all knowledge* of it. As the *Critique* will not unveil the advent of Truth throughout universal History, dialectical Reason signifies no more than knowledge—dialectical activity—of human *praxis*, which is itself dialectical.

II

The Practico-Inert; or, the Hell of Daily Life

Why is there something rather than nothing? This question, which was *the* question of traditional metaphysics before Kant and then Bergson suggested that it made no sense, admits of no answer. Why has humanity a history? This is Sartre's question. It is an inevitable question within his philosophy but, as a transcendental question, it remains no less paradoxical than the traditional one. We have the experience of multiple societies and of changing institutions: from this diversity and these changes the historian or sociologist looks for their modalities and causes. But why must the philosopher look for their *basis* or deduce their *a priori necessity* by means of conceptual analysis?

The question results from the conjunction of Sartrism and Marxism or, if you like, of existentialism and historicism. Sartrism, we have said and we shall have to repeat, has free and translucent consciousness as its starting point and immutable principle; it is exempted from doubt or critique, it is the model for dialectic, or better, is dialectic in essence; it is temporalization, project, and, by reference to an objective that transcends the order of lived experience and external reality, comprehensive apprehension of the given. Sartrean consciousness plays with the same freedom as the God of Descartes; it has no need for others to be fulfilled itself. *Probably for the first time a philosopher discovers the dialectic in solitude.*

If it is true that consciousness is self-sufficient, and history must come to it from without, first of all as an obstacle or a negation. Freedom immediately becomes enslaved by participating in becoming. The birth of history is mixed with the fall. The project of humanity is the recovery of its freedom in and by History. But this freedom, which would mark the end of History (or of pre-history), is possessed by the consciousness of each individual from the beginning and *cannot* entirely be alienated. The Sartrean scheme goes from individual paradise (the freedom of translucent consciousness), which is both lost and preserved, to another paradise, the paradise of the project. It passes into this collective paradise by way of the fall into the practico-inert or History. These two tendencies or origins of Sartre's thought are juxtaposed rather than united.

The for-itself has nothing to do with others (hell is other people). But the Marxist, through a glass darkly, sees the reconciliation of men (thanks to conquest of nature) beyond the class struggle (thanks to the development of the forces of production); he ignores the solitary and sovereign consciousness.

*   *   *

How does the *Critique* get from Sartrism to Marxism, from monologue to dialogue, from the individual consciousness-dialectic to the dialectic of consciousnesses? This transformation, it seems to me, takes place in three moments, each designated by a concept: *materiality* (or *alterity*), *plurality*, and *scarcity*.

The first moment, the analysis of the organic totality and of need, it seems to me, contains nothing to modify Sartrism or what property pertains to it. It is simply a matter of translating the structure of the for-itself into biological language. Living being constitutes an organic totality. It experiences a need and this need reveals a lack suffered by the organic totality, a lack that constitutes its negation. 'It is the first totalizing relation of the material being that is man with the material whole of which he is a part . . . Need is the negation of the negation to the extent that it is denounced as a *lack* within the organism; it is positivity to the extent that by means of it the organic totality tends to preserve itself *as such*' (p. 166). Why does need appear as the negation of the negation? To the extent that we have understood the argument, need reveals a lack, a gap in the organic totality and this negation can be negated in turn by inorganic, material elements. The organic totality is manifest as a totality and makes the material environment appear, at infinity, as the total field of its possibilities for satiation (p. 166). This contradiction between organic and material totality (living being maintains and reconstitutes itself by appropriating what satisfies its needs from the environment, and it appropriates an inorganic material, oxygen, in order to fill in the gaps of the organic totality) underlies the original and permanent status of man or, more generally, of living being. Such a being is in danger in the universe and must make itself from inert matter if it is to continue to exist and modify the material environment. 'A man in need is an organic totality who perpetually turns himself into his own tool in the external environment' (p. 167). 'The action of the living body on inert matter can be exercised directly or by the mediation of another inert body. In this case, we call the intermediary a tool' (p. 167). Organic function, need, and *praxis* are strictly tied together in a dialectical order: with the organism, in fact, dialectical time has entered into being, since living can persist only by renewing itself; this *temporal* relation of the future to the past through the present is nothing other than the functional relation of totality to itself: 'it is its own future beyond a present of reintegrated disintegration' (pp. 167–8).

The schema of intelligibility, characteristic of dialectic and consciousness (or of the for-itself, in *Being and Nothingness*), is thus discovered along with organic totalities and so with living being. Living being presents a structure identical to consciousness itself, an identity that gives Sartrean philosophy an appearance of materialism. 'And so, to the extent that, (1) the body is a function, (2) the function is need, and (3) the need is *praxis*, it can be said that *human labour*, that is to say, the original *praxis* by which the body produces and reproduces its life, is *entirely* dialectical; ... the unity of the project gives a quasi-synthetic unity to the practical field, and the most important moment of labour is when the organism uses its own inertia (a man *bears down* on a lever, *etc.*) in order to transform surrounding inertia' (pp. 173–4).

This analysis, which brings to light the dialectical structure of living being itself, leaves room for a formula in which Sartrism and Marxism appear to be completely reconciled: 'dialectic', defined as 'logic of labour', means 'determination of the present by the future, change of place between the inert and the organic, negation, contradictions overcome, and negation of negation: in short, continuing totalization. Such are the moments of a labour, *whatever it may be*' (p. 174).

Perhaps this reconciliation is more apparent than real. The dialectic of need, present in all living beings whether vegetable or animal, is not *per se* self-conscious. The identity of structure between life and consciousness does not necessarily imply identity of being or of essence. Assuming that this identity is postulated or affirmed, the result would be either a kind of metaphysics of consciousness diffused throughout life or even, in an opposite direction, a devaluation of consciousness into an epiphenomenon of the dialectic of life, which would be un-conscious of itself at lower levels.

Moreover, this biological interpretation of consciousness and labour on the basis of need plays no role at all in the course of critical experience (that is, outside the fundamental opposition between the organic and the inorganic, or of consciousness and materiality). Sartre avoids the question: why are there organic wholes rather than simply inorganic matter? *Provisionally*, he considers the question non-scientific. What he says amounts to a decree that 'if there are organic wholes, their type of intelli-gibility is dialectical' (p. 175). But this proposition is not with-out some difficulty for the theory of dialectical Reason: in fact, if the dialectic constitutes the schema of intelligibility appro-priate for organic wholes, and if living beings constitute organic wholes, biology itself is dependent upon dialectical Reason. This will not fail to surprise biologists who, even if they retain some elements of a holist philosophy, are convinced that the Reason operating in biology does not differ from the Reason of other natural sciences.

Let us pass over the eventual consequences of this biological translation of the constitutive dialectic of the for-itself, and establish the fact that a dialectical structure does not demand the plurality of living beings: once again, dialectical structure is discovered at the highest level of abstraction and in the labour of an isolated individual. It is not just a matter of an abstrac-tion however, nor even of an abstraction that is dangerous, at least to the extent that it may suggest a molecular vision of society, the origin and essence of liberalism, which falsely intends 'to apply the principle of inertia and the positivist laws of externality to human relations' (p. 179). The discovery of the other, which, in *Being and Nothingness*, assumed a tragic character—the gaze of the other makes me an object—becomes, in the *Critique*, the second moment of critical experience, a *neutral* and non-tragic moment. Labouring men discover each other without being disclosed as either friends or enemies. They recognize their humanity reciprocally and thus the totalizing *praxis* that defines each of them. Each becomes an object within the universe totalized by the other, (a transposition of objectification by the gaze as in *Being and Nothingness*), and each can serve as the instrument for the other's project. But, the immediate recognition of the humanity of the other creates a reciprocity that neither implies nor excludes either cooperation or struggle.

As labourer and as *praxis*, 'man is a material being in the midst of a material world. He wishes to change the world that crushes him, which is to say, to act upon the material order by means of matter, and thus to be changed himself' (p. 191). Nobody appears simply as 'man' but only in such and such a role: roadworker, gardener, or intellectual. Each one has his own project to change the world and to be changed himself; each one integrates the project of the other in his own project since his own project totalizes the whole world; each one is separated from other people since he follows his own project; and each one also recognizes the being of the project in the other person, that is to say he recognizes a humanity similar to his own. The objectification of each by the other is nobody's goal, but it is the consequence of this fundamental structure. 'The goal is the production of a commodity, a consumer good, a tool or a work of art' (p. 192). Since each one is a project, perfect reciprocity[1] demands the fulfilment of four conditions: (1) that the other be a means to the same extent that I am myself; (2) that I recognize the other as *praxis* even if I integrate him into my totalizing *praxis*; '(3) that I recognize his movement toward his own goals in the same movement by which I

[1] *See* Appendix, Note B.

project myself toward mine; (4) that I discover myself as object and as instrument of his goals by the same act that constitutes him as an objective instrument for my goals' (p. 192).

The reciprocal recognition of individuals as labourers, *praxeis*, and totalizing projects leaves the positive and negative alternatives open: either reciprocal acceptance of the project of the other (or exchange) and cooperation of projects (which, nevertheless, remain distinct) or, on the contrary, reciprocal refusal of projects or struggle, which is initiated on the basis of a mutual recognition or reciprocity, but which is no longer confused with a fight to the death. It is not true that each consciousness seeks the death of the other (p. 192). Having become *praxis* or labour, consciousness recognizes the other and is fundamentally affected himself by this recognition, but is ever separated from the other by the singular totalization of his own project.

I am busy writing at my desk and I look through the open window; I see a labourer in the garden and a roadworker in the street. Each of us sees the world through the totalization of his own project. Each of us can also communicate with the other two, and exclude the third from this relation. The third man, in turn, can constitute himself as mediator between the other two. The gardener and the roadworker may communicate by the intermediary of the writer. The roadworker and the writer may find a common language by the intermediary of the gardener. The gardener and the roadworker may cast the writer back towards the solitude of the intellectual, outside of labourers' society. Each in turn can be the third-man mediator without being elevated, at this moment of critical experience, into a leader or a judge. What does this analysis indicate? It seems to me that it suggests two objectives: on the one hand, it seeks to substitute an elementary sociality, equivalent to the state of nature that is neither peaceful nor bellicose and that, by a kind of indirection, thereby allows the integration of a Marxist eschatology back into Sartrism, in place of the tragedy without appeal and without conclusion that is the struggle of consciousnesses where each seeks the death of the other; on the other hand, it seeks to introduce interpersonal relations that present the same dialectical nature as individual *praxis*. Relations among projects must depend on dialectical Reason and therefore must appear as internal relations at the same time as relations constitutive of the organic totality. But simultaneously, the totality of these relations will never exist save in the totalization effected by an individual: society is never identical with an organic totality. It is a totalization and not a totality.

This second moment brings us to the matter of partial unities such as the unity in the exchange or cooperation of two projects, unity in the struggle of incompatible projects, unification in my perceptual field of the gardener and the roadworker, who sometimes only know each other by way of me and sometimes exclude me from their dyad. Matter serves as the milieu and the instrument for these *praxeis* who recognize each other in their separation and in their possible cooperation. Neither matter, from which is extracted whatever satisfies needs, nor plurality constitutes negativity, the motor of the specifically historical dialectic, that is to say, a cumulative movement over time. A third term, which is necessary to give birth to history, is still missing.

Consciousness, even having become *praxis* by the intermediary of need and labour, remains positivity, freedom, project, and totalization. So that something like history turns up, a negative principle, which is the negation of this freedom but which is constitutive of humanity itself, is required. This negation is called *scarcity*.

Let us stop for a moment. *Does* History have materiality or scarcity as its basis? The Sartrean reply presents no equivocation: the bare relation to materiality does not characterize human history in its singularity, that is, as a *single-handed adventure*. It is the relation to both matter and scarcity that gives 'History, taken at this level, a terrible and hopeless meaning; in fact, it appears that men are united by this inert and demonic negation that takes their substance (that is to say, their labour) from them in order to turn it back against everyone in the form of *active inertia* and totalization by extermination' (p. 200). Why this demonic negation? Because it is a *contingent* fact that scarcity reigns over our planet and tyrannizes humanity. 'Without scarcity, one can perfectly imagine a dialectical *praxis* and even a dialectical labour. In fact, nothing would prevent the products necessary for the organism from being practically inexhaustible. But even so, a practical operation would be necessary to wrest them from the earth' (p. 201).

Before we examine the role of scarcity[2] within the critical experience or in the interpretation of social existence—which amounts to the same thing because critical experience follows the movement that, at the transcendental level, goes from individual *praxis* to *History*—let us recall the different features, so abruptly introduced, needed to launch the dialectic. Scarcity is a *fact* and not a *necessity*. Sartre affirms, as the above quotation makes clear, that labour does not imply scarcity. At first sight, this affirmation is surprising since labour takes time, and no one has unlimited time at his disposal. If products were 'inexhaustible', necessity would not encroach upon man externally, from the environment. It may be objected that products could not be inexhaustible without space itself being unlimited, an hypothesis incompatible with the planetary environment of a living species. Let us go beyond this objection: the contingency of scarcity results from the possibility of *conceiving* but not of *imagining* a humanity relieved from the curse of ceaselessly eliminating a fraction of itself. 'The entire human adventure, at least up to the present, is a relentless struggle against scarcity . . . Three-quarters of the world's population are undernourished even after millennia of History' (p. 202).

The scarcity that rules over the whole of human History, in the sense that History and humanity would be other than they are in a material environment of 'unlimited products', does not yet make the development of societies necessary, as continued existence at a level of extreme poverty or in certain archaic social forms bears witness. 'History is born from an abrupt disequilibrium that sends cracks through every level of society; scarcity establishes the possibility of human history, and only its possibility, in the sense that history can be lived (by means of the internal adaptation of organisms) between certain limits as in an equilibrium. So long as one remains at this level there is no logical absurdity (that is to say, no dialectical absurdity) in conceiving of an earth without History, where human groups

[2] *See* Appendix, Note C.

vegetate, remaining within the cycle of biological repetition, and producing their lives with rudimentary techniques and instruments in perfect ignorance of each other' (p. 203).

Why does Sartre attach so much importance to scarcity and to its contingency? The contingent nature of scarcity allows him to retain the contingency, or at least the non-necessity, of History, and thus indirectly to retain original freedom as an irreducible characteristic of man himself. Since man and freedom are combined, the collective adventure of humanity must retain the same characteristics as freedom. Necessity comes to men from materiality; the contingency of necessity, even if the necessity of this contingency appears at every instant, protects freedom right from the beginning of the historical dialectic.

As the protection of original freedom, scarcity also contains its future blessings. If scarcity provokes the war of all against all and the class struggle, if man has become his own enemy because there are not enough resources to go round, it follows that the development of productive forces can progressively triumph over scarcity and thus over the class struggle and the exploitation of man by man.

Finally, and this appears to me to be essential, scarcity radically alters the nature of reciprocity, the interaction among *praxeis*. At the moment before the critical experience, *praxeis* recognize each other, even if this recognition, being positive or negative by turns, tolerates conflict as well as exchange or cooperation. Reciprocity is not less human in either case because each *praxis* recognizes the other as such, as being separated but identical in its essence. Transcendentally, 'without this human relation of reciprocity, the inhuman relation of scarcity would not exist' (p. 202). Or again, in more precise terms, 'in pure reciprocity, the Other-than-me *is also the same*. In reciprocity *modified by scarcity*, the *same man* would appear as radically Other, as man-against-me, *le contre-homme*, the anti-man; he is the bearer of the threat of death for us . . . In fact nothing, neither wild beasts nor microbes, can be more terrifying for man than another intelligent, carnivorous, and cruel species who would be able to understand and frustrate human intelligence and whose goal precisely would be the destruction of man' (p. 208).

Man in the milieu of scarcity becomes a danger to man, a threat of death. There is not enough room for everyone in their common dwelling-place, the earth. Some of the living must perish, and perish at the hands of their fellows. Each internalizes the condition of scarcity, and sees in others, an Other, an anti-man, something inhuman from whom death will come. Not that all the conflicts between individuals and groups have an immediate cause in the economic order, but scarcity transforms the other into an anti-man, and consequently gives rise to violence and struggle. 'We therefore consider that scarcity, even at the level of need and by means of need, is lived in practice by Manichean action, and that ethics is manifest as a destructive imperative: evil *must be* destroyed. It is at this level as well that *violence* is defined as the structure of human action under the reign of Manicheism and within the framework of scarcity' (p. 209).

Materiality and scarcity constitute, as it were, the ontological foundation or the transcendental origin of the class struggle, itself the social expression of the fact that *lupus est homo homini, non homo*[3] when there is scarcity of food, or tools, or resources and therefore a surplus of men, and some are condemned to disappear in order to make room for others. Does not this transcendental foundation bring Sartre, perhaps unconsciously, back to the Darwinian struggle for life where Marx and Engels sometimes saw a confirmation of their own theory, where the class struggle seemed to them to be an expression of biological competition? Even if there were no doubt about the similarity, Sartre would not subscribe to such a reconciliation. He wishes to resolve a problem that is asked of his own philosophy: why, *in principle*, does man recognize another as a man? And *in fact*, why does he deny it at each instant? How is *praxis*, pure activity, reduced to inertia? And from where does this passivity that negates him, but ends up constituting him, come? Why does History unfold as violence without man being by nature violent? (Man, having no nature, is violent only as an historical being.) Scarcity, the *deus ex machina*, answers all these questions: 'Violence, as the constant inhumanity of human behaviour, is internalized scarcity; in short, it is what makes each person see

[3] Plautus, *Asinaria*, II, 4, line 495 [Tr. note].

scarcity in each Other, and the principle of Evil in everyone else' (p. 222).

Sartre wonders if this theory of scarcity is in agreement with Marxism or not. An affirmative reply appears possible, at least in one sense. In the *German Ideology*, Marx and Engels in fact call forth a vision of life after the Revolution, and write that if poverty continued 'the filthy business would start up again'.[4] It is a Sartrean text: need created poverty and poverty created struggle; the development of productive forces and the victory over scarcity create conditions indispensable for socialism. Having noted the commonality of Sartrism and Marxism, we must add that it is confined to this commonplace idea, and that two important differences appear at this point of the critical experience.

Scarcity in the form of disproportion between needs and resources is part of the thought and language of bourgeois economics. 'The analytical study of the institutions of scarcity is called political economy' (p. 225, note). Marxism itself starts neither from scarcity nor from a Robinson Crusoe attitude at grips with the material environment, but from forces and relations of production, from social formations. From there, Sartre must show that the transcendental and dialectical analysis of scarcity has nothing in common with the analysis of bourgeois economics but, on the contrary, that it 'sets negativity into motion as an implicit motor of historical dialectic, and that it gives the dialectic its intelligibility'. The essential discovery of Marxism in fact remains: 'labour, as historical reality and as the use of tools determined within a social and material milieu that is itself already determined, is the real foundation of the organization of social relations.' But the transcendental analysis *establishes the foundation* for the discovery of Marxism: '*in the milieu of scarcity*, all the structures of a determined society rest on its mode of production' (p. 225, note). In a more or less detailed and believable way, Engels tried to reconstruct the origin of the class struggle on the basis of the disintegration of the primitive community. He did not look for a 'dialectical

[4] Cf. Marx and Engels, *The German Ideology*, tr. R. Pascal (London: Lawrence and Wishart, 1938), pp. 24–5; *Werke* (Berlin: Dietz Verlag, 1969), vol. III, pp. 34–5.

principle of intelligibility'. But then, Marx and Engels had a
tendency to impute to capitalism responsibility for the surplus
of men, whether in terms of an absolute surplus that Malthus
argued was a function of the fertility of the human species, or a
relative surplus that was created by the development of productive forces such that fewer labourers were necessary to obtain
the same product. Marx did not see the function of scarcity as
the negative unity by which all men and all societies were integrated into the same History as enemies of each other. Neither
Dühring nor Engels discerned that man was violent in History
and not by nature.

By giving the class struggle a transcendental foundation and a
principle of intelligibility in scarcity, has Sartre consolidated
Marxism as he believes and claims? In Marxism, scarcity
appears as a kind of watermark, as a counterpart to the necessary development of the forces of production. More important
than scarcity, however, is surplus, the surplus of production
that, compared with the incompressible needs of the labourers, is
appropriated by the owner of the means of production, whether
a slave owner, or a capitalist. The Marxism of Marx deals less
with scarcity, which is considered to be a constant of the human
situation, than with surplus, whose mode of extraction and
distribution varies from regime to regime. The increase in
surplus, and not poverty, leads many Marxists who are in
power, notably in the Soviet Union and in China, to deny that
there is a problem of over-population when socialism has been
instituted. This has been the official doctrine of the People's
Republic of China for many years.[5] More generally, if violence
will only disappear with an end to scarcity, when will scarcity
end? If man is violent by nature, he would condemn History
to eternal violence. If he is violent in History and 'by means of
the fact of scarcity', he retains the hope of escaping violence if
scarcity could be overcome. But how to overcome scarcity
except by limiting births, and thus by the elimination of those
who could have lived? Or else by eliminating those who are
already alive?

*   *   *

[5] This doctrine has been abandoned today.

We already know the three transcendental conditions of History: materiality, plurality of consciousnesses, and scarcity. And scarcity, so to speak, unifies the other two: living beings need matter to live and, because of the number of living beings, matter becomes scarce and each being becomes a potential enemy of another. Or again, the reciprocity of *praxeis*, an individual's being recognized as such, is transformed to non-recognition: the *praxis* of the other is a threat to my life, and becomes anti-dialectic and inhumanity.

Of these three terms, the third and most important one plays no explicit role in the analysis of the historico-social world. Once and for all, it conditions the violence and inhumanity of the historico-social world, without which it would not otherwise be visible. Scarcity is everywhere present but appears nowhere by itself. On the other hand, the first two, *matter*, upon which *praxis* makes its mark or imprint and which becomes *worked-upon matter*, and *plurality*, wherein each *praxis* finds himself both lost and isolated, are themselves manifest at each moment as both causes and expressions of the alienation of consciousness and of the practico-inert in which freedom is trapped.

First let us translate the principal ideas into a more common language. *Praxis* or *labouring consciousness*, objectifying itself in matter, is defined as a free project. Now, the machine, a symbol of worked-upon matter, may perhaps represent the free project of a consciousness, at least in the sense that it has been conceived and constructed by a consciousness. But once in place, it becomes the destiny of labourers who become the servants of worked-upon matter (but matter worked upon by others). The machine commands and the labourers obey; they serve the thing that others have created, matter that others have humanized. This machine does not only reduce free *praxeis* to the level of servants and slaves of matter, it transforms the relations of production and deprives them of occupations by turning them into useless and superfluous labourers. According to the inhumane logic of materiality, it strikes randomly at the peasant who is thrown off land that has become unprofitable, or the artisan who cannot compete with industrial goods. Since Marx's day, we have used a 'strange language' where 'the same proposition ties finality to necessity so indissolubly that we no longer know if it is the man or the machine that is the practical project' (p. 230).

According to the Marxist formula, man makes his history on the basis of given conditions. Now, 'the given conditions' are revealed to us by critical experience: at each moment they are mixed with worked-upon materiality, with matter upon which *praxis* has put its mark, an impression that is passively retained by it. *Praxis* has been objectified, and it is with respect to this objectification that *praxis* thrusts itself towards new project, overcoming what is given and reorganizing the milieu.

'Matter, which is the receptacle of practices made passive, is indissolubly tied to lived *praxis*, which at once adapts itself to material conditions and internal significations. *Praxis* renews or *re-constitutes* the meaning of material conditions by going beyond its given meaning in order to transform it' (p. 237).

Let us now consider the entrepreneur rather than the labourer. In a certain way, he also submits to the tyranny of the machine that at each instant upsets the conditions of labour and that, being better used by his competitors, threatens him with failure. He is not defined simply by the proletarians he exploits but also by members of his own class, men who are other than him as well as the same as him. Each other exists as Other with respect to each because all are slaves of the same mechanism of competition. The liberal calls this circular or recurrent alterity the market. Sartre describes it with horror. Reification is not 'a metamorphosis of the individual into a thing as too often one might believe; it is a necessity imposed on members of a social group through the structures of society to maintain his membership in the group and through it, his membership in the whole society, as a kind of molecular edifice. What he lives and does *as an individual* and in the immediate remains genuine *praxis* or human labour; but a kind of mechanical rigidity haunts this concrete task of living and places the results of his act under the jurisdiction of the alien laws of addition-totalization. His objectification is modified from without by the inert power of the objectification of others' (pp. 243–4).

The tyranny of the machine or worked-upon matter and the

tyranny of these strange laws, which steal from individual *praxis* the mastery and the meaning of its own action, appear to me to be, in a quasi-popular language, Sartre's interpretation of alienation and *reification*, of the fall into the practico-inert. Of these two tyrannies, one has a Marxist resonance, but the other sounds as much Sartrean as Marxist. The dispersal of *praxeis*, the relations among entrepreneurs who are subjected to the same constraints but yet are strangers to one another, each with a project that is incompatible with the projects of the others (all the projects being the same, namely, to adapt to the machine and actualize a project)—this molecular structure appears to Sartre, if not inhuman in the way the capitalist-proletarian or colonialist-colonized structures are inhuman, at least *reified*, and to that extent inhuman. *Praxeis* are not united in a single project comparable to individual *praxis*. And individual *praxis* is, and remains, the model of the dialectic and of freedom.

Materiality as the mediation between consciousnesses, and seriality as the molecular structure of sociality, constitute the principles that govern the fall into the practico-inert, the origin of alienation, and the creation of mass society. Everyone becomes the slave of worked-upon matter. The humanization of things leads not to the 'thingification' of men but to their subservience to others and to their isolation. In this sense, the practico-inert, even though disclosed by the critical experience, is not equivalent to a moment of the dialectic but to a moment of the anti-dialectic: necessity and the anti-dialectic of the practico-inert are understood in terms of freedom, or the constituting dialectic.

We have been dealing, so far, with the theme of the subservience of *praxeis* to materiality and seriality in a simple and semi-popular language. Let us return to a language closer to that of our author, which, therefore, will be more philosophical but perhaps also more obscure. On page 248 of the *Critique*, Sartre situates himself vis-à-vis Heidegger in the following terms: 'How to establish the basis of *praxis* if, in fact, only the inessential moment of a radically inhuman process must be seen in it? How to show *praxis* to be a real and material totalization if the whole of Being totalizes itself through it? Man would then become what Walter Biemel,[6] commenting on Heidegger's books, said: man was "the bearer of the Opening of Being". This reconciliation is not incongruous. If Heidegger has praised Marxism, it is because he sees in this philosophy a manner of showing, as de Waelhens[7] said, speaking of Heideggerian existentialism: "that Being is the Other in me . . . [and that] man . . . is only himself by way of Being which is not himself." But all philosophy that subordinates the human to the Other-than-man, whether it be an existentialist or Marxist idealism, has the hatred of man as its foundation and its consequence; History has proved both cases. It is necessary to choose: man is first of all himself or first of all Other-than-himself. And if the second doctrine is chosen, one is very simply the victim and the accomplice of real alienation. But alienation only exists *if* man *is first of all action*. Freedom is the basis of slavery and the direct link from internality, an original type of human relation that establishes the human connection with externality.'

This text, which is but one of dozens of others of the same kind that I could cite, confirms and illustrates the intransigence of Sartre: the authentic Sartre, the philosopher, forms a strange contrast with Sartre the political opportunist. The one concedes nothing to Marxism, at least nothing important to him, while the other concedes everything, or nearly everything, sometimes to Stalin, sometimes to Thorez, sometimes to Togliatti, and sometimes to the *enragés* of the student Commune. The first Sartre will concede, *en passant*, and with indifference, the evident truth of the analyses of *Capital*. On the other hand, when it is a matter of freedom or of consciousness, he opposes the determinism and materialism usually associated with Marxism with an unconditional objection. The primacy of action over Being appears to the philosopher as the foundation of *his own* humanism. As for the analyses of *Capital*, he knows nothing and wishes to know nothing of the respective merits of planning or the Market. He sees inhumanity inevitably and irresistibly emerge from what he holds to be a philosophical error. He seems neither

[6] Walter Biemel, *Le Concept du monde chez Heidegger* (Louvain: Nauwelaerts, 1950), pp. 85–6 [Tr. note].

[7] Alphonse de Waelhens, *Phénoménologie et vérité. Essai sur l'évolution de l'idée de vérité chez Husserl et Heidegger* (Paris: P.U.F. 1953), p. 16 [Tr. note].

to believe nor to be disturbed that errors of political or sociological analysis might more easily give rise to the use of inhumane means in the service of a grandiose goal. Later on, at
the end of the chapter devoted to the fall 'of free individual
praxis into the practico-inert', he once more differentiates the
philosophical meaning of his enterprise from human destiny.
Here we can see some formulae that distinguish the same idea:
'The experience of the practico-inert [is] what each of us does
in his work as in public life (and, to a lesser extent, in private);
in sum, it [characterizes] our daily life' (p. 372). Thus we have
two contradictory experiences: that of free *praxis*, the translucent experience of each individual by himself, and that of
the universe of activity–passivity, which constitutes a field that
individuals, defined on the basis of their function and class,
cannot leave. 'Can we therefore move, according to circumstances, from the translucent consciousness of our activity to
the grotesque or monstrous apperception of the practico-inert?'
Sartre replies to his own question: 'not only can we, but we
constantly do do so. There is no doubt that at the moment of
labour—and, to the extent that it lasts, even in the case of a
minutely divided task—the simple necessity of a control or, in
the total bondage of the individual to the specialized machine,
the necessity of *one eye* or *one hand* waiting for automation, action[8] still appears, *at the very least*, as the adaptation of the
body to an emergency situation ... Vulgar Marxists have
calmly done away with the moment of individual *praxis* as the
original experience of the dialectic, or, in other words, as the
dialectic being realized in practical experience. *They did not see*
that it is necessary to preserve the fundamental reality of this moment or to
do away with the reality of alienation' (pp. 372–3).[9] Alienation presupposes the moment of original freedom and translucid *praxis*.
Otherwise, it would but remain the experience of the practico-
inert, the activity–passivity that we live out each day, and
could not be recognized as the experience of bondage.

Then again, 'the moment of freedom, as unifying and translucent practice, is the *moment of the trap*. By being set up as free
and individual, *praxis* continues, so far as it itself is concerned,

[8] Of course, the word action here refers to free individual *praxis* [R.A.].
[9] Emphasis added.

to realize the world of the other by itself, and for everyone'. By becoming conscious again of our freedom within the practico-inert, we are courting the danger of not recognizing that this freedom affects our bondage, that it reproduces the alienated world, and that it constitutes the 'fundamental mystification'. But it is not free *praxis* that constitutes this mystification. This mistaken experience of freedom is not of the act but of its materialized result. Within materiality and seriality, the dialectic is necessarily transformed into anti-dialectic, and freedom into bondage. However, individual *praxis* remains the original moment of the experience and at each instant it retains the capacity of taking itself up again, even though, within the practico-inert, it only exerts itself in order to negate itself, and only acts in order to submit, in one form or another, to bondage in the world of things and of men reduced to molecules.

Must it be said that all objectification leads to alienation? 'Shall we return to Hegel, who makes alienation a constant characteristic of objectification, whatever it is? Yes and no. In fact, we must consider whether the original relation of *praxis* as totalization of materiality, which is understood as passivity, obliges man to objectify himself within a milieu not his own and to present an inorganic totality as his own objective reality. This correspondence of internality with externality is what originally constitutes *praxis* as the relation of the organism to its material environment. And there is no doubt that man, as soon as he is no longer denoted simply in terms of the reproduction of his life, but as the ensemble of products that reproduce his life, discovers himself as *Other* within the world of objectivity. Totalized matter, an inert objectification that perpetuates itself as inertia, is in fact a *non-man* and even, if you like, an *anti-man*. Each of us spends his life imprinting his malignant image upon things, an image that fascinates and misleads man if he wishes to understand himself *by means of it*. Moreover, he cannot be other than the totalizing movement that ends in *this* objectification' (p. 285).

This last, very fine phrase gives a pathetic accent to objectification-alienation; it is effectively fatal, in both senses of the term. In the *Critique*, alienation certainly constitutes a constant characteristic of objectification. Of the yes and no, it is therefore the yes that Sartre first of all agrees with. However, it does not follow that this objectification-alienation marks a return to Hegelian thought as distinct from Marxism. Sartrean alienation is defined in ethical and even sociological terms. Consciousness, the pure act, translucid freedom, are all necessarily projected into the world of things and multifarious individuals: the meaning of his act escapes him and he is caught in an inert materiality that negates his own essence, namely pure creation and translucidity. Thus, alienation does not disappear, as in Hegel's philosophy, with the suppression of the dualism between subject and object, or between consciousness and the world, and with the absolute knowledge of the Wise Man who thinks the system and thinks himself as the thinker of prior systems. The Sartrean suppression of alienation, assuming it remains possible, demands a transformation of interhuman relations, not a return of spirit to itself once it has completed the cycle of possible creations.

Even more, the reference to *Being and Nothingness* accentuates again the anthropologico-social signification of Sartrean alienation. It is no longer a matter of the odyssey of consciousness; it is no longer even a question, as in *Being and Nothingness*, of the vain ambition of the for-itself, to attain the brute solidarity of the in-itself. '*Praxis* certainly provides its own light, that is to say, it is always consciousness (of) self. But this non-thetic consciousness can do nothing against the practical affirmation that I am what I do (and am the one who escapes myself by constituting myself immediately as another). The necessity of this fundamental connection allows one to understand why man *projects himself*, as I said, into the milieu of the in-itself-and-for-itself. Fundamental alienation does not come about, as *Being and Nothingness* may wrongly have led us to believe, from a pre-natal choice. It comes from the univocal internal correspondence that unites man, as a practical organism, to his environment' (p. 286, note).

I am, authentically, my act. But even though (in a non-thetic fashion) I remain conscious of my act, I only attain self-consciousness as a result of this act, a result that, being inscribed upon matter, strips and reveals me to myself as being other than myself. This analysis would be more convincing if my act were defined by any kind of contents whatsoever, apart from its projection into materiality. Now, this act, this pure freedom, this translucid *praxis*, appears, as such, to be stripped of all contents. *Qua* for-itself, it is nothing. It alienates itself by projecting itself into materiality but, outside of this projection, it *is* only to the extent that it *is not*; or again, it is a permanent possibility of negating the real and projecting itself towards the future, a projection that only realizes itself in materiality and therefore at the price of alienation.

A second remark: this alienation by means of projection into materiality owes nothing to scarcity. Once again, scarcity seems necessary less for the origin of history than for its (possible or necessary) end. Because the organic totality must make use of the matter it needs from the environment in order to keep going, and because it does so by labour, it follows that man cannot avoid objectifying himself, nor can his self-objectification avoid giving rise to a kind of alienation. It substitutes a self-consciousness-within-things, which reflects to each one a distorted and deceitful image of himself, for pure self-consciousness. The demonstration of necessary alienation *without recourse to scarcity* makes the end of alienation much more difficult.

* * *

The analysis of the practico-inert[10] contains four principal moments, which in turn determine four concepts: *exigency*, *interest*, *social-being*, and *collective*. It goes without saying that we are not concerned with four historical moments. The analysis is situated at the transcendental level, and hardly deals with historically successive stages of the fall. These four concepts must take us from *individual praxis* to the *socialized individual*. It seems to me that throughout these pages Sartre gives himself a number of objectives, which are not explicitly formulated but which can and must be distinguished Here and there he wishes to tackle Marxist themes and always he wants to show the compatibility between his own themes and those of Marxism. In addition, he takes *individual praxis*, unconditional but empty freedom, as his starting point. Man, according to him, has

10 *See* Appendix, Note D.

neither nature nor essence: he *is* freedom and freedom is nothing determined. It is the unlimited power of negation, neither good nor evil, neither moral nor immoral, but a pure choice. The second objective of the transcendental experience seems to be the recovery, on the basis of *praxis*, of socialized man in his daily existence. By illustrating or by describing the diverse aspects of the human condition within the practico-inert, Sartre does not intend to give up all claims to the specificity of understanding and intellection, and thus his claims for dialectical Reason. We are following the stages of the conquest of consciousnesses by worked-upon matter, and we are discovering that enslaved or conquered consciousnesses, integrated into social ensembles, remain comprehensible or intelligible. Finally, perhaps the last term, social ensemble, which refers to classbeing, inspires the whole movement. For a long while Sartre had been discussing the relations between class and Party in his occasional writings. By means of transcendental analysis, the *Critique* establishes the truth of this relationship.

Let us begin with the concept of *exigency*.[11] In a first and superficial reading, Sartre defines exigency as the result of the dialectic of *praxis* and materiality. The machine, the work of one or several men, commands the *praxis* of other men. These men serve the machine rather than are served by it; they are bound to the orders that the machine itself gives them, and they must obey because lack of maintenance and operation means that the machine will stop and the totalized organisms, the men, could no longer continue to exist. Within the organic milieu, *praxis* must first of all live and assure the reproduction of life. Within the social milieu, service to the machine becomes the equivalent of a categorical imperative, because if men did not obey it, they would not survive. By accepting death, freedom to disobey becomes, at this stage of analysis, devoid of signification. *Praxis* as such, as organic totality, has the exclusive goal of maintaining its own life: it cannot refuse.

The theme of man in bondage to his works and the servant of his own machines gives rise to some well-known variations. Sartre deals with it with the assistance of his own vocabulary and within his own system. It does not matter whom the

[11] The texts of greatest clarity are found on p. 253.

machine orders around; consequently, the worker who is ordered around is reduced to doing a job which equally anyone, no matter who, could do. He is condemned to a 'universal task' that has become other than himself, which is to say that he has been stripped of his particularity. Other men than him have thought, willed, and built the machine that orders him around: thus, he obeys men other than himself. Finally, having become worked-upon matter or machine, the *praxis* of these others who *make demands* of him has been transformed into an inertia or passivity to which the alterity of its servants submits.

Neither the theme nor its variations present any particular originality, but the concept of *exigency*, nevertheless, has a philosophical function in the *Critique*. It introduces a principle of command into an anthropology that otherwise has none. If the freedom of each consciousness is equally total, why can one consciousness *legitimately* give orders to another? 'What a man expects from another, when a relation is personal, is defined in reciprocity, because expectation is a personal act . . . No *praxis* as such can even formulate an imperative simply because exigency does not enter into the structure of reciprocity' (p. 253). If we agree that in the *Critique* the relations of *praxeis* constitute the equivalent to the state of nature as found in some classical seventeenth-century philosophies, we say that freedom, which is equal in everyone because it is total in each, excludes the authority of man over man. The categorical imperative comes from outside, from the machine or from materiality, but it comes necessarily because projection into materiality and the anti-dialectic necessarily follow from *praxis* itself.

Submission to worked-upon matter thus represents the original form of alienation and the rupture of reciprocity between consciousnesses. But as this consubstantial submission to life in society appears indispensable for his survival, man in society obeys the machine in the same way that he eats in order to live. Thus, the origin of the categorical imperative blends with the origin of bondage. The definition of *praxis* and the relation among *praxeis* is, by its own inevitable structures, going to confer a grimacing and demonic face upon society itself.

Exigency represents the substitute practico-inert, the practico-inert alienated from the categorical imperative. *Interest* seems to be the Sartrean substitute for *property* (as, for example it is used by Jean-Jacques Rousseau in his hypothetical reconstruction of the gradual development of humanity) and for *egotism*, as was presupposed by economists or liberals in order to explain the social order and to justify positive organization. 'Considered in itself, in his simple and free activity, an individual has needs and desires; he is a project; he realizes his goals by his labour; he has no *interest*' (p. 261). Man only acquires an interest by mixing himself with things. The property-owner, who identifies himself with his possessions, has interests. Likewise the director of a factory and, indeed, every man who has his being outside himself in the practico-inert. 'Interest is being-entirely-outside-of-oneself-in-a-thing *insofar as it conditions praxis* as categorical imperative.' The exigency of the machine or the social system constituted around machines in service to them is defined for *praxeis* by categorical imperatives. Seeing that such and such individuals are identified with things or fragments of the social system, they have *interests*; they form a society of interested men, opposed to each other, others for each other and yet united by their essential alterity. 'The relation of *interest* therefore contains, at the level of individual interest, the massification of individuals as such, and their practical communication through the antagonisms and the harmonies of the matter they represent' (p. 268). On the basis of this definition, the analysis returns to the competitive milieu and the abstract representation of the economy as seen by liberals. But this competitive milieu becomes 'always another negation and always the same negation of each by everyone and of everyone by each' (p. 265).[12]

Towards what does this transcendental deduction of the concept of *interest*, which we have rather roughly summarized, lead us? According to his own formula, Sartre wishes 'to get rid of hedonist and utilitarian hypotheses'; in other words, he wants to refute a certain conception of the human species that holds man to be condemned by nature to the struggle of all

---

[12] Another startling formula of Sartre is the following: 'Interest is the negative life of the human thing in the world of things insofar as man reifies himself in order to serve it' (p. 266).

against all. Once again, here is the fundamental logical succession: 'either, "each follows his own interest," which means
that the division of men is *natural*, or the division of men, being
the result of the mode of production, makes interest (whether
particular or general, individual or class) appear as a real
moment of inter-human relations' (p. 277). If the first hypothesis is admitted, two consequences result from it: interest and
the interested man remain natural, opaque, and unintelligible
data. The intelligibility of human history is abandoned. In the
second place, 'the whole of history sinks entirely into the absurd,
to the extent that conflicts of interest are its motor; in particular,
Marxism is no more than an irrational hypothesis.' If the antagonisms of interest are basic, the mode of production is
responsible not for the class struggle as such, but only for the
form that this struggle is dressed up in during each historical
period.

Once again Sartre's demonstration has the same intention: to
eliminate human nature, to exclude the *natural* cause of rivalry
among men and groups, and to establish a radical heterogeneity
between a Darwinian or liberal conception of man (in his eyes,
the struggle for life of the Darwinians and the competition of
economic subjects derive from the same inspiration) and his
own. He finds fault with Marxists who 'hesitate between the
law of interest and the Marxist conception of history, that is to
say, between a kind of biological materialism and historical
materialism. They invest need with all sorts of shadowy opacity.
When they render it perfectly *unintelligible*, they call it by an
unintelligible name: objective reality. And, being satisfied, they
consider this inert and dark force, this externality within internality, to be interest' (p. 277). The priority of existence over
essence is translated in the *Critique* by the primacy of *praxis*, the
pure act, over all determinations that limit and disfigure it. The
interested man gives rise to the confusion between *praxis* and
materiality, and to the confusion between property, into which
the individual is assimilated, and the collective beings of which
he must be a participant or which are realized in and by him.
'It is not the diversity of interests that gives rise to conflicts
but, to the extent that worked-upon matter is imposed upon
struggling groups as an independent reality by means of the

temporary impotence that gives rise to their conflict-relations, it is conflicts that produce interests' (p. 278).

The interest of the proletariat is not an immediate *datum*; it does not arise from the fact that proletarians exist in greater or fewer numbers and with more or less comparable conditions of life. Rather, it arises from the conflict with capitalists and through this conflict. The owners necessarily act according to the law of their own interests or, in other words, with a view to the prosperity of their business: they have the *same* interest since they all intend the same object, but they are *different* since the same object puts them in opposition to each other. To the extent that they must transform the factory, lay off redundant workers or reduce salaries in order to preserve the profitability of their business, they cannot avoid harming the proletarians, who like-wise are the same and different, the *same* because of the passive commonality of their destiny, *different* because, according to their contract and level of qualification, the interests of one diverges from those of another.

On the basis of this alienation within materiality, this forma-tion of individual and collective interests within and through conflict, the analysis proceeds through the successive levels of *Social Being, Collective Being*, and *Social and Collective Being*. In ordinary language, we say that each *is* his social being or, in other words, that he retains within himself or that he has inter-nalized the conditions within which his existence unfolds. These conditions result first of all in the '*crystallized practice* of preceding generations' (p. 289). 'Following Hegel, we have said in *Being and Nothingness* that essence is past and surpassed being. And in fact, this is first of all the true being of the worker since he has been prefabricated in a capitalist society by means of already crystallized labour, labour already done. And his personal *praxis*, as a free and productive dialectic, moves in its turn beyond this prefabricated being by the very movement that *praxis* impresses itself upon matter or upon the machine-tool' (pp. 291–2). Free *praxis* continues to exist in relation to the past that has become essence. But this freedom, being spread out within the practico-inert, cannot transcend the past because the past, submitting *praxeis* to the exigencies of machines, has already limited the possible future, and condemned the project of man. By his service to the machine, he is transformed into an anti-man, so that he can never create anything beyond what has been offered to him by the past. The individual remains free, but within the practico-inert. He will never succeed in leaving the hell of inertia that has filtered into him while he was being trapped within sociality.

Thus, inalienable freedom is reconciled with the necessity of alienation (and alienation introduces the necessity of the anti-dialectic). Each one freely makes himself a worker, but, despite the diversity of these free decisions, everyone together is seen to achieve the social being of class: 'one worker reads, another militates, another finds the time to make a scooter that yet another one buys; another plays the violin, another works in the garden. All these activities are constituted upon the basis of particular circumstances, and constitute the objective particularity of each. But at the same time such activities merely realize class-being for each individual to the extent that, in spite of themselves, they remain within the class framework of unsurpassable exigencies' (p. 294).

Just as each individual, by freely choosing his particular destiny, does not transcend and cannot transcend his class-being, so too individuals who are part of a defined and similar situation do not transcend an alienated condition, either in their practice or their theory. And so we find that the anarcho-syndicalism of the professional workers cannot move beyond itself: 'It was necessary to improve one's knowledge and skill within the trade, to be instructed, to teach manoeuvres . . ., to fight, to forge workers' unity, and to draw near to the day when power is seized . . . They have identified the real man and think him achieved with the professional worker. And this false identification (false not with respect to the bosses, but only with respect to the masses) was an unsurpassable limit because it was *themselves* or, if you prefer, it was the theoretical and practical expression of pure practico-inert relations with other workers' (pp. 298–9).

Such an analysis, apart from its vocabulary, presents neither originality nor difficulty to the sociologist. Sartre never grows tired of multiplying examples to demonstrate and confirm his two ontological theses: First, the freedom of *praxis* continues to exist, even within the practico-inert, and second, reality is under the jurisdiction of dialectical Reason and escapes from analytical Reason. The discovery of our social Being is terrifying because it reveals to us our ignorance of ourselves. For the group as for the individual, 'inert Being can be defined by the kind of practical option that makes one ignorant of what one is' (p. 301). But, 'this prefabricated objectivity does not prevent *praxis* from being free temporalization and *effective* reorganization of the practical field in the light of goals discovered and established during *praxis* itself' (p. 301).

Sartre devotes a lengthy note (pp. 301–3) to other concepts, such as *value*, that pertain to the practico-inert. Value also harbours within itself the duality of translucid freedom and inertia. It is distinguished from exigency because it does not translate the pure and simple imperative of the machine. Value retains from pure *praxis* the translucidity of freedom achieving itself, but it also keeps within it the inertia of the practico-inert. The system of values that the thinkers of each epoch elaborate results from *praxis*, but from *praxis* that discovers itself in the world of alienation. Values simultaneously deny and confirm the alienation of *praxis* from itself. Values are tied to the existence of the practico-inert field or, in other words, to hell, as negation of its negation. The analysis that we have roughly summarized seems to have the following objectives: to protect the autonomy and the relative positivity of value-systems (ethics are critical of the social order even while they justify it), and to overcome the unrefined antithesis of infrastructure and superstructure by showing the origin of values in the fundamental structures of individual or collective *praxis*.

The transcendental deduction situates the concepts of social sciences, brings to light essential serializations, recovers the freedom of *praxis*, confirms the role of dialectical Reason, and leads us to class-being, *exis* not *praxis*: 'the *inert* (unsurpassable) *relation* of an individual with his class comrades on the basis of certain structures' (p. 304). At this moment of the dialectical experience, class is part of the practico-inert.

From *class-being* we pass on to the last concept of the practico-inert, the *collective*. In Sartrean jargon it is defined as 'a relation with a double meaning: that of a material, inorganic and worked-upon object and of a multiplicity that finds its unity in itself coming from without' (p. 319). In common language, all social ensembles that receive their unity externally and that leave the individuals who compose them effectively separated from each other and solitary within a mass, can be called collectives. A radio audience constitutes a collective because they receive their transitory and passive unity from the outside and from materiality. The competitive market also constitutes an example of a collective because each buyer and seller plays his role, and the entire ensemble is part of a system that determines their conduct without uniting their will. The market is a de-totalized totality, existing as a kind of dispersion. It is neither a state of nature nor a simple model, but the specific modality of relations among individuals within the practico-inert. In many manifestations, such as panic, public opinion also represents a collective. Carried away by the same anxiety, individuals do not act in common, but they undergo the same impulsion or the same feeling in their alterity (the separation of *ego* and *alter*). In the widest sense, the entire socio-economic system can be considered as a collective or a *social object,* unified and multiple, unified in its multiplicity.

In the last analysis, the practico-inert is indistinguishable from the world within which our daily life unfolds: it is at once infernal and banal. 'The field of the practico-inert exists. In sum, it surrounds us and conditions us. I have only to glance out the window where I will see cars that are men, cars whose drivers are cars, a municipal policeman on the corner directing traffic and farther along an automatic timer regulating the same traffic with red and green lights. A *hundred exigencies* ascend from the earth towards me: pedestrian crossings, notices telling me to do this and forbidding me to do that. There are collectives: the branch of the Crédit Lyonnais, a café, a church, an apartment block; and there is a visible seriality as well: men making a queue in front of a store, instruments proclaiming in their stiff, frozen voices the way in which they are to be used as pavements, roads, taxi stands, bus stops, etc. . . . . A little later I will go down into the street and be *their thing.* I will buy this collective, a newspaper, and the whole practico-inert that besieges and specifies me will suddenly be discovered *on the basis* of the whole field, that is, the entire Earth, . . . as the Elsewhere of every Elsewhere, or the series of all the series of series' (pp. 362–3).

Banality of hell or hell of banality. Why this grotesque or monstrous transfiguration of our everyday world? Because my total and translucid freedom is trapped in the inertia of social beings, a prisoner of materiality that is itself an expression of other *praxeis*. Each one is other than the others, and each submits to the exigencies of the machines and is lost in an indefinite series. Each is alienated in the sense that he remains free but only exercises his freedom from within limits fixed by the ensemble of the practico-inert. The practico-inert, the anti-dialectic, is only unveiled by critical experience, and only reveals its meaning to dialectical Reason. Analytical Reason confuses this anti-dialectic with reality itself. But if man cannot escape, he remains forever damned, condemned to hell. Faced with the constituting dialectic (or individual *praxis*) and the practico-inert (or the anti-dialectic) where to find salvation if not within a *collective praxis* capable of protecting individuals from both materiality and solitude?

III

The Rock of Sisyphus; or, from the Bastille to the Kremlin

We have followed the first dialectical movement, where dialectic is transformed into anti-dialectic without *praxis* losing its freedom, even though trapped in a world of reified things. In this chapter we shall deal the second dialectical movement, which goes from the practico-inert to constituted *praxis* and begins with rebellion. Each of us *is* his social being, but he remains free within and by means of the way that he makes himself what he is. Bourgeois or Jew, I freely take my bourgeois or my Jewish being upon myself.

A celebrated example provides a simplified and symbolic illustration of the matter within which *praxis* is trapped. From his window the writer sees a line of people, waiting for a bus, across from the Church of Saint-Germain-des-Prés. This queue of men and women displays the main characteristics of *serial* assemblies. The individuals are physically close to each other but they remain a collection of solitary people. They have nothing in common save an intention that unites and opposes them. Their unity comes from without, from the machine whose services they await and whose driver will enforce and interpret the law. The materiality that gathers them together, *i.e.* the bus they all want to catch, blots out the particularities that make you and me unique and irreplaceable human beings. Each one is reduced to the quality of 'bus rider', every one is united by this quality, but in alterity, because the seat that one takes will be unavailable for another. Just as men who must sell their labour on the market are the same in their alterity—they fulfil the same market function, but the behaviour of each one de-

pends upon that of another, and his in turn upon yet another
and so on, without there ever arising a totalization within a
common action—so too the bus passengers become, so to speak,
rivals within and because of their identical (not common)
intention, to find a seat on the bus. Who will get aboard?
The first ones in line, in the order of their arrival. There is no
consideration of urgency, no care for the qualitatively different
needs of the worker or the woman of the world. Scarcity—
everyone waiting cannot get aboard—imposes a selection, a
selection that is, so to speak, anonymous in that it retains or
eliminates atoms, not qualitatively distinct human beings.

Thus the queue of bus passengers provides us with a symbolic
and simplified characterization of the series: unity comes from
outside, by way of *materiality*; it exhibits a molecular *structure*
(they are together but they look past each other) and *scarcity*
(not everyone will get a seat); *selection* seems to be the decree of a
pitiless and senseless destiny: six seats and ten passengers for the
bus, four will have to catch the next one.

This example simplifies almost to a caricature the analysis of
the series. The crowd that stormed the Bastille fully achieved the
assembly antithetical to the *series*, namely, the *group*. The bus
passengers, capitalists, consumers, and radio listeners have no
common *project*. Each one has, *in a certain respect*, the same project,
but it is an individual one: to catch the same bus, to pay the
lowest possible wages, to buy the same merchandise, to listen
to the same voice. These identical wishes are assembled, either
in proximity or at a distance, but without being united. They
separate those who come together, leaving each to himself, to
his own intentions, to the solitude of his own project, which is
always, in its ultimate intentions, different from that of another
person as his is from a third, and so on. On the other hand, the
crowd that stormed the Bastille has or, better, *is* a common
praxis; it seeks the same goal, vibrates with the same emotions,
and acts with the same heart.

To be precise, consciousnesses do not fuse. By its very essence,[1]

---

[1] From time to time I employ the word 'essence' even though neither
man nor consciousness properly speaking has an essence in Sartre's philosophy. I mean by this term, the consubstantial characteristics of consciousness, the identity of consciousness with freedom, solitude, etc.

Sartrean consciousness remains permanently condemned to solitude at the same time as it is condemned to freedom: the one implies the other. But this individual solitude does not exclude the community of action. It is within and by action, and by action alone that the *we* is constituted, where each consciousness lives the same project and intends the same object. 'Everyone to the Bastille' replaces 'each in his turn'. There are no turns and no roles because single roles have disappeared in the heat of combat. There is no selection because there is room for everyone. Within the practico-inert, numbers meant selection; but within the group-in-fusion, number becomes the principle of strength, of pride, of confidence. 'Here is more, and more and more!' Who has not experienced these mass demonstrations when the crowd discovers itself as it swells and bursts forth?

No hierarchy and no organization is to be found within the group-in-fusion. Between A and B, who both animate the same project, C becomes the third-man regulator. But at the next moment B can become the third-man regulator between A and C. Complete equality results from the community of action, from the spontaneity of each and everyone, and from the mediation among individuals less by a particular person than by the group itself, by the common project that brings them together and this time unites them.

Freedom, which defines individual *praxis*, does not disappear from this common *praxis*, the first stage of the constituted dialectic. The group gives birth to freedom, to a resolution that circumstances can favour but not determine. On the one hand, scarcity contains no intrinsic intelligibility or rational necessity but is merely a contingent fact that makes history be born. On the other hand, the rebellion that tears the individual from the practico-inert, that creates the group from the series it dissolves, gives birth to human freedom. 'The essential characteristic of the group-in-fusion is the abrupt resurrection of freedom. Not that it has ever ceased to be the very condition for action and the mask that covers alienation, but we have seen that it has become, within the field of the practico-inert, the mode in which the alienated man must live his sentence in perpetuity, and ultimately, it is the only way he had to discover the necessity of his alienation and his powerlessness. The irruption of rebellion as the liquidation of the collective does not *directly* remove the sources of alienation laid bare by freedom, nor does it remove freedom suffered as powerlessness; a concatenation of historical circumstances, an explicit change of the situation, a risk of death, violence is needed. The silk-weavers are not united *against alienation and exploitation*: they are fighting to change the constant decline of salaries, that is to say, in short, to preserve the *status quo* . . . But against the common danger freedom tears itself away from alienation and affirms itself as common and effective action. Now, it is precisely this characteristic of freedom that brings into being in each third person an apprehension of the Other (the former Other) as *the same*. Freedom is my particularity at the same time as it is my ubiquity. In the Other, who acts *with me*, my freedom can only be recognized as *the same*, that is, as singularity and ubiquity' (pp. 425–6).

The analysis of the group is pursued at length because Sartre as usual, wishes to bring to light simultaneously the *ontological*, *epistemological*, and *ethical* structure of the group, the decisive stage of the critical experience. The *ontological structure* includes the relation between individual *praxis* and other *praxes* within the two cases of the practico-inert (or the *series*) and the community (or the *group*). The *epistemological structure* shows that only dialectical Reason grasps the totalizing dialectic; the opposition between the totalization in action and the object totalized remains (in fact the *group* is not *my* object; it is the communal structure of my action). Within the *ethical structure*, freedom tears itself away from alienation in and by means of the common project, the group-in-fusion, the rebellion.

Let us stop for a moment here. Freedom tears itself away from alienating passivity, or alienation within passivity, only by action. Action, in turn, only comes to the fore when there is an external threat or aggression, and thus is actualized by rebellion and struggle. The group begins to exist by discovering an enemy for itself. Even at the time of *Being and Nothingness*, the ethics that Sartre wished to write, but which he has provisionally abandoned, was turning into a politics.[2] What lesson can be learned

[2] According to Contat and Rybalka, *Les Écrits de Sartre* (Paris: Gallimard,

from ethics become politics or from politics become the condition for, if not equivalent to, ethics? Incontestably, it is a lesson of activism, and perhaps a lesson of violence. Since man is alienated within the practico-inert, which resembles the daily life of each of us, humanity begins with rebellion. Goetz attains his humanity at the end of *The Devil and the Good Lord* by killing two of his brethren. The theory of the group contains a kind of foundation or transcendental deduction of a philosophy of violence at the same time as the class-struggle in the Marxist sense.[3]

Why does the revolutionary crowd that captured the Bastille appear to Sartre as a rupture with passivity and the dawn of humanity? Because, for the first time, individuals escaped from the passivity of their *collective being*. So long as they accept their condition, they freely make themselves what the crystallization of former practice made them. With rebellion they transcend both their being and their solitude. They act in common and form the first group, the fighting group, which is first in the order of the critical experience, but is essentially first as well. The terms *action, violence, and fighting* if not exactly interchangeable do, it seems to me, irresistibly call upon one another. Common action or constituted *praxis* surges forth in reply to an experienced threat; it is only achieved in fighting against an equally active externality and so inexorably involves violence, only this time it is not passive violence inscribed upon the practico-inert, but active violence that becomes self-conscious by discovering the violence it suffers rather than by discovering the impossibility of living an impossible life.

In addition, the constituted dialectic is developed in successive moments that are comparable to the successive moments of the practico-inert (or the passage from dialectic to antidialectic). It seems to me that Sartre distinguishes four principal moments: first is the *oath*, which creates the situation of terror-brotherhood; then comes the *organization*, which marks the first stage of the formation of the group-in-fusion; the organization hardens

1970), pp. 425 and 735, Sartre will write this ethics after his book on Flaubert.

[3] Certainly Marxism is *not* a philosophy of violence. The question is whether by basing Marxism upon *humanity achieved by rebellion and the oath* Sartre does not end up with a philosophy of violence.

into an *institution*; the instituion first arises as *authority*, and later becomes *hetero-conditioning* and *bureaucracy*.

The group-in-fusion, the revolutionary apocalypse, the storming of the Bastille, represent, so to speak, the perfect moment, the ideal type of freedom being achieved with others: no leader, no organization, 'a practical, non-substantial "we", a free ubiquity of me as an internalized multiplicity' (p. 420). 'In the Other who act *with me*, my freedom can only be recognized as *the same* as his, which is to say, as both particularity and ubiquity' (p. 426). As violence against the outside enemy and hope against the violence materialized within the practico-inert, the revolutionary crowd symbolizes the effort of humanity to overcome the past of crystallized practices and to refuse to suffer bondage to seriality and materiality.

Perfect moments do not last.[4] The ubiquity of the group in each individual, and of the common project in all, the total absence of leaders and organization mark the utmost limit of fusion, the first but transient term of the constituted dialectic. In order that the group continue to exist, it must fear its own dissolution at the same time as it fears its enemies. I have freely joined the group, I am part of it, I have acted with it and in it. But if I am to keep my freedom whole, I may not be able to guarantee it in spite of myself. Sartrean freedom, like Cartesian freedom, never fetters itself; at each instant everything is at stake. Even then, when I freely decide to choose my side, my companions, and a cause. I must fear the future. Or, if you prefer, I cannot be sure that I will act tomorrow as I wish today that I ought to act then. My freedom obliges me to dread my own treason and prevents me from binding myself except by an oath that authorizes others to castigate me in case of desertion. I will have willed in advance the sanction that will fall upon me. It will express my *oath-bound freedom* since, being unable to determine my future, I can only bind myself by transferring to the group my sovereign freedom of self-preservation. I do so by calling upon the oath of each one as witness.

[4] The reader will recognize the 'perfect moments' as having appeared in Sartre's *Nausea* and in Merleau-Ponty's *Humanism and Terror*, tr., John O'Neill (Boston: Beacon Press, 1969). Sartre used to speak of 'perfect moments' with his classmates at the École Normale Supérieure.

It is a fraternal group because each one recognizes himself in the other and recognizes the other as the possibility of being recognized by him. But it is a terrorist fraternity since the group receives the mission to perpetuate everyone's oath and to eliminate without pity any real or potential traitors, all those whose courage flags, who will be tempted to treason, who will despair of fighting. Spontaneity creates the perfect moments of the revolutionary apocalypse; the oath prolongs the free rebellion over time. It guarantees duration to this rebellion and introduces an element of inertia into it.

The rebels keep within themselves the poison that would preserve them from their own weakness and guarantee their own faithfulness. Rather than run the risk of treason, they would freely choose death. And so the rebels tie down their freedom and consecrate their commitment by means of the oath, by an anticipated submission to the punishments that the group, which has become sovereign by the will of all and terrorist by the necessity of fighting, will itself inflict upon those who may one day refuse to obey their own will right up to its final consequences.

The first moment still leaves us at the level of the group-in-fusion. All the *praxeis* are acting together and constitute the group. 'I have freely consented to the liquidation of my person as a free constituting *praxis*, and this free consent returns to me as the free primacy of the freedom of the Other over my own freedom, which is to say, as the right of the group over my *praxis*' (p. 450). The group is neither organism nor material totality. It is devoid of positive existence and being and is only assured of itself by coercion and terror. In the absence of a sensed external danger, terror as such becomes the substitute which holds the group together and maintains the unity of individuals within the group.

Once its long-term existence is guaranteed by the terror-brotherhood, the fighting group must submit itself to a second necessity, a second movement of the critical experience of the constituted dialectic, *organization*. Within the crowd that stormed the Bastille there were neither leaders nor followers: there was no division of labour and hardly any allotment of tasks unless by accident and then for only a short time. Each in turn commands and obeys, each watches and acts, loads the cannon or shoots his gun. The group is organized with effectiveness in mind. Nevertheless, it does not fall back into the practico-inert.

The analysis of a football team in action allows us to discern the radical distinction between *collective being* and *team action*. In any group, after the lyrical illusion or the perfect moment has passed, individuals must not all do the same thing but each must do the task that will most effectively assist the common enterprise. The common enterprise does not disappear into the organization in the way that any common intention vanishes from those whose unity comes from the outside by the intermediary of a *passive being*. Such a situation would be identical with the field of the practico-inert, as in the example of the bus queue. The organization of a *group* at this moment resembles more the organization of a team: all for one and one for all. After the group-in-fusion, the team provides us with a second example of common action and egalitarian reciprocity among *praxeis* that preserves the freedom of each member.

Within the *group*-in-fusion, each individual *could* do anything. No one essentially or definitively fulfilled a defined role or a specified function. This lack of distinction gives way to a precise distribution of functions, laid down in advance for each person. The centre-halfback receives assignments that do not coincide with those of the centre-forward, the defenders know what they must do to guard the goal, and the others count on them to do it. This differentiation of individual projects remains *mediated* by the common project. The common project continues to exist because the team still has a single objective, to defeat the other team by shooting the ball into their adversaries' goal. Moreover, within the common action, the team player does not alienate his freedom. Within the fixed framework of imposed obligations, he retains a margin of autonomy, and executes and interprets what he is to do. He is a functionary in the proper sense of the term, a man with a function. He is not trapped in passivity, for his function joins him to the ensemble without degrading him to a robot. Simultaneously the two correlative notions of *right* and *duty* appear. Each has the right to demand the co-operation of the other to the precise extent that the other has the duty to furnish it. Once again the transcendental deduction lays the foundation for political concepts or discovers the authentic meaning in them.

No one may make rights and duties emerge from *praxis* or freedom. He who believes in his rights appears in *Nausea* as the swine *par excellence*. Freedom no longer can impose duties as it does within its own pure and unmotivated realm. Rights and duties *presuppose* a common project and cooperation among individuals mediated by it.

Reciprocity excludes any priority between either right or duty. What the team or the common enterprise gives me a right to, I have the duty to lay claim to, not in a legalistic spirit, but because I wish to accomplish my assignment. During a period of shortage, the man who undertakes heavy labour will receive a greater ration than the others: it is a right rather than a privilege because he needs more food in order to serve the community.

The team is made up of players in action. It never has the same shape for more than a moment, and constantly is being organized, disorganized, and reorganized again. Each player totalizes it in his consciousness. None of these fugitive totalizations is crystallized in totality since none among them benefits from a value greater than the others. The team exists only within and by means of innumerable ever-changing totalizations, where each responds to the other and where they all have the common enterprise as a mediation.

At this point an objection raises itself, as it were, of its own accord. What makes the *exigencies* of the machine different from the *duties* imposed upon team members? The machine demands a division of labour, a differentiation of jobs, and also a reciprocity of workers' *praxeis*. Each responds to the other and they all adapt themselves to each other.

The first reply will be that football players are defined by their *action* and not by their *being*. The workers bear within themselves a class-being that makes them proletarians. Each one has his own way of doing so, but they are all within the field of the practico-inert, at least when they are not tearing themselves away from passive alienation by rebellion, by the common rebellion that reinforces the oath. Granted. But the football players become professionals and so cannot avoid becoming wage-earners. In that case, they too retain their class-being within themselves and take on their professional status within a field of alienating passivity. But then again, the workers also constitute an action-team when at work: one for all and all for one.

Where does the difference between the work-gang and the working team come from? I can see two possible answers. First, the organization remains an oath-bound group. In order to prevent their inalienable freedom from being used against their present will, the members of the group have declared in advance that possible desertion is criminal, and so have recognized the legitimacy of the punishment they might receive. It is the common enterprise (which the oath, 'the beginning of humanity' (p. 453), solemnly consecrates) that preserves the characteristics of the *group* in the working football team. The second difference, therefore, is that the work-gang takes on this characteristic only when it sets itself up as an autonomous unit with a common goal, the construction of socialism, and, rather than obey the engineers and managers, discovers itself to be an oppressed and exploited class opposed to the owners.

In other words, an organized group such as the football team remains essentially different from the work-gang insofar as it expresses a common will and a free decision perpetuated by the oath, despite the differentiation of tasks. But this difference threatens to disappear progressively as the organization ossifies into an institution. If the oath was agreed to not by me but by those who preceded me, what do we find if not a Sartrean equivalent to the Rousseauean contract? Can the oath keep its integrity if it is not directed to a fighting group? Does not the work-group, like the football team, need an enemy if it is not to sink back into the practico-inert?

Can we find another answer to the objection by comparing the way that the football player and the labourer fulfil their respective functions? The former has a margin of initiative or interpretation to deal with that the latter lacks. If this line of thought is followed, Sartre meets up, curiously enough, with F. A. Hayek.[5] Hayek also distinguishes freedom from

[5] See F. A. Hayek, *The Constitution of Liberty* (London: Routledge and Kegan Paul, 1960) and my essay, 'La Définition liberale de la liberté:

non-freedom in terms of the margin of autonomy left to the individual. Where the law, the general rules, do not forbid the individual from choosing an effective combination of means, he freely determines his own action. On the other hand, a detailed and precise command makes its executor a mere arm of the director. It remains to be seen what functions within a modern system of production would tolerate freedom of interpretation.

Before moving on to the next stage of the critical experience, let us emphasize the radical heterogeneity between *organization* and *organism*, a heterogeneity that is thrown into relief by the evidence of the preceding analysis. The organization exists only by means of the multiple and diverse totalizations of its members. It does not constitute an object nor a totality in the way of a living organism. The organic conception of society once again makes the mistake of not taking individual *praxis* to be the exclusive ontological origin of all human reality. The organization is totalized within and by means of the intention of a *praxis*. It only becomes a totality by congealing into a quasi-thing, by escaping from the individual consciousnesses that make it and unmake it at each instant. It is a totality ceaselessly detotalized and retotalized.

This last remark allows us to grasp the logic of the transition to the following moment. The conflict of the individual and the collective is not resolved and cannot be. Organization has no ontological status and cannot have any. 'A double loss, to which one has agreed, is the manifestation of one's *being-in-the-group*, of being right inside it: it is to be unable either to leave or to integrate oneself in it. In other words, it is to be able neither to dissolve the group in one-self (because of sworn inertia) nor to be dissolved in it (because of its practical unity being the absolute contradiction of an ontological unity). However, the *single-being* of the group does exist: it is the sworn inertia that is *the same* in each one, which is to say, one's own freedom has become other by means of the mediation of the Other' (p. 566). 'The profound contradiction of the group, which the oath has not succeeded in resolving, is that its real unity is common *praxis* and, even more exactly, the common objectification of its

à propos du livre de F. A. Hayek, *The Constitution of Liberty*,' in my *Études politiques* (Paris: Gallimard, 1972), pp. 195–215.

praxis . . . For non-groups and for other groups (rivals, adversaries, allies, etc.) the group is an object. It is a living totality. And, as we have seen, it must interiorize this objectivity' (p. 567).

'The group is made in order to act and is unmade by doing so' (p. 573). It is organized with a view to effectiveness, but it risks being dissolved under the pressure of organizing itself. It is no longer a matter of a threat that defers eventual desertion from the fighting group by individuals who are unable to take the rigours of battle or, on the football ground, of the undisciplined star who shows off rather than contributes to the success of everybody. A more subtle and more insidious danger threatens the team, the petrification of the organization into an institution, and of the genuine functionary into a man of the institution and into an institutionalized man. How does this conversion or, better, this fall, operate or threaten to operate? In ordinary language we say that the functionary behaves like a man of the institution from the moment when he no longer expresses his own self by fulfilling his function. He no longer achieves what is essential in himself but substitutes, so to speak, the conditioning of others. Here we have already returned to the practico-inert. Certain practices necessary for the organization are given the status of practico-inert. From now on, common *praxis* is imposed upon individual *praxis*. Individual *praxis* takes common *praxis* upon itself, but only by submitting to it. Or again: from the active passivity of the oath, we slide towards the passive activity revealed in our analysis of the practico-inert. 'We have seen active passivity as the regular product of sworn inertia and as the condition of common activity. And we have also seen the experience of passive activity within the practico-inert field as the result of alienation. The institution within a declining group must be considered as the *transition* from one to the other' (p. 583).

Active passivity: the individual makes himself passive by means of activity. He freely decides to restrain his own freedom and to punish in advance or to instruct others to punish all violations of his oath. Passive activity: the worker is alienated but he keeps his freedom by taking his alienated condition upon himself in one way or another. The worker is situated within serial powerlessness that removes not his individual freedom but his freedom to transcend his bondage. The institution marks the moment when the active passivity of the oath turns into the passive activity of the individual trapped within the practico-inert and condemned to live freely his slavery. Again, the purge shows clearly the terror-brotherhood, but, 'within the purged Convention, the "collective" appears from below as the impossibility for the group to be subject (contrary to what Durkheim thought), and the extent of its reality is in direct proportion to this same impossibility. Because of this, it will have its own structures, its own laws and its own rigidity.' (p. 577).

The institution is going to uncover for us two other concepts essential for political order, *authority* and *sovereignty*. Within the group-in-fusion, everyone takes turns giving orders. The leader is here or there, he or I. He is picked out by others rather than himself since he commands only because he is recognized as leader by others. The common objective that animates all the members of the group-in-fusion makes each one of them a (possible) third-man regulator between me and anyone else. But organization has apportioned the jobs so as to ensure effective action against the enemy or with a view to the common enterprise. Before the organization, the oath had guaranteed the continuation of the revolutionary apocalypse. The oath gives a common being to the organization and prevents it from getting lost in the practico-inert even when the organization ossifies into an institution. The institution, which reinforces the advantages of the organization, also increases its dangers, namely the growing alterity among members of the group. The more individuals are differentiated, the more they forget their oath in order to restrict themselves to the performance of their function, and the more they need a special 'agency' to maintain the group and be responsible for giving orders. Such an 'agency' does not successively pass from one member to another, as in the group-in-fusion, but belongs permanently to a specialized institution. Before reaching that point, however, let us reflect upon the nature of sovereignty within the Sartrean philosophy of freedom.

Free *praxis* constitutes the equivalent to the *state of nature* of the classical seventeenth-century philosophers. In the state of nature or at the level of individual *praxeis*, sovereignty, authority, and power cannot exist and, on the whole, no one legitimately possesses more than anyone else. The seventeenth-century philosophers allowed for natural inequality of individual abilities, while Sartre starts off from the essential equality of freedoms. He agrees with them, however, in attributing to each individual the same sovereignty as to another. 'Man *is sovereign*. And, to the extent that the material field is also a social field, the sovereignty of the individual is extended without limits over all individuals. These material organisms, these individuals, must be unified as his means within the whole field of his sovereign action. The only limitation to the sovereignty of a man over all Others is simple reciprocity, which is to say, the entire sovereignty of each and everyone over him. This primitive relationship, when it is lived outside all institutions, reappears to constitute every man as an absolute for any other man . . .' (p. 588). If it is agreed to assimilate the (Sartrean) *institution* with the *civil society* of the seventeenth-century philosophers, the primitive relations of *praxeis* become equivalent to the relation of men within the state of nature.

Then where does sovereignty, authority, and power come from? From the group and thus from the oath. It is by means of the oath that *praxis* is freely tied down. It is with a view to being victorious that the group is organized. It is in order to compensate for this forgotten oath, and a weakening of the common being that the organization is petrified into an institution. And finally, it is in order to prevent dissolution into seriality that authority bursts forth and is justified. '*Authority* only is manifest in its complete development at the level of institutions; institutions, that is, the rebirth of seriality and powerlessness, are necessary in order to consecrate Power and assure it the right of permanence' (p. 587). Authority rests on inertia and seriality to the extent that it constitutes the sole common weapon effective against factors of dispersion.

How does the absolute sovereignty of individual *praxis* accord with the authority of a specialized agency, namely, the authority of a leader over the whole group? Strictly speaking, the sovereignty of the leader remains a quasi-sovereignty since the sovereignty of *praxis*, which is inseparable from freedom, never disappears. But by means of the oath, by means of freedom-terror, each individual submits himself to the authority of the group and to the power it exercises over its members. The sovereignty of Power and its authority results simply from the anchoring of quasi-sovereignty in an institution and a leader. By the oath I have alienated my sovereignty for the benefit of the group in the same way that Rousseau alienated it by the *Contract*. Alienation within the terror-brotherhood threatens to establish a philosophy of violence, just as alienation by the contract threatens to establish a philosophy of democracy, eventually a totalitarian democracy.

The end of successively circulating quasi-sovereignties and the incarnation of quasi-sovereignty in one man arises from the threat of seriality and dispersion. Sovereignty 'is the institutional re-internalization of the externality of institutions or, to the extent that institutions are reifying mediations between men made passive, it is the institution *of one man* as the mediation among institutions' (p. 595). Or again: 'The institutional group, or constituted reason, the counterfeit dialectic already divided by seriality, is grasped within the practical unity of the sovereign as constituting reason' (p. 596). At the same time, this quasi-sovereignty arrogates an absolute power to itself in order to fight against dispersion. It treats members of the group (must we still speak of a group?) as objects and employs force legitimately. It would be better to say that it defines itself as integrative force. 'In this sense, force is at once the right and the duty of authority: it is the concentration of Terror in a single man as the struggle against seriality' (pp. 602–3).

This theory of sovereignty brings us to a theory of the State, which belongs 'to the category of groups institutionalized as specified sovereignty' (p. 612). Among these groups, the State has the job of manipulating inert serialities. Within a given society, which is composed inextricably of groups and series, the State is neither legitimate or illegitimate: it *is*. I obey because I cannot do otherwise, which is what confers a serial pseudo-legitimacy on the State. It would only be legitimate if I recognized myself in it. The third man who cannot be overcome, the leader, exercises a legitimate quasi-sovereignty from the moment he exercises it within the group, aims at a common goal, and unites individuals within a common enterprise that remains their own. On the other hand, from the moment that group falls apart or that groups and series are mixed together, the State or the institutionalized group has lost its legitimacy, which only the original oath, lived within the group, can confer upon it.

By way of this digression, Sartre gets back to a Marxist theory of the State, which holds it to be a 'mediation between conflicts internal to the ruling class, insofar as these conflicts threaten to weaken the ruling class *vis-à-vis* the classes they rule. It incarnates and realizes the general interest of the ruling class over and above any particular antagonisms and conflicts of interest. The ruling class *produces its own State*' (p. 611). The State, as we know, does not possess the sovereignty peculiar to the revolutionary group. For, the sole genuine sovereignty (or legitimacy of authority), has its origin in freedom and thus in common *praxis* and the oath. From the perspective of the critical experience that we have attained, the institutionalized group that is the State responds to the needs created by the threat of dispersal. It acts upon seriality by domination, it manipulates the series, and it inserts itself as an alienating *praxis* into the practico-inert.

The ruling class need the State. They need it even if the State attains some autonomy with respect to the ruling class and in this way obtains the passive acceptance of the State on the part of the oppressed. *It thinks of itself* 'as the nation itself, and it tends to become, as the institutionalized and sovereign group, the inventor of objects common to everyone and the planner of operations that allow it to reach and manipulate all the series . . .' But, for all that, it does not overcome its own contradiction: it wishes 'to carry out its policy as the means of developing the milieu of sovereignty rather than put its sovereignty to the service of a policy' (p. 613).

This Marxist-inspired theory avoids the vulgar formulae of the class State and restores some autonomy to the institutionalized group, the unifying *praxis* whose decisions are conditioned by the interests of the ruling class but, nevertheless, do not account for all State action.

Two consequences flow from this analysis: a new concept, extero-conditioning, and a comparison between the bourgeois State and the Soviet State. State *praxis* essentially consists in manipulating the series. In ordinary language this means using propaganda, advertising, spreading more or less false information, sloganeering, and so on. The institutionalized group acts. It has an objective, and this objective consists in eliciting such and such a behaviour from individuals. But in reality this behaviour amounts to each one assuming a false consciousness of freedom because it coincides with the behaviour of others. By its action, the group determines the conduct of each individual by means of the behaviour of the others, and thereby creates the fascinating illusion of totalized seriality.

A show of this kind as practised in the United States illustrates the mechanism of extero-conditioning.[6] The organizer, the manipulator of the series, informs the public of this week-end's top ten records. The announcement is enough to set off a new round of sales. A jury gives a book a Prix Goncourt and at least a hundred thousand people buy the winning book, but not because they are particularly interested in it, nor because they judge soundly. They buy it because *others* (the jury) picked it out, because others by the thousands are going to get hold of it too. The weekly top ten and the Prix Goncourt share the common trait of extero-conditioning: each individual buys because others have also decided to do so, each individual remains fascinated by the false totality of the series. The top ten records become a type-list, the illusory expression of the totalized series, just as the winning book seems to be chosen by common *praxis* when in fact each individual submits passively to the *praxis* of the manipulator, and is mediated by the series and by the fascination of the totalized series.

Advertising, as propaganda, plays upon extero-conditioning. The radio-listener will buy the popular record and feel guilty or feel that he lacks taste if he does not get it as soon as everyone else. The same is true at a higher level: the propaganda manipulator will pour out his racist advice by multiplying its signs and expressions. To each individual he will spread the image of

[6] Should we say 'extero-conditioning' (p. 613) or 'hetero-conditioning' (p. 624)?

the others' anti-Semitism and by this process will double everyone's anti-Semitism, as each individual resists less and less this passive serial movement that initiates common practice.[7]

The sovereign group, the manipulator, and the State add to the leader's hold over the series, over individuals trapped within the practico-inert. He 'increases the powerlessness of each one all the while maintaining the deceitful façade of the totalizing ceremony' (p. 623). In order to maintain and reinforce his power, he tries hard to maintain seriality and to prevent organized action, for which military parades provide a caricature. By its very perfection, organization results from the transcendent action of the sovereign, and the extero-conditioned status of everyone. The State, as such, acts by undertaking the extero-conditioning of the governed.

At once this explains how the bourgeois States sometimes appears to be less oppressive than the proletarian one. The State, a sovereign group with a specified function, does not run without a bureaucracy, without a hierarchical organization petrified into an institution. Even though at its lower levels the bureaucracy would be in contact with the masses, it may not serve as a mediation because it separates the series from *a sovereign group* that has the maintenance of the series in powerlessness and alterity as its object and political goal. 'Within the world of the Other, which is the world of government', there is no authentic communication between the *praxis* of the governed and the *praxis* of the sovereign group. The bureaucratic hierarchy becomes the diabolical universe of suspicion: 'with each degree of hierarchy, each one is a *possible* sovereignty over agents at a lower level, or each one is a *possible* third-man regulator (by taking the initiative in agitation and the formation of a group). But each one *repudiates* these possibilities, because of distrust towards his equals and fear of being suspect to his superiors' (pp. 625–6). By faithfulness to his oath he is constrained to inertia towards his equals in order to obtain the inertia of others. 'His organic individuality dissolves within him

[7] Nothing would be easier than to explain the revolutionary crowd by means of extero-conditioning, as counter-revolutionary authors have done. Sartre postulates a difference in nature between the revolutionary crowd and the non-revolutionary rioters.

as an uncontrollable factor of multiplicity; along with his peers, he melts into the organic unity of a superior caste, finding no other guarantee against his individual freedom than the free individuality of another' (p. 626). The bureaucracy marks the extreme form of the institutional petrification of the sovereign group, the total suppression of humanity save at the top of the hierarchy. The affirmation of a practical sovereignty of man over man and the concerted maintenance of the status of the practico-inert at the bottom necessarily implies the ossification of man at all levels except that of prince. The critical experience ends with the dialectical interpretation of Stalinism.

The bourgeois democratic State more easily resists this total bureaucratization. To be sure, an electoral system, whatever it is, results in the practico-inert and extero-conditioning. The State has only the legitimacy that arises from its acceptance by the masses. There cannot be less legitimacy than 'when the State is an apparatus of constraint within a society torn by class-conflict. Bureaucracy, the constant threat of the sovereign, can be more easily avoided within a bourgeois State than within a socialist society in the making; . . . within a society at a delicate point in its existence . . . when the class struggles, in all their forms are animated perpetually *against* the status of seriality (both for the oppressor *and* for the oppressed) the conduct of the sovereign will become a policy' (p. 627). Let us not forget that 'a particular contradiction opposes the sovereign group (masquerading itself as the unity of the individual and the universal) to the ruling class, which produces and sustains it (pays for it) as its own apparatus. As we have seen, the dependency of the sovereign is certain, but so too is this perpetual affirmation of autonomy at every echelon' (p. 628). Of course, Sartre immediately adds that 'these considerations do not tend to prove the superiority of the group with sovereignty in the bourgeois democracies, but to show that it sucks its life from the social contradictions that it expresses' (p. 628).

Despite this reservation, the analysis reveals Stalinism to be both the necessary result of bureaucracy and its internal contradiction; that is, it reveals the absurdity of the notion of the dictatorship of the proletariat. 'The very notion of it is absurd. It is a bastard compromise between the sovereign and active group and passive seriality' (p. 630). The sovereign group can never be constituted as a superorganism.

The sovereign group rules over the passivity of the series by means of this same passivity. 'Bureaucratic terror and the cult of personality once again show the relation of constituting dialectic to constituted dialectic; that is to say, they show the necessity for a common action as such, . . . to reflect practically on itself in order to control itself and ceaselessly to be united under the unsurpassable form of individual unity. It is *true* that Stalin was the Party and the State.' But this same truth one day precipitates an even more basic truth: 'the violent contradiction' between two dialectics, that of the constituting dialectic or individual *praxis*, and that of the constituted dialectic or common *praxis*. Constituted Reason, from the group-in-fusion to the cult of personality, derives its intelligibility from constituting Reason, or individual *praxis*. But individual *praxis* sets limits to constituted Reason. It tears itself away from the practico-inert only by rebellion, is never constituted into a quasi-organism, and, in order to act effectively, must concentrate its action in institutions and ultimately in a man, thus condemning everyone else to the bondage they had avoided during the perfect instant of the revolutionary apocalypse.

Does the dialectic find the proof of its truth in circularity? In any case, it is an immobile circularity:[8] assuming it to have been achieved, why should post-Stalinist democratization produce a quasi-mediator between the series and the groups any more than or any better than the sovereign group?

*　　*　　*

The dialectic or constituted Reason brings us back to the starting point, namely, to the constituting dialectic or constituting Reason, and we seem to have gone round in circles. But this outcome should imply a cyclical vision of history, an indefinite repetition of the same 'useless passion'. In order to free itself from the practico-inert, freedom rebels. In order to perpetuate its rebellion, it swears to be faithful to itself and binds itself by its own oath. In order to triumph over its adversaries it

[8] Sartre's second volume is to put all these universals into movement.

organizes and institutionalizes itself. In order to act, it transfers responsibility for common *praxis* to a quasi-organism. Ultimately, the revolt of everyone results in an all-powerful and free single man.

In another sense, the dialectic simply results in bringing the real history of collectives and groups to light. Constituting *praxis* and constituted *praxis* represent the abstract moments of the critical experience. It is left to us to combine these abstract moments, and in particular to do so in the case that most directly interests Sartre, class. After all, the *Critique* aims, among other things, at giving a philosophical foundation to the role of the party with respect to class. This relation is transformed into a relationship between *Being* and *praxis*.

During the preceding discussion, we have twice met the term class. First it was used when discussing passivity, whereby each individual is in his class and vice versa. The situation in which he finds himself, the conditioning by worked-upon matter and seriality, determine the proletarian as much as his own free acceptance of his condition, a freedom that, apart from rebellion, does not break away from the bondage of his social being. During the second dialectical movement, the group appeared. Now, the group differs from class-being, as the *praxis* of passivity, just as the unity of action differs from the unity of dispersal. As the proletariat finds itself ranged against the aggression it suffers and against the owners who exploit it, it becomes a common will and organizes itself to resist and fight. But the *group* takes to distinct forms depending upon whether it is the beginning or the end of the constituted dialectic. 'The trade-union *is* the *objectified, externalized, institutionalized* and sometimes *bureaucratized* working class, but is unrecognizable in its own eyes and comes to fruition as a pure and practical schema of union' (p. 646). Let us take the copula, is, in its full meaning. The trade union *is* the working class. It does not represent it; it incarnates it. Representation and elections bring us back to the series and thus to the practico-inert. But the trade union *is* the working class as Stalin *was* the Party. The trade union has already passed through the stages of the constituted dialectic long after the initial and decisive moment that constituted it as radically other than the serial and passive class-being. In other words, the trade union remains the working class to the extent that it keeps within itself the common *praxis* that, at the moment of rebellion or the group-in-fusion, achieved the union of individual *praxeis* towards a single objective.

Between class-being, the more or less common condition of workers in dispersion, and the trade union, the objectification of the schema of action, there always continues to exist, at least *in posse*, the fighting group, workers united against their oppression and their oppressors in a common *praxis*, prior to any organization and outside any institution. 'We therefore will be led, as a synchronic determination, to consider the working class, at such a moment in the historical process, as a group within an institutionalized organization (the "cadres"), as a grouping-in-fusion, or as an oath-bound grouping (the constitution of the soviets in 1905 appears to be intermediate between the oath-bound group and the organized group) and *at the same time*, as still inert seriality (within certain sectors) but deeply penetrated by the negative unity of oath-bound groupings' (p. 647).

In some respects, this triple reality of class tells us nothing that earlier experience has not already made known to us: proletarian *exis* or class-being is present in each individual, as each individual is found in it. There is the *fighting-group*, common *praxis* with its primitive *élan* in the group-in-fusion, and there is the *trade union*, or objectified and institutionalized *praxis*, which remains the incarnation of the working class to the extent that it keeps within itself something of the common *praxis* or of the oath that perpetuates the revolutionary apocalypse. It is enough for us to add that there is no temporal priority of *exis* or *praxis*, of class-being or of the fighting group, and we are left only to put these three terms into their dialectical relationship. The fighting-group is always threatened by organizational or institutional degeneration at the same time as by serial dispersion. The trade union is also threatened by petrification that would transform it into a sovereign group and radically separate it either from the workers within the practico-inert or from authentic individuals the moment they assume and achieve their humanity by breaking out of their slavery. Of the three terms, the fighting group benefits from a kind of privilege, for it is produced and defined as a *mode of existence*, a 'free environment of free human relations'; 'on the basis of the oath', it produces 'man as a free common individual'; it is '*the absolute goal* as pure freedom that frees men from alterity' (p. 639). The group-in-fusion is the fundamental form and guarantee of any oath-bound group (p. 642). Nothing in these analyses deflects us from the second dialectical movement, which, with the revolutionary apocalypse, establishes the beginning of humanity in rebellion and the oath, that is, in common *praxis*.

But the dialectic of these three terms introduces a relatively new concept, that of the common field, which is not to be confused with the practico-inert and which leads us, in turn, towards another concept, that of the *praxis-process*. The common field is reduced neither to the practico-inert nor to *praxis* but it permanently includes a double dialectic. By the first, the constituting dialectic turns itself into anti-dialectic, and by the second, *praxis* tears itself away from the practico-inert and risks declining into a petrified institution. At the same time, on the common field appears a *social reality* that is neither *exis* nor *praxis*. *Praxis-process* is intermediate between the two and participates in them both. It is the class itself as the dialectic of *being, group*, and *institution*. 'The working class is neither pure pugnaciousness, nor pure passive dispersion, nor a pure institutionalized machine. It is a complex and mobile relation among different practical shapes, each of which sums it up completely, and each of whose genuine bonds is totalization (as a movement leads by each one in the others and returns from each one toward the others)' (p. 652).

According to the body of doctrine from the *Critique* (but not according to the party), this analysis establishes the primacy of the group. For, after a fashion, the party does reproduce in itself the dialectic of the fighting group and the institution, even though Sartre takes the trade union and its 'staff', its permanent bureaucracy, as his examples of the institution and the sovereign. The soviets and not the Stalinized party are defined as the fighting group. 'The group defines the struggles it will participate in and its own exigencies: it discovers itself to have a certain internal "temperature" with respect to its own serial external being. It is the class that suffers, but more exactly, and more importantly, it is the class that fights. In it the class that suffers has been overcome towards the fighting union. It discovers the fighting union as a serial totality to the very extent that the group totalizes itself by means of the dissolution of seriality' (p. 653). The group, within which *praxeis* are unified into a common will, is formed on the basis of the dispersion of the workers. The workers find their unity within the group, which finds in them a multiplicity that is threatening to it. Some workers at each moment risk forgetting the struggle and their common objective and falling back into passivity by being satisfied with what they can obtain *hic et nunc*, each for himself with no consideration of the whole.

Where is Sartre heading? Towards the understanding of plurality–unity, of immanence–transcendence, of class action that sometimes appears as the revolutionary apocalypse and sometimes as trade-union sovereignty and that, *qua* action, is defined only by the negation of seriality or the passive being of workers trapped within the practico-inert. Fighting groups, trade unions, or parties, and non-oath-bound workers (workers who have not sworn fidelity to the fighting group), each constitutes the working class. But they also constitute it by their own internal dialectic. Now, the contradiction between the group-in-fusion and trade-union sovereignty cannot avoid being raised at one time or another. The trade-union perceives the group as 'a particular determination of class (and thus as limitation and finitude)'. Meanwhile, 'the group-in-fusion sends union sovereignty on holiday' (p. 655). The apocalypse-class becomes self-conscious as a fighting group and rejects the institution of the trade union or the party as petrification and seriality. The rigidity of the institution seems to be as treasonable as the dispersion of passive workers.

This dialectic, internal to the class or constitutive of it, remains intelligible, but it raises questions. The understanding of individual *praxis* and of common *praxis* sends us back to a subject: the actualization of this understanding takes place on the basis of a project of a subject. When *praxis* is constituted by the dialectic of seriality, group, and institution, where do we find the subject? Where is the project? And how could understanding grasp the unity of this project? Working-class action can end up with a result that responds to no one's project. At the same time, the positivist point of view acquires its truth. It is that 'the negative limit of constituted dialectical Reason, just as, in fact, (in, moreover, numerous but rigorously defined cases) the objective process, considered at one level of History and from beginning to end, appears in itself to be the non-dialectical result of an internal dialectic that is destroying itself' (p. 659).

Outside this hypothesis, which would mean the end of the total process of understanding, the dialectic of the three terms, which reciprocally determine seriality, the revolutionary apocalypse, and the institution, constitutes the working class as an on-going but incomplete totalization. 'Action is controlled in the sense that, for example, the series (as a national collective) is arbiter and mediation in the conflicts between local leaders and "spontaneously" formed groups: that means that final action (whether it be organized *praxis* or apparently non-understandable disorder) is a three-dimensional process where each one finds its meaning within the other two' (p. 665). Evidently the situated witness of the historian manages to totalize this on-going totalization (properly speaking, a totalization without a totalizer), which is to say that he understands it.

If the three-dimensional totalizing dialectic provides an understandable or intelligible account of the nature of the working class, an account that is wholly present in each of these dimensions, then what is at issue is less a process than a *praxis*, since, by its complexity in n+1-dimensional social space, totalization eludes both the agents and the witness. The process outlines the limit of an understanding that threatens to disappear sometimes into anti-dialectic (pure seriality) and sometimes into non-dialectic (analytical Reason, juxtaposition of facts, and cause-and-effect relations).

In the case of *praxis-process*, the absence of a subject would allow a lack, an emptiness in the unfolding of dialectical experience to subsist, if there did not appear another solution to the problem of the subject, a principle of the intelligibility of class other than the three-dimensional dialectic: this other principle is the enemy. The intelligibility of class derives from the class struggle, but inversely, the class is constituted by *praxis* out of its dispersion and into the multiplicity of its dimensions with a view towards struggle, because it finds another, oppressive, and exploiting class opposed to it, namely the bourgeoisie.

An analysis of the bourgeoisie and the trinitarian dialectic of totalization should help us here in the analysis of the working class—with, it seems to me, one essential difference.

The bourgeoisie has a class-being within seriality, as has the working class. The bourgeois live their being in dispersion. Each one has his-being-outside-of-himself and others make him what he is. At once the same and other, they discover their alterity by discovering the similarity of their condition, which is to be condemned to competition and to rivalry, enclosing each one in a constraining and solitary *praxis*. It is represented by the State, the equivalent to the sovereign institutions of the working class, rather than by organizations of employers

What is missing, because the bourgeoisie have neither the number nor the will to transcend the reality that creates the apocalypse of the group-in-fusion, is the fighting group and its spontaneity. The bourgeoisie live within seriality or in dispersion within the petrification of the sovereign institution. It deals with the masses or it manipulates them, but by using extero-conditioning. It sets fascist groups or the 'forces of order' into motion.

The bourgeoisie have no less a practice than the working class: it too *is* a *praxis*, but only by its relationship to the working class. Bourgeoisie and proletariat only exist as classes or are constituted as *praxeis* against each other. As a collective, the bourgeoisie are dispersed within seriality in the same way as the working class are. As a sovereign group, it has its being outside itself in the State while the working-class being is in the trade union or the party. The bourgeoisie can only turn itself into a fighting group against the workers' passivity or against the revolutionary apocalypse. Bourgeoisie-*praxis* is a will for oppression before being a process of exploitation.

Accidentally Sartre has stumbled upon the controversy between Eugen Dühring and Fr. Engels over the respective priority of oppression and exploitation, of politics and economics, and of violence and surplus value. Now, from all evidence,

even though Sartre treats Dühring as an 'imbecile',[9] he turns
up on Dühring's side in the debate. He intends to refute
sociological and economic determinism in order to affirm
once more the ontological and epistemological priority of
praxis.

We already know of this priority, and we know it is finally
based on scarcity: as scarcity conditions his milieu, man is the
enemy of man. Hostility precedes exploitation. The process of
exploitation develops the meaning of the class struggle within a
common field. One meaning of the class struggle, and not the
least important one, arises, if not from new ideas, then from their
unperceived implications. The objective and material contradictions are situated on the anti-dialectical level that the
constituting dialectic slides towards and eventually turns into
(pp. 670–1). The sociological analysis of the capitalist system
thus only represents a second moment of History. On the other
hand, every analysis of colonialism in terms of the inevitable
unfolding of a process, every theory of the kind that speaks of
the '*clochardisation*'[10] that results from the meeting of two
civilizations, is said to omit what is essential, the *praxis* of the
colonialist. 'The racism that the Algerian colonialist *intends* is
the conquest of Algeria; what he imposes and produces is the
everyday policy that re-invents and actualizes it at each moment through serial alterity' (p. 672). '*All relations* between
colonialists and colonized people through the colonial system
are the actualization of the characteristics of the practico-inert
introduced and defined by common actions. Or, if you like,
they are relations that sociology and economics must resolve
within History as well' (pp. 673–4). 'The term "*clochardisation*"
and the pseudo-concept that it hides become perfectly useless:
modestly, they both seek to return us to *process*. But the only
intelligible reality, the *praxis* of men, sends them both on
holiday, and brings us back to two quite distinct kinds of
action: past action, action surpassed, and present action' (p.
674). And, in conclusion: 'thus we have shown, in the simple

[9] I wonder if he has read him.
[10] This term, which comes from the derelicts or tramps of Paris, *les
clochards*, was introduced by Miss Germaine Tillon during the days of the
Algerian war and, at the time, raised a considerable debate.

example of colonialization, that the relation of oppressors and oppressed was *a struggle* from one end to the other, and that this struggle is a double and reciprocal *praxis* that, at least up to the phase of insurrection, ensures the rigorous development of the *process* of exploitation' (p. 687).

I have used so many quotations because what is involved is a central theme of Sartrism rather than Marxism. 'I have wished to study the practice of the colonial system in order to express by a simple example the importance that there can be in re-placing by History economic and sociological interpretations, that is, in a general manner, putting in the place of History all sorts of determinisms . . . There should be no more game-playing with the precise and true words *praxis* and *struggle*, . . . which means that their significations are rendered into discourse, and *praxis* is defined as the organizing project that overcomes material conditions towards an end, a project that is impressed by labour upon inorganic matter as a reshaping of the practical field and as a unification of means with a view to attaining the end. And it is necessary that the class *struggle* is understood in its most complete sense; in other words, even when it is a matter of economic development within the same country, even when the proletariat is constituted from the most miserable levels of the peasant class, even when the worker "freely" sells his labour-power, exploitation must be inseparable from oppression just as the seriality of the bourgeois class is inseparable from the practical apparatus it provides itself with. Economic explana-tions are false because they make exploitation a certain *result*, and only a result, rather than show that such a result could neither continue nor could the process of capital be developed if they were not upheld by the *project of exploitation*' (p. 687).

Let us stop for a moment. Does such an interpretation, the subordination of exploitation to oppression, of the struggle of *classes* to *struggle*, of the process of exploitation to the project of the exploiter, and of social determinism to human wills, correspond to the authentic intention of Marxism or of Marx himself? The correspondence seems dubious to me. Marx tried to show the capitalist as the prisoner of capitalism, the incarna-tion of capital, and the accidental personification of a non-human force. Elie Halévy used to say that Marxism taught one

to detest a regime rather than men and that, in this sense, in
depersonalized the class struggle. Capitalism called forth
hatred, but not of the capitalists. Sartre reverses things. He
imputes the inhumanity that he observes in the colonial or the
capitalist regime to the projects of colonialists or capitalists.

As the critical experience progressed, Sartre has said and we
have repeated that individual *praxis* constitutes the principle
and the model of the constituting dialectic. Why does individual
praxis bring us to an historical philosophy based upon the class
struggle and violence? In *Being and Nothingness* pessimism derived from the original relation of consciousnesses, each one
objectified by the gaze of the other and by this objectification
torn away from itself and deprived of its freedom. Each for-
itself made an in-itself of the Other and thereby took his most
deeply rooted meaning from him. The *Critique* begins from
individual *praxis* and discovers the environment of scarcity
within which each *praxis* must be the enemy of the other: there
is no room, no food, and no life possible for everybody. Since
man is the enemy of man, how can history escape from a reign
of violence?

Even if this individual dialectic establishes foundations for the
reign of violence, it does not establish the intelligibility of historical processes. How can we pass from the microscopic intelligibility of individuals to the macroscopic intelligibility of the
dialectic of a common field, and the three dimensions of
seriality, group, and institution? The class struggle provides an
intermediary since each class constitutes itself by struggle into
a *praxis*-process, *praxis* against another class and process without
an individual or common project.

'Man is violent—in *all* History and up to the present day
(up to the suppression of scarcity, if it takes place, and if this
suppression is produced *under certain circumstances*)—against
anti-man (that is, against just any other man) and against *his
Brother* in so far as he has the permanent possibility of himself
becoming an anti-man. And this violence . . . is called *terror*
when it defines the very bonds of fraternity. It is called oppression when it is exercised over one or several individuals and
when, as a result of scarcity, it imposes a status upon them that
they cannot transcend' (p. 689). *Terror or oppression:* violence

of the revolutionary apocalypse so as to perpetuate the liberating project, or violence of the dominating class so as to perpetuate oppressive domination: *tertium non est*. So long as scarcity lasts, each must choose his violence, and none may choose
non-violence except by making an exit from history or by
blinding himself to his own destiny.

There is an apparently pitiless destiny in store for the 'tender
hearts' of the liberals, which is, however, indispensable for the
intelligibility of History. Either what matters in society are
social strata and serial being, in which case society is lost in a
transient seriality and an inert dispersion, and History itself
loses all intelligibility, or the relations between classes are
effectively antagonistic, and in that case, each class gives unity
to the other. The reciprocity of antagonism assures the unity of
classes by a *praxis* and at the same time, it assures the macroscopic intelligibility of History as class struggle. 'Our History is
intelligible to us because it is dialectical, and it is dialectical
because the class struggle produces us as transcending the
inertia of the collective towards dialectical fighting groups'
(p. 744).

Struggle and reciprocity within antagonism gives the unity of
a project to each class, which constitutes a dialectic of three
dimensions, seriality, group, and institution. But if these projects collide violently with each other and only impose themselves on the other by violence, why choose one rather than
another? Hobbes did not become a partisan of one side or the
other. Why prefer the violence of the terror-brotherhood that
ends up with the cult of personality to the oppressive and diffuse
violence of bourgeois democracy? But then again, we must add a
theoretical question to this moral or political one. All partial
understanding of a project and thus all understanding of totalization presupposes that the project be grasped. But, how can
the contradictory projects of the classes be totalized? How,
either in reality or in knowledge, can we imagine a totalization
without a totalizer?

Sartre gives several replies to the first question: why choose
one camp, the working class, rather than the other? Human
truth, he says, is found on the side of the victim; the look of the
unfortunate makes us conscious of our privileges by revealing

their intolerable injustice. Under the gaze of the dehumanized other, *praxis* gives to itself the object of realizing humanity in everyone and in each one. Affirmation of the evident, unarguable, and unsurpassable truth of Marxism, repeated numerous times, justifies his political choice.

In spite of all, these two motives remain extrinsic to the *Critique*. Since oppression precedes exploitation, nothing can guarantee that after the revolution the working class, incarnate in its institutional sovereign, will use violence less and respect men more. The superiority of socialism over capitalism is easily deduced from the analysis (whether it is true or false) of the relations of production within one or another regime. But since exploitation has its source in oppression, the very demonstration of the superiority of socialism over capitalism seems almost impossible.

The *Critique* contains innumerable arguments in favour of this thesis. At the end of the part dealing with Constituted Reason, the comparison between bourgeois democracy and Stalinist bureaucracy turns rather in favour of the former (pp. 627–8). The impossibility of a dictatorship of the proletariat and the in-depth identity of all institutionalized sovereign groups would urge us to condemn the revolutionary enterprise as vain, to the extent that, in order to construct socialism, it continues on into bureaucratic petrification, which in turn is only repaired by turning towards a revisionism and perhaps even a revisionism dedicated to serial democracy.

Elsewhere Sartre himself recognized another obvious fact: since alienation follows from seriality and materiality, no revolution will ever eliminate the final causes of alienation. 'To what extent will a socialist society be rid of atomism *in all its forms*? To what extent will collective objects, the signs of our alienation, be dissolved in a genuine intersubjective community, where the only real relations will be of men and among men? And to what extent will the necessity for all human society to remain a detotalized totality keep up the cycle of recurrence and escape, and consequently maintain unity-objects as limits to true unification? Must the disappearance of capitalist forms of alienation be identified with the suppression of all forms of alienation?' (p. 349 fn. 1).

While refusing to accept the innocence of any process, Sartre agrees in general with what is today a rather ordinary proposition, namely that industrialization cannot avoid costing millions of lives. 'And no doubt it will be said to us that accumulation (as a process) could not but cost millions of human lives, that it demanded the misery of the worker as a condition for social enrichment. *No doubt this is true in general*,[11] but we know that it is never entirely true in detail' (p. 738). Could not the same be said of the socialist revolution? And if it could not avoid 'the indissoluble combination of bureaucracy, terror and the cult of personality' has not Stalin gone beyond the necessity at least as much as the nineteenth-century bourgeois? Does one not imitate the bourgeois who calls the oppressed person an anti-man who 'deserves his oppression', if one denounces the Trotskyite as a traitor deserving the most severe punishment? Has not Stalin gone farther in the transfiguration of oppression than even the most self-righteous bourgeois?

Outside the Marxist analyses, which are held, by hypothesis, to be true but which are neither confirmed nor denied by the *Critique*, I see but a single valid motive for preferring the proletariat to the bourgeoisie and the terrorist violence of one to the sly violence of the other: *l'esprit de classe*, class spirit.[12] Between *exis*, a manner of being, and *praxis*, effective action, Sartre slips in *objective class spirit* as a common way for class-being to take on signification. The bourgeois all take part in the spirit of the bourgeoisie so long as they have a common will or a common *praxis*. Each individual on his own within his inert solitude internalizes the idea that makes him a member of his class. Let us not follow this analysis, which is rather subtle, and contains many pertinent remarks on *la distinction* which is at the same time the ideology and the spirit of the bourgeoisie. Let us stick to a successful and well-known formula: 'The bourgeoisie of the second half of the century adopt an attitude of laicized Puritanism toward life whose signification is immediately oppressive:

[11] Emphasis is added.
[12] We have translated Sartre's *esprit de classe* as class spirit, but as Aron makes clear here and in the following chapter, the implications range from those contained in the Gallicism, *esprit de corps* to the Hegelian *Geist*. [Tr. note].

distinction is anti-nature. The bourgeois is *distinguished* by having suppressed his needs within himself . . . Now, this *praxis* is oppressive first of all because, by means of it, the bourgeois affirm their Being-Other in comparison with the exploited . . .' (p. 717). 'I immediately see in distinction the practice invented by the heir of bourgeois wealth who wishes to affirm his right to inheritance against the exploited classes at the same time that he wishes to deny the so-called privileges of blood from the former dominant classes; . . . his right must be a desert to which he was born, and a birth that he deserved . . .' (p. 719).

On the other hand, the objective spirit of the working class marks him out for a revolutionary project. 'Now this practical *understanding* of the workers' actions by workers (however obscure it may be and however erroneous it remains) is precisely the *objective spirit* of the working class in so far as it has been invented as a measure of extreme urgency and a necessary negation of its sub-humanity . . . It is the attempt to get rid of alterity everywhere . . . He who says: "I shall do no more than the others, so as not to compel them to do more than they can, and so that an Other does not compel me to do more than I then can,"—such a person is already a master of dialectical humanism, not as a theory but as a practice . . .' (pp. 742–3).

The objective spirit of the working class is manifest as dialectical Reason in the struggle against the bourgeoisie. Reciprocity–antagonism or, in ordinary language, the class struggle, constitutes the foundation of the intelligibility of History. Perhaps in the absence of scarcity, history would be intelligible without reference to a dialectic that is mixed up with class struggle. But history that produces internalized scarcity owes its intelligibility to an action that itself unites men against other men, the oppressed against their oppressors, both being unified within the fighting group. Once more, dialectic, intelligibility, and hope are blended with the characteristics of violence.

IV

Practice-Oriented Ensembles; or, Between Marxism–Leninism and Leftism

---

To what extent does the critical experience whose development we have followed in the preceding two chapters answer the questions raised at the beginning of this study? And in particular, how has it answered the most important question: 'Under what conditions is knowledge of a *single* History possible?'

We have available only the first volume of a work that is to contain two. This volume brings us to the threshold of history but does not cross it. All authors since Hegel, both neo-Kantians and analysts, have declared the problem of historical totalization, of a true interpretation of the total movement of ideas and events, to be insoluble. Only the second volume, which will probably never be written, would allow us to judge Sartre's success or failure.

The class struggle, the last moment of the critical experience, is insufficient to establish the totalization of a *single* History, for it is a totalization without a totalizer, a totalization without absolute knowledge. This totalization without a totalizer must simultaneously give a *single* meaning and be shown to be both final and true. 'I have given the example of Malthusianism with the intention of showing the *minimum* meaning that the *class struggle* must have in order for it to be described as the motor of History (rather than say simply that this motor is found within the economic process and its objective contradictions' (p. 730). In other words, historical totalization on the basis of the class struggle presupposes that the class struggle must not only be the cause or the principal cause of the human adventure, but the cause that reveals or creates *meaning*, a cause and a reason at the same time, one could say. 'History is intelligible if the different practices that can be discovered and specified at a particular moment of historical temporalization would appear in the end as being both partial totalizings and as being joined with, and established in their very opposition and diversities by means of an intelligible totalization from which there is no appeal' (p. 754). An 'intelligible' totalization perhaps; but why 'no appeal'? How could a totalization be without appeal during the course of historical time before the final instant?

The first volume has neither established the truth of Marxism nor even the possibility of Marxism as the Truth of History. 'It is not the real history of the human race that we wish to restore; it is the *Truth of History* that we will try to establish' (p. 142). Neither this Truth nor even the possibility of such a Truth has been established. Individual consciousness, always situated within the historical field, cannot totalize History.[1] An external observer does not and cannot exist, at least not outside of God (who, for Sartre, does not exist, and who would, by his existence, do some damage to the foundations of the *Critique*, that is, to the freedom of the for-itself or *praxis*).

Let us elaborate a little upon the distinction between a *static* and a *dynamic dialectic* or, better, between a *repetitive* and a *cumulative dialectic*. Sartre makes this distinction for himself, but only in passing: 'The dialectical experience within its regressive moment can provide us with only static conditions for the possibility of a totalization, that is, of a history' (p. 155). The inverse and complementary experience must be 'the ability to show us if social contradictions and struggles, common and individual *praxis*, labour as the producer of implements and the implement as the producer of men, the rules of work and of human relations, etc., comprise the unity of an intelligible and therefore oriented totalizing movement' (*Ibid.*).

'The inverse and complementary experience' is again concealed in the mists of the future. Let us not pretend to describe it even though it could be conceived. The *Critique* tells, as a sort of philosophical novel, the odyssey of consciousness alienated

---

[1] It can have a totalizing vision of the human past, but only one among other possible visions.

within the object, and lost within the practico-inert, within materiality and seriality. Then it is torn from its slavery or, better yet, from the snares that surround and enclose it; it re-conquers itself by rebellion in order to fight against its alien-ation and finally, to win. But it loses its reasons for winning. So as not to fall under the blows of its enemies, the rebellion becomes revolution; revolution survives only by organization and then by institution; the State and the Sovereign are born or re-born from the triumphant revolution, betrayed by its triumph. Consciousness liberated by rebellion little by little falls back, by way of the intermediary of common *praxis*, into the practico-inert. The second volume must open another per-spective: Sisyphus will have pushed his rock to the top of the mountain. The rebellion will have ended in the reciprocal recognition of *praxeis* and not in the reconstitution of the series or the return fall into the practico-inert.

Is this cumulative dialectic and this happy ending to the class struggle possible? Do the necessary connections, which the critical experience is to reveal, and which, effectively, it has revealed (hence the inevitability of the cult of personality), allow us also to establish the possibility, if not the necessity, of the cumulative dialectic and the historical advent of Truth? To try to reply to these questions, let us recall that the *transcendental analysis of sociality* is what constitutes the essential part of the *Critique*.

* * *

Sartre gives numerous definitions of the critical experience: we have chosen the one that appears to be the closest to what it effectively is. The goal of the critical experience is to establish the ontological status of collectives. Such an enterprise is typically Sartrean and not at all Marxist. Paraphrasing Kant, one might say: how are collectives possible within a philosophy that in the final analysis knows but a single kind of evidence, the evidence of consciousness, a philosophy that postulates a translucid individual consciousness, which is betrayed by bad faith and which is not subordinated to an unconscious, as its model of intelligibility? Where are these collectives located? Since the for-itself, or *praxis*, or individual consciousness, remains the ultimate and exclusive principle of understanding and action, in what does the social, as such, consist? The difficulty is readily seen: the freedom that Sartre attributes to consciousness (to *his* consciousness) resembles that which Descartes granted to God. But the Cartesian God does not live in society. The Sartre-man or Sartre's man does. From *No Exit* to the *Critique* the existential theme has not changed, even though he gives it innumerable variations. It is a theme that Marx, who learned of it by meditating upon Hegel, did not long retain. According to Marx, man is ontologically social; he has not been trapped within the practico-inert but has been historically alienated within his own works. The class struggle and the revolution would open up the hope of reconciliation with his fellow-men.

The theory of *practice-oriented ensembles* or the transcendental analysis of sociality allows for two interpretations of unequal depth, the one sociological, the other properly philosophical. According to the first, the theory of practice-oriented ensembles is equivalent to a *descriptive typology of the forms of sociability*, to use the language of Georges Gurvitch, or as Sartre himself writes, of *fundamental socialities* (p. 305). This descriptive typology, which is perfectly adequate for sociology,[2] does not fulfil the project of the philosopher. He wishes to *establish its intelligibility* by clarifying it. In fact, he seeks to continue the dialectical experience that proceeds from empty consciousness, with no content other than the vertiginous absolute of freedom, to socialized consciousness. He wishes to continue a second moment as well, from socialized, and therefore trapped consciousness, to the repossession of freedom. From empty consciousness to the practico-inert, passing by way of *exigency*, *interest*, *value*, and *social-being*; from freedom within the group-in-fusion to the cult of personality, passing by way of the *oath*, *fraternity*, *terror*, *organization*, *institution*, and *Sovereign*—such are the two dialectical moments of the critical experience.

[2] 'These considerations, which ordinarily are enough for sociologists evidently cannot establish the intelligibility of fundamental *socialities*. One must get rid of vague descriptions and try to carry the dialectical experience on to that point where intelligibility *is* established' (p. 305).

Of these two interpretations, it is obvious that the author is more interested in the second one, which gives originality to his enterprise. The transcendental analysis of sociality has three functions according to this second interpretation: first to clarify the ontological status of collectives, to bring to light their reality as well as their unreality, and to recall once again that consciousness, even when trapped within the practico-inert, remains ontologically *constituting praxis, freedom, for-itself.* In the second place, it has the function of uncovering the transcendental origin of sociological and philosophical concepts such as *exigency, interest, value, fraternity, terror, organization,* etc. Finally, it has the function of clarifying the nature and tracing the limits of dialectical Reason that are only applicable to a reality that is itself dialectical.

The second function, what I have called the transcendental deduction of key concepts, has a precise signification within the framework of the Sartrean problematic. An ethics was to follow *Being and Nothingness.* Sartre, it seems, finally recognized that *Being and Nothingness* did not lead to an ethics. Perhaps he felt that an ethics was excluded by contemporary society, that within the world of alienation, no ethics save the ethics of rebellion is possible. Or, to express the same idea in other terms, the *Critique* substitutes a politics for an ethics as the sequel to the ontology of *Being and Nothingness.* Over the ages, sociality has been mixed with alienation within the practico-inert; humanity does not begin, or does not begin again except within and by means of rebellion. The ethics of Sartre has suddenly become a politics, but as this politics has rebellion as its expression, it suggests an ethics since it tends to extol revolutionary action as such. Only the reference to universality prevents this ethics–politics of rebellion from sliding into the fascist cult of violence.

Simultaneously, by means of the transcendental deduction, the consequence of the discovery of the fundamental concepts of all sociology and all politics (*interest, value, fraternity, terror*) is to disqualify, as ethical or political philosophy, theories that in principle employ one or another of these concepts. Because of the *Critique,* ethical or economic theories that use the concept of interest undergo a critique that is close to both the Kantian and the Marxian critiques. The *Critique* unmasks them and situates them: those who elaborate a theory based upon the concept of interest are not themselves conscious of expressing an alienated humanity or of conceptualizing a practice and an interpretation of practice that presupposes a consciousness already trapped within the practico-inert, a prisoner of materiality. The transcendental deduction of sociological and political concepts indirectly perpetuates the primacy of politics over ethics and establishes rebellion as the sole morally valid retort to the alienation of consciousness within sociality.

As for the third function of the transcendental analysis, it reminds us of an idea constantly implied by the exposition of the preceding chapters: Reason must be dialectical because, first of all, reality is. Ever since Vico, all those who have reflected upon history (within a certain line of thought) have in one way or another upheld a sort of kinship between the nature of reality and the mode in which reality is appropriated by consciousness. This kinship, in the case of Sartrism, unfolds with the evidence of the ontological theses of *Being and Nothingness*, which are assumed in the *Critique*. Individual *praxis* achieves the first totalization at each instant of its existence. The consciousness of the actor and that of the spectator appear as being of the same genre because each one is in turn knowing and acting, because knowledge and action are parts of the same movement. There would only be a dialectical knowledge of nature if nature as such were dialectical.

Farther on, we find once more the philosophical functions of the transcendental analysis of *sociality*. Let us now consider this analysis at a lower level, the level of those mediocrities, the sociologists, and consider sociality as a *descriptive typology of practice-oriented ensembles*. Then we shall look for the relations of this typology with the ontological status of collectives and the transcendental deduction of concepts.

The descriptive typology of practice-oriented ensembles is organized around the dichotomy series-group: at one extreme we find the bus-riders waiting in a queue in front of the Church of Saint-Germain, and at the other, the crowd drunk with its unanimous strength, the group-in-fusion that stormed the Bastille. The first example symbolizes the practico-inert, the second, rebellion and the birth of Prometheus. We also find a more complex, if less symbolic, distinction between the three terms: *class-being* as *exis* or manner of being, *institutionalized group*, for example, the trade union, and finally the *fighting group*, strikers, soviets, and eventually the party itself provided it retains something of its initiative and first activity.

The dichotomy series-group, the opposition between the inert assembly and the crowd in action manifestly has a signification of political as well as philosophical import. This dichotomy establishes the basis for the distinction between class as being and party as action, or in other words between *proletarian exis* and *communist praxis*. A class *is*, a party *does*.

Can a typology of practice-oriented ensembles that is instructive for the sociologist be dragged from this opposition, which, translated into ordinary language, suffers neither from obscurity nor from excessive subtlety? Such a question can be divided into two sub-questions: are all the ensembles that are understood in terms of the practico-inert genuinely of the same type? Does the fact that they are subsumed under the category of the practico-inert add something to our knowledge or to a strictly sociological elaboration? And, in the second place, to what extent is the radical opposition between series and group, between *exis* and *praxis* fruitful and usable? Can real ensembles be unhesitatingly assigned to one side or the other?

The category of the practico-inert, as we know, is defined philosophically, and perhaps, it must be said, ontologically, as anti-dialectic, as the alienation of *praxis* within materiality and seriality. It is a dialectical not a sociological category. This does not constitute an objection since, to be accurate, Sartre is not satisfied by descriptions that are adequate for sociologists. It remains to be seen whether the translation into technical jargon of data easily accessible to the unprejudiced observer contributes to clarity or confusion. Of course, jargon gives a touching accent to the description. The practico-inert, which differs not a bit from our ordinary world, appears to the obscure clarity of seriality and materiality as a sort of hell and, in a sense, the most infernal possible hell because those who live in it ignore their accursed plight.

Let us consider some of the practice-oriented ensembles that are part of the practico-inert: the passengers waiting for their bus, the industrial workers who are within their class as it is within them, 'a common inertia as a synthesis of multiplicity', the buyers and sellers of merchandise in the market, a radio audience, or newspaper readers, changes of opinion that sweep away hundreds of thousands, millions of individuals, the whole of the capitalist economic regime. What have we learned by following the subsumption, with frequent reference to materiality and seriality, of these diverse collectivities under the same category? What do these practice-oriented ensembles have in common that takes on a diabolical appearance in the Sartrean vision?

These ensembles all owe something to the exigencies of machines. The bus creates *exigencies* to which the passengers submit themselves. It is the same with the assembly-line workers at the Renault factory, or the radio or television set, and finally, the same obtains with the whole economic system, stuffed with machines and, as a whole, comparable to a machine, worked-upon matter. These machines retain a human imprint, and men put up with the tyranny of their own works.

The second element common to all these ensembles comes from seriality, itself an equivocal concept because it displays at least three different meanings: *passivity* (or impotence), *alterity*, and *reification* (or molecular structure). Whether you wait for a bus or turn on the radio, you put up with a wait or a listening. You are free to turn off the switch and no longer hear the voice. But, by doing this, you remain impotent because the voice you do wish to hear, that you wish to answer, continues to resound in other ears. It is intolerable and invincible since others will hear it if you turn it off. Workers in the factory, buyers in the market, and listeners to the radio put up with their impotence half-consciously, in opposition to machines that demand their ration of living labour, that force their way into living-rooms, that make consumers buy, and without which the 'economic machine' would not work.

This passivity is accompanied by alterity. The people waiting for the bus are others for one another, strangers to each other. Likewise, the scattered radio audience who are listening at the same time *together* participate in the show. Or again, alterity inevitably insinuates itself into relations among workers because each one suffers the exigency of the tyrannical machine, each one is part of a business together with others, each one is part of one hierarchical group among others, and each one is part of one sector of production among others. In his own place, at his own level, each worker becomes other than the other. The audience do the same thing and yet are not united, other than as a result of innumerable and isolated decisions that have neither been willed nor predicted. Alterity gives them their false identity: everyone is the same as a buyer and everyone is other because they ignore each other and are different in all perspectives but one. Whatever the practice-oriented ensemble, nothing is more easy to detect in it than alterity. In the *Critique*, this single concept offers multiple significations, which Sartre does not take pains to distinguish, but which do not coincide at all.

In its first and strongest sense, alterity implies that man becomes other-than-man for man. In ordinary language, a man does not recognize the humanity of his fellows: man becomes a non-man for man, the colonized for the colonialist, the worker for the bourgeois. At one extreme, all discrimination can be considered as an attenuated form of this refusal of man to recognize man. At its other extreme is found the weakest meaning of alterity: if I passively listen to the radio, I succumb to inertia, I cease to be free and creative, I become other than myself within the collective. Stronger and weaker meanings are scattered between these two poles. At each instant, inexorably, the other makes me what I am not, his look objectifies me and strips me of my own face in order to make it my-face-seen-by-the-other, he does away with my act and twists it by totalizing it within *his* experience. Perhaps, in a sense derived from its first meaning, I am condemned never to grasp my own being except as it is outside myself: having been called a Jew by my milieu, I become responsible for what *another*, also forcibly inserted within the collective *the Jews*, has been able to say or do. Within this collective, which the other has created by attributing to it an *exis*, perhaps a fictitious one, I vainly chase after a myself whom I will never catch up with. I am condemned to the labours of Sisyphus if I chose to take it upon myself, and I am a deserter if I refuse or ignore it.[3] In short, most collectives, having been constituted by a social situation—workers, colonialists—present but a fleeting unity, a totalization by means of recurrence, and, from this fact, a totalization that is never completed. The worker[4] is never this one or that one, but always an other, and another of this other, since the totalization is only stopped or is only achieved at the moment when a will, a *praxis*, will have unified these others, even within their alterity, with a view towards a project. I do not claim that this enumeration of the meanings of alterity is exhaustive; I wished only to illustrate how, as a translator or a painter, by using a few words with an ontological and moving resonance, Sartre substitutes his own disgusting, viscous, infernal world for a world given in common to mortals.

The third meaning of seriality refers to its molecular structure, or to the solitude of the individual among his fellows. Each of us remains alone as he waits for the bus, when he travels in a train-compartment with strangers, when he watches the television screen at the same time that thousands of others also watch it, when he buys bread or meat in a supermarket —the merchandise all prepared, standardized, anonymous, reflecting in advance, so to speak, the anonymity of an interchangeable buyer, an atom in a collective dubbed 'customers' or 'consumers'. 'At this level we discover that inanimate matter is not defined by the actual substance of the particles that make it up (such particles could be inert or alive, inanimate or human), but by the relations that unite them among themselves and with the universe. We can also distinguish the Nature of reification under this elementary configuration: it is not a metamorphosis of the individual into a thing, as too often one might believe; it is a necessity imposed upon members of a social group through the structures of society to maintain his

---

[3] 'In fact, the Jewish-being of each Jew, . . . the *perpetually-being-outside-of-himself-in-the-other* of members of this practico-inert grouping,' is clearly not a 'group' (p. 318).

[4] 'At this moment the *common-being-of-class* is no more, for each one, than *being-in-the-midst-of-class*. That is, in fact, the *being-elsewhere* of each one in so far as he is constituted as *Other* by the progressive series of Others and the *Being-Other* of each at his place in the series, in so far as he constitutes the Others' (p. 356).

membership in the group and through it his membership in the whole society as a kind of molecular edifice' (p. 234).

This ontological–literary description of the undisturbed social condition, or of the flattened society[5] has as its goal, we know, to introduce rebellion and the humanity of rebellion, which is to say, violence. But if we neglect for a moment the politico-philosophic finality of this description, the transfiguration of daily life, or if you prefer, the critique of daily life, what typology of these serial ensembles would a sociologist, with nothing but a phenomenological intention, sketch from these texts? I see at least four types of series or serial ensembles.

First of all is the type that Sartre uses to introduce the very notion of series: the line of passengers at the bus stop. Of course, these passengers ignore each other, each remaining alone in the midst of the others, and, once the bus is full (the pitiless necessity of scarcity!), the extra passengers will wait for the next one, and so on. Such a series is, from all evidence, part of modern daily life; as such, it presents no terrifying or infernal characteristics. Must I prefer conversation with these strangers on the bus to silence? The question has provided a theme for innumerable novelists from Jules Romains to Butor. The series, a random collection of individuals *who have nothing to do together*, scarcely constitutes a collective. It has no qualitatively distinctive name unless it appears as the symbol of an existence that is less capitalist than anonymous.

In the same way, the numerous and dispersed radio and television audience submit more or less passively to the voice that drums in their ears and the pictures that captivate their eyes. How could it happen otherwise? There may be a moral or an aesthetic critique of mass-man or tyrannical machines. This critique, stripped of its vocabulary and detached from the dialectical movement that goes from *praxis* to the *practico-inert*, does not display a great deal of originality and scarcely contains a lesson. Unless one permanently lives collective *praxis*, and thus lives the combat and the exultation of combat, the individual must accept a molecular status, which simultaneously creates the condition for *private life*.

The third serial ensemble, the market mechanisms with their

[5] Herbert Marcuse would say a one-dimensional society.

innumerable buyers and sellers, is effectively defined by seriality and molecular structure, by the separation of one act from another, and by the result, the behaviour of all, a result which no one sought. We all know the theory of the 'invisible hand'. Whether or not he adheres to liberalism, the economist must at one time or another leave individual behaviour-patterns to themselves, with the result that they will seem more or less necessary. This necessity, which arises from the absence of a project common to these atoms, as well as from the absence of a leader who, sovereign-like, manipulates the complex relations of these atoms, also contradicts the Cartesian or Sartrean freedom of each individual. When does the invisible hand offer the best solution? When does the *social mechanism*, the economy become a *human machine*, appear preferable to voluntary organization and planning? The answer will not emerge from an existential or ontological analysis.

Movements of opinion, the Great Fear, constitute another type of serial ensemble: innumerable individuals allow themselves to be swept away by a sentiment that they take part in, *passively*, so to speak, by an emotion aroused from the outside, which is progressively amplified in each one by the very fact that it involves a greater number of individuals. However, this human wave remains more passive than ever. It undergoes its own ecstasy outside itself. It is wholly absorbed by its blind fury, where beforehand it was peaceful and dispersed. Nothing provides it with an objective or orients it towards one.

Finally we come to the fifth type, which is the most interesting both for Sartre and for us, and which is the one towards which all the analyses were heading: *class-being*. The collective, the working class, is defined by an *exis* and not by a *praxis*, by a way of being and not by a doing or by a project. The consciousness of each worker is defined *qua* worker. In other words, he has within him, in one degree or another, the *exigencies*, *values*, *ideologies*, and *aspirations* more or less common to those who live the workers' condition. Is it a matter of slavery, of a fall into the practico-inert, or is it very simply a question of what sociologists describe or analyse under the name of socialization? Is it anything other than the process whereby the individual, never a universal man but always a socially particularized being, internalizes both the imperatives issued from the surrounding society and the exigencies imposed by his situation, by reactions to his situation, and to other situations in the surrounding society?

The five serial or collective assemblies that I have just enumrated do, certainly, present some similarities: looked at in a certain perspective, they all reveal an element of inertia, impotence, and individual solitude, of constraint by the machine or by the objectified work that invites a moving description of critique of mass, rationalized society, and indeed of society as such.

Description or critique express feelings that the individual feels with more or less force or frequency: the feeling of suffering the irresistible and insatiable pressure of a social mechanism created by everybody and directed by no one, the experience of the lonely crowd, the feeling of being a prisoner without being able to identify the jailer since he is mixed up with society itself. The jailer is everyone and no one, the machine and the bureaucracy; it is you and I, since together we take turns in fulfilling the roles of prisoner and jailer.

According to the circumstances, this expression, alienation, may assume a *social* or a *religious* signification. It sustains the critique of modernity, the nostalgia of narrow and warm communities, of personal relations within small circles where each is and remains irreplaceable for the other. It also occasionally transposes a religious experience into social terms: the feeling of being thrown with no reason into a universe that existed before I entered it, whose inexorable and arbitrary rules are imposed on me without my being able to escape from them, even if I wanted to, since they are instilled in me and have become my very being, which is at once me and other than me.

The Sartrean ontology, like that of Heidegger, recovers the accents and themes of religious thought, of man abandoned, knowing not where to be taken nor whence he comes nor whither he goes. But with this difference: that this non-meaning and this consciousness of non-meaning do not lead to salvation but to resolute and lucid acceptance of his condition. 'Man is a useless passion.' The bondage of *praxis*, of total freedom, within a knot of ties and collectives does not contradict the analysis of *Being and Nothingness*, although it is not to be deduced from it.

Man 'is born free', Jean-Jacques Rousseau wrote; he is free
(or better, he *is* freedom) writes Sartre. And Rousseau continued, 'everywhere he is in chains'. In Sartrean language,
everywhere he is enslaved. Why this bondage?

Of the five examples of serial assemblies that we described
above, the last one, *class-being*, answers our question. Man
'everywhere is in chains' because Sartre has chosen to interpret
the process of socialization at the transcendental level as a
process of alienation or enslavement.

At the beginning is found not *human nature*, as with Jean-
Jacques Rousseau, but *man without a nature* or, in other words,
the pure and total freedom of an empty and translucid consciousness. Now, all the men we know belong to a class, a society, a
religion. The most ordinary sociology teaches us that there are
men and not a universal man, societies and not a single society.
This is so even if biology identifies the limits and variations of
individuals who belong to the species *homo sapiens*, even if
psychologists discern the fundamental impulses always and
everywhere present in the depths of consciousness or in the unconscious, and even if ethnologists distinguish constant elements
of the human mind or the social order. Just as consciousness is
empty, so too is the origin of the transcendental analysis a freedom within emptiness by means of emptiness. (As with the
freedom of the Cartesian God, consciousness escapes even the
necessity of the True.) The filling of consciousness by social
beings (class-being, nation-being, etc.) becomes alienation or
enslavement. The fall into the practico-inert simply amounts to
an emotionally moving description of the inevitable process of
socialization.

Class-being certainly does not enter into the Aristotlean
conceptual system. Nor does genus or species: all workers do
not have the characteristics that we attribute to workers any
more than all Jews have the characteristics that an observer
attributes to them, whether he does so out of goodwill or
hostility. But this *class-being*, this *exis*, corresponds exactly to
Max Weber's concept of *ethos*, where, in a given situation, men
have internalized the imperatives and ways of thinking and
acting that derive, without absolute necessity, from the milieu
into which they were born. The collective results from the

internalization of the social by the individual. The worker is in a class because the class is in him. The Frenchman belongs to France because France has made its mark on him (it is up to the sociologist to decide if and to what extent, if any, class-being differs in nature from nation-being). In the eyes of the sociologist socialization does not signify enslavement since he knows only socialized men.

To admit of the equivalence between the practico-inert and enslavement leads inexorably to the impossibility of liberation, even though Sartre has the opposite objective in view. The warping of the analysis derives from a categorical and typically Sartrean affirmation, (p. 420): 'The free development of a *praxis* can in fact only be total or totally alienated.'[6] How could a *praxis* be developed if not on the basis of an internalized *exis* and from objective exigencies? In spite of himself, Sartre returns at times to the formula with which Marx reproached Hegel: all objectification is alienation. Let us recall a fragment of a text we have already quoted: 'Shall we return to Hegel who makes alienation a constant characteristic of objectification whatever it is? Yes and no. In fact, we must consider whether the original relation of *praxis* as totalization of materiality, which is understood as passivity, obliges man to objectify himself within a milieu not his own, and to present an inorganic totality as his own objective reality. This correspondence of internality with externality is what originally constitutes *praxis* as the relation of the organism to its material environment. And there is no doubt that man, as soon as he is no longer denoted simply in terms of the reproduction of his life, but as the ensemble of products that reproduce his life, discovers himself as *Other* within the world of objectivity. Totalized matter, an inert objectification that perpetuates itself as inertia, is, in fact, a *non-man* and even, if you like, an *anti-man*' (p. 285). Of the *yes* and the *no*, the text rather justifies the *yes*, even though, in contrast with Hegel, alienation by worked-upon matter replaces the origin and meaning of alienation as the result of all objectification.

[6] In normal language he would have had to write: 'The development of a *praxis* can only be totally free or totally alienated.' Such appears, to me at least, to be the meaning of the phrase.

All men are at once free and enslaved: free since nothing can remove from consciousness the freedom that constitutes it, and enslaved since they suffer the constraints of materiality, and of industrial and social machines. Once socialized, they bear within themselves the *exis* by which one collective defines itself and which the other transforms into an object.

Two examples hold Sartre's attention: the workers and the Jews, the first because of its political significance, the second because of its exemplary value as a limiting case. Must we say it is the same thing to be a Jew or a worker? Yes and no. There would only be a radical difference if Jewry was reduced to what others imagine it to be. If the Jew defines himself exclusively by the fact that Others call him a Jew, if my Jew-being is the result of the look that Others cast upon me, then the collective, *the Jews*, become radically original, or nearly so. To be sure, the game of mirrors between collectives is met with in all cases. Class-being also contains elements that arise from internalization by the workers themselves of judgements brought upon them by the bourgeois. Workers make themselves workers because the bourgeois see them as such. And in the same way but by reaction, the bourgeois take upon themselves or deny the attitudes that the workers or the petit-bourgeois adopt concerning them. But the situation, whether that of the worker or of the bourgeois, is objectively given, whereas the situation of the Jew results exclusively from the opinion of non-Jews. The sole-being-common-to-Jews is that which results from being considered as such by others. In fact, the Sartrean analysis in *Portrait of the Anti-Semite*[7] essentially relates to un-Judaized Jews who only accept their condition out of self-respect and without spontaneously feeling anything that distinguishes them from their fellow citizens. Religious Jews or Jews who are attached to their traditions bear within themselves a being of a quasi-nation, comparable to class-being.

I use the term quasi-nation through lack of a concept to designate adequately the condition of the Jews whose religion is inseparable from their nation but who have lived for centuries

---

[7] Sartre has, I see, recognized the inadequacy of his analysis on this point. [R.A.]. *Portrait of the Anti-Semite*, Tr., E. de Mauny (London: Secker and Warburg, 1948) [Tr. note].

in the diaspora, that is, within non-Jewish political entities. No other abstract term, such as ethnic group or religious community, provides a better description of this singular destiny of a collective without equivalent. In the end, the being-of-Jews informs individual Jews only from without, as an arbitrary designation of the milieu. It is subject to no other internalization by members of the collective, and consists in nothing other than this designation, which is more often deprecatory than commendatory.

This analysis of *exis* or *class-being*, an abstraction made with reference to the practico-inert, accepts that the analyses of sociologists themselves are essential. It has the merit of dissipating illusions of *essentialism* or of national stereotypes. We all have a tendency to transform class-being, whether proletarian or bourgeois, into things or essences, to provide them with a consistency such that the individual would be integrally determined by his participation in the collective. By inadvertence we all employ the language of national stereotypes: *the* Germans, or *the* Jews, or *the* Americans are this or that.

The *class-being* that Sartre takes as symbolic of passivity within the practico-inert represents, to my eyes, one collective among others, one expression or characteristic of the socialization of consciousness or of the individual, and no man, no consciousness, can exercise his freedom (or his *praxis*) save from a social situation, itself internalized by exigencies, imperatives and values. God alone would choose eternal values and eternal truths. Every consciousness attains an already socialized self-consciousness or, if you like, an *oath-bound* self-consciousness immersed in the practico-inert, achieved by refusal or acceptance on the basis of a collective being that it bears within itself. Or, if one prefers Sartrean language, non-thetic self-consciousness is socialized: consciousness become self-consciousness is not attained in a void but by reflection upon what it bears within itself.

Moreover, the class-being that we have analysed up to now in terms of situation, internalization of the situation, and the gaze of others that influence the consciousness that individuals have of their situation and themselves, leads within the Sartrean dialectic to another concept, that of *esprit de classe*, class spirit,

half-way between *exis* and *praxis*, between passivity and freedom: individuals—or only certain individuals?—of this collective themselves *wish* to conform to a *way of being*, and they transform their destiny into their destination. In this way Sartre
rediscovers the concept of *class spirit*, which was a classical concept in the social sciences of yesterday, if not of today. To be
sure, he does not speak of the *spirit of a nation*, and perhaps he
would reject this notion by arguing for the opposition between
the objective situation that determines class and the absence of
a situation common to all members of a nation. But it is enough
to place a nation among nations, to awaken the internalization
of certain values, of certain modes of conduct, and of a language,
in all members of the national collectivity in order to acknow-
ledge that it is in individuals as they are in it. It is all very well
for those for whom the proletariat has no fatherland to hold that
education intends to diffuse national consciousness as a govern-
mental method of mystification by which the ruling class endeavours to maintain its rule, but between the spirit of a class
and the spirit of a nation, when all is said and done, there is
only a difference of degree.[8]

Now, with the concept of the spirit of a class, Sartre provides
himself with the means to commit, with a good conscience,
the very error of essentialist thought or of national stereotypes. In fact, from the moment when class-being becomes class-
spirit, when an idea or an ideology of the collective animates
the way in which individuals live their situation and, so to
speak, passively assume it, nothing is left to limit the arbitrariness of the interpreter. Without indulging in any 'empirical'
study, and by means of a simple intuition or by his privileged
position, Sartre decrees that the bourgeois refuses humanity
to the proletariat, that he values what he isolates from common
humanity, that the objective spirit of the worker is, of course,
exactly opposed to that of the bourgeoisie, is the door to universality, etc. Let us leave these echoes of the pink library of
populism, as revised by our Marxo-existentialist, where they
belong.

What is important to us is that Sartre, by this detour, has

[8] In any case, this is true at the Sartrean level of transcendental analysis.
Empirical sociology more or less accentuates these differences.

managed to imitate those whom he denounces. The bourgeois, or the objective spirit of the bourgeois, becomes no less a carica-ture than the worker, or the spirit of the worker, as seen by the most reactionary of bourgeois. Henceforth the bourgeois is defined by the wilful and thus the conscious (having been done in bad faith) negation of the humanity of the worker. In the same way, the colonialist is defined in the eyes of the anti-colonialist by his project of oppressing and exploiting the indigenous popu-lation, by refusing him any humanity. The concept of the *project of the colonialist* transposes into existential language na-tional stereotypes or essentialist prejudices. Which colonialists take on this project? Or make it their own? Project is not philosophically equivalent to essence, but, in practice, it lends itself to the same abuse. Nothing was more striking to me when reading *Portrait of the Anti-Semite* than the increasing resemblance between the anti-Semite as seen by Sartre, and the Jew as seen by the anti-Semite. The anti-Semite, and the *colonialist* and *bourgeois* as well, defined, right to their very being, by their pro-ject or their objective spirit, ultimately turns towards us a face as disgusting as, in their own eyes, are their antagonists. Is it true that the anti-Semite is wholly revealed in his anti-Semitism? Does anti-Semitism corrupt everything in him? Or, does the colonialist attitude to the indigenous population or that of the bourgeois to the workers always amount to an ideal-typical nature that lends itself to pseudo-phenomenological description? Phenomenology used to have to pay attention to the concrete and to particularities. Now it ends up offering the best justification for caricature portraits that harden relations between collectives and between the socialized individuals who themselves suffer this hardening.

In fact, seeing that each individual takes on his own social specificity and is given the project of achieving the idea or the ideology of his collective, relations between collectives tend to take the place of relations between persons. One might say that relations between persons undergo at each instant the deforming influence of representations that the members of each collective have of the other. Peter no longer communi-cates with Paul, but Peter, conscious that he is bourgeois, does communicate with Paul the worker, in whose presence he experiences a feeling of uneasiness, of guilt, of superiority. Such appears effectively to be the social tragi-comedy, the hell created collectives, inserted in each consciousness, and crystallized as stereotypes or prejudices through which individuals judge and act. The phenomenologist transfigures whatever nuance of attitude that a majority of the collective has assimilated into their essential *project* or *class spirit*. Seeing that the members of the collective want to be different from the others, they effectively declare their own superiority, as equality within difference seems foreign to social beings, and the comedy turns into a tragedy. All differentiation becomes hierarchic. In the extreme, the superior denies the humanity of the inferior. It is enough to take the limiting case, to substitute for consciousness of superiority the refusal of humanity to the other, in order to discover the social universe of the practico-inert available for Sartre's inspection and proposed by him for ours. The hellish universe of *Being and Nothingness* has been modified by the *Critique*: objectification by the other is completed by the insertion of collectives into individual consciousness and by the objectification of collectives by each other, which results in the loss of value of both. But once in this universe that Sartre has made so hellish—by assimilating all socialization into the fall into inertia and passivity, by declaring the alternative to be either total freedom or total slavery, by confusing the will for differentiation or superiority by which each collective asserts itself as regards others, with the negation of the humanity of the other—how is man going to get out of it? Is the group going to open a way to salvation? Will the radical opposition of the series and the group be justified as a typology or as an onto-logico-existential alternative?

*   *   *

Let us take as a starting point the apparently commonplace and innocent distinction of *exis* and *praxis*, of class-being and class-*praxis*.

I bear a class-being within myself, and I recognize it objectified in the other's look and remarks. He makes me be present where I am not, he makes me responsible for what I do not do, he makes me bound to others whom I ignore. I can accept, flee, or ignore the fate that others impose upon me because they only see me as an example of a Jew or a member of the working or bourgeois class. For the Jew in an overwhelmingly non-Jewish society, rebellion constitutes neither a hope nor a possibility; there will only be the choice between running away or accepting the Jewishness that the 'discrimination' of the surrounding world imposes upon him. On the other hand, the oppressed or exploited class has the choice between *submission to inertia*— to accept the working-class collective, the dispersion and multiplicity from which class-being is constituted by an objectifying and incomplete totalization, which is to say, bondage— and *rebellion*, common action for which the group-in-fusion represents the transcendental origin and, apparently, the pure and exemplary form. Sartre appears to me to be the first philosopher in the West to have admired without any reservation the revolutionary crowd, and the head, on the tip of a pike, of the warden of an almost unused prison. He is the first to have hailed the group-in-fusion as providing the individual's access to authentic humanity.

The model of the dialectic in Sartre's eyes is not the dialogue and the relation *between* consciousnesses, but solitary consciousness, the totalization, by the gaze of what is presented to it, the unification of a field thanks to the project that brings data together with a view to a future. Free as the God of Descartes, sovereign in itself since it is only waylaid by its own bad faith and is not enslaved by the unconscious, and yet uncertain of itself since it is never what it is, since it is nothingness and absolute at the same time, consciousness or individual *praxis* only leaves its proud prison in order to lose itself, so to speak, in the crowd. The God of Descartes—the consciousness of Sartre— must resign itself to its isolation or be degraded. Before 1940, Sartre's notion of consciousness seemed to be oriented towards the first option; since existentialism became a humanism, consciousness has chosen the second. But at the same time, it has chosen the humanism of violence. If humanism begins with rebellion and fraternity-terror, it also begins with violence. A fascist philosopher would easily subscribe to this thesis of the 'beginning of humanity'.

Psychologically, the movement from for to against, from solitary consciousness to the group-in-fusion, from individual consciousness as the principle of all social reality to the crowd swept away towards a common objective by a spontaneous will, is easily explained. Sartre's admiration for the Sorbonne students' commune in May, 1968, and the admiration for the Sartrean analysis of the group-in-fusion that Epistémon feels, both find a place within the logic of the *Critique*, for it is a philosophy of revolutionary spontaneity more than of Marxism–Leninism, even though the book tries to justify them both. The justification of Marxism–Leninism only appears at the end of the Sartrean dialectic, very close to the fall back into the practico-inert.

Nevertheless, it remains true that the revolutionary crowd has the ephemeral nature of perfect instants: as a fighting group, it must be organized to win. What conditions does it keep to within the organization to safeguard the humanity it makes use of in rebellion?

It seems to me that the *Critique* gives the football team as a model of an organization that both escapes from the practico-inert and maintains the freedom of *praxis*. Each player retains a margin of initiative even though together they are all aiming at the same goal. Each freely responds to the initiative of his fellow-player, each one relies on everyone, and everyone relies on each one and yet without anyone having to alienate his autonomy for the sake of a Sovereign. If the *team* is contrasted with the *stratum*, the distinction between *exis* and *praxis* very clearly appears: the *stratum* of factory workers or middle-level employees constitutes only a way of being and does not represent a way of doing or a collective action. But, let us substitute for the *stratum* of factory workers, workers who work together in a small workshop. Must we consider them as part of a *team* or a *stratum*? They too, like the team-players, orient their work towards each other. Probably each worker has less initiative in the execution of his task than does the football player, even though the football player submits to discipline and strategy (the coach being responsible for strategy). Does the work-team in a small workshop belong to the same category as the playing-team or does it remain within the practico-inert? It seems to me to be difficult to decide simply on the basis of an analysis of organization. The work-group resembles the fighting group organized with differentiation of jobs and accentuation of organizational authority. After the revolution, the work group can neither disappear nor fundamentally change its nature, even though the philosopher must discover an essential difference between labour organized under an oppressive regime and labour organized in revolutionary fervour.

The theory of the *oath*, it seems to me, answers this problem and provides us with a principle by which the two kinds of organization can be differentiated. The *oath* holds the same place in Sartre's philosophy that the contract does in Rousseau's. It is the principle of all social order that could possibly be considered human. But this same fact is equivocal and perhaps unavailable to empirical observation. Neither the oath nor the contract as such are original or historical events. To be sure, revolutionaries and each revolutionary party, in a certain way, renews the oath of fidelity that establishes fraternity and accepts terror in advance. In this sense, each revolutionary group, each guerrilla team effectively renews the oath of fraternity on its own account. Rousseau's contract escapes experience even though every expression of national will and resistance to foreign oppression constitutes the equivalent to the contract; the will to *live* together corresponds to the will to *fight* together, and the city to the class. Between the oath and the contract, there is an essential similarity, namely the idea that society is born from an original freedom, or from a constituting *praxis*, and that the power of man over man, or rather, the very existence of collectivities in principle derives from an essential unanimity. Before the regime fixed the rules according to which some exercise an authority over all, it is necessary for everyone to have subscribed to these same rules and thus to the collectivity itself. The *we*, the creator of the free collectivity, is found by Sartre in the group-in-fusion of the revolutionary apocalypse and by Rousseau in the contract.

The opposition between the crowd that stormed the Bastille and Rousseau's popular assembly illustrates at a lower level the contrast between their memories or historical myths. The one

dreams of 1789 or of 1917, the other of popular assemblies in
the agora or the forum, of the bourgeois cities that were still
alive during the eighteenth century. At a higher level, the
opposition corresponds to that between war and peace, violence,
and law. The act that gives rise to the city, according to Rousseau, is a contract that commits all the citizens totally and
definitively; the act of birth of the group and of the eventual
free society is an oath by which each pledges his fidelity to all
and legitimates in advance the sanctions that will punish him
in the event of treason. Man before the contract possessed freedom. He cannot alienate it except by a free and therefore voluntary and peaceful act, the contract. Man before the rebellion is
trapped within the practico-inert. He cannot tear himself away
from it save by a violent rupture, rebellion. By the contract,
the citizen accepts in advance the fact that he is forced to be
free, that is, he is forced to remain faithful to the commitment
that made him a citizen. By the oath, the revolutionary submits in advance to the rigours of discipline and the purge. He
distrusts his own inalienable freedom (man *is* freedom) but,
knowing that he risks betraying his oath, he freely pledges that he
will pay the price of his treason and that he wishes to be
punished. The one ends up with the sovereignty of law and the
other with the reign of terror.

Is this a return to the opposition between Hobbes and
Rousseau, between a state of nature defined by the war of all
against all and a state of nature wherein flowers the joyous and
anarchic freedom of each individual? In a sense it surely comes
to this. Scarcity makes man enemy to man; man has no nature
and thus, as pure freedom, deserves no qualification, neither
that of good nor evil. But, as he fights against scarcity everything happens as if man was for man a wolf.[9] Apparently the
contrast continues to exist: according to Hobbes, society is
constituted by submission to the Sovereign, a submission that is
freely agreed upon by individuals who prefer obedience to the
threat of violent death. By the revolutionary oath, on the other
hand, freedom renounces itself voluntarily for the sake of
effectiveness and combat, but it does not alienate itself; not

[9] As it happens, the wolf is a badly chosen symbol since, in fact, wolves do
not kill their own kind when they overcome them.

disposing of its own future, freedom authorizes others to do so. Incontestably there is a contrast, but one easily explained since one wishes to exorcise the demon of civil war while the other wants to keep it going, in life and in glory. Yet, let us not forget that fraternity-terror ends up in the cult of personality: 'It is *true* that Stalin was the Party and the State. Or rather, that the Party and the State were Stalin' (p. 630). 'Historical experience has undeniably shown that the first moment of socialist society in the making can only be—to consider it on the still abstract level of power—the indissoluble compound of bureaucracy, Terror, and the cult of personality.' In short, the revolutionary group monopolizes *praxis* and force for itself, and is institutionalized in an ensemble of series. The absolutism of Stalin within the cult of personality cedes nothing to the absolutism of Hobbes' Sovereign.

A difference does remain: the revolutionary group, which monopolizes action, continues to incarnate the rebellion and the oath. If it no longer incarnates it, it ceases to belong to the constituting dialectic and it falls into the practico-inert. By this shift we return from Hobbes to Rousseau: a legitimate power presupposes consent, the will to live together that the contract symbolizes. In the *Critique*, it presupposes the equivalent of this contract renewed each time or, in other words, the renewal of the oath. But how is the renewal or the non-renewal of the oath to be discerned?

A legitimate order unfolds from Rousseau's contract since the citizens are unanimously committed to submit themselves to the majoritarian law. There is nothing comparable in Sartre since the procedures of formal democracy (elections and representation) are part of the serial and the practico-inert, imply heteroconditioning, and exclude the total flowering of freedom. Consequently, institutions and the revolutionary group monopolizing the State are only differentiated from despotism pure and simple by their origin (they incarnate the free and unanimous oath of the revolutionaries) and their project (if it is admitted that Stalin prolonged the revolutionary project of the group). But how to know if he was going in that direction? Strictly speaking, the persistence or non-persistence of Rousseau's contract in real institutions lends itself to an objective or rational determination: the majoritarian law and the constitution. As a legal act, the contract is prolonged by the rule of law. But, as it is the consecration of a revolutionary act, how will Sartre's oath be prolonged? Who can say if or to what extent Lenin's companions judged themselves bound by their oaths to recognize the proletariat and the party in Stalin? Even more, if 'the internal contradictions of the socialist world bring into relief, through the immense progress accomplished, the objective exigency of a debureaucratization, a decentralization, and a democratization' (p. 629), the question that immediately arises is to know how this 'democratization' will differ from Western democracy, and how it will avoid the fall into seriality and hetero-conditioning, in short, into collectives characteristic not of one social regime in particular, but of sociality as such.

Once again we have the choice between two replies: the difference continues to exist either thanks to the substitution of teams for inert collectives (but there are 'teams' in all societies, and all practice-oriented ensembles cannot assume the form of teams), or it continues by means of the persistence of the revolutionary oath even during the epoch of the cult of personality. But who can decide which? To define a regime indefinitely by the project of its founders is to commit the error that Marx imputed to bourgeois or idealist historians: to judge a man or a regime in terms of the idea he has made of himself and not in terms of real being (every reservation being made with respect to the definition of this 'real being').

To be sure, the fall back into the practico-inert does not begin with organization but with the institution. The institution appears at the same time as the crystallization of a hierarchical order that takes a distance, so to speak, with regard to individuals. How could the *organization* not slide towards the *institution* and in turn, how could the institution not slide towards the *sovereign group*, towards the State, which is neither legitimate nor illegitimate, where individuals obey because they cannot do otherwise, and where they find no recognition? The two things are one: either the *organization* necessarily becomes an *institution*, and in this case the fall back into the practico-inert obeys an inexorable dialectic of decline, or this fall can be avoided. In the first case, man does not leave the cave, does not leave his slavery. At most, he succeeds in brief sorties towards the sun of the Bastille, towards the revolutionary fête, towards the communion of battle, the ephemeral but exalting moments, the memory and emotion of which he preserves during the grey days within the practico-inert, during the long wait for the next sortie. This is a doctrine of permanent revolution in the proper sense of the word rather than that of the Trotskyites. Man does not avoid his solitude and slavery save in rebellion that is always conquered, sometimes by victory, sometimes by defeat. In the second case we should still indicate, if not define precisely, the organizations, indeed the institutions, that would represent the perpetuation of rebellion and the elimination or at least an attenuation of inertia, atomism, and seriality, which seem inseparable from a complex, diffuse, and multifarious society.

Sartrean thought oscillates between the two terms of this alternative; in its depths it is closer to the first than the second. It is forced to suggest the second so as not to move too far from Marxism–Leninism, while always recalling the first in its most heartfelt desire. 'To what extent will a socialist society be rid of atomism *in all its forms*? To what extent will collective objects, the signs of our alienation, be dissolved within a genuine intersubjective community, where the only real relations will be those of men and among men? And to what extent will the necessity for all human society to remain a detotalized totality keep up the cycle recurrence and escape, and consequently maintain unity-objects as limits to true unification? Must the disappearance of the capitalist forms of alienation be identified with the suppression of *all* forms of alienation?' (p. 349). To this last question, common sense and Sartre both reply *no*. Sartre has provided arguments irrefutable to common sense. Materiality, seriality, and inertia constitute the immediate givens of sociality and especially of modern sociality. *Praxis* develops itself with total freedom only by negating sociality, that is, in combat. Once more we arrive at a philosophy of violence.

In truth, Sartre remains much more Sartrean than Marxist in the *Critique*. By the distinction of three terms, *class-being* (the working class as *stratum*, as unity of situation, as non-totalized unity of multiplicity), *institution* (workers' trade unions), and *fighting group* (soviets), he lays the philosophical foundations of the party, establishes a basis for the organized recovery of the soviets, and endows them with a dignity that he withholds from the class and the trade union. But this distinction at the level of sociological description provides no originality compared with that to be found in Lenin or the empirical sociologists. The link between the party and the fighting group (that is, rebellion in its initial phase, the group-in-fusion) permits a philosophy of the spontaneity of the masses to combine with an indirect and reticent justification of the totalitarian party. These compromises with Marxism–Leninism do not conceal the Sartrean pessimism of *Being and Nothingness*, which, despite all his politically inspired concessions, appear throughout the *Critique*.

By pessimism I mean the fatality of alienation, a new expression of the contradiction of the for-itself and the in-itself, a contradiction unaccompanied by any resolution. 'Fundamental alienation does not come, as *Being and Nothingness* may wrongly have led us to believe, from a pre-natal choice. It comes from the univocal internal correspondence that unites man, as a practical organism, to his environment.'[10] This formula, which is obscure for the non-specialist, serves to conclude an analysis that is itself perfectly clear: 'the practical agent [man] is an organism [a living being] that transcends himself by action and that, in the objective grasping of himself discovers himself as an inanimate object, the result of an operation whether it be a statute, a machine, or his own particular self-interest . . . This inert materiality of man as the foundation of all self-consciousness is therefore an alienation of knowledge at the same time as it is a knowledge of alienation.' What revolution could bring an end to this 'fundamental alienation' resulting from the projection of *praxis* into materiality, a materiality that, as an intermediary, is the means that *praxis* is known to itself, but that is also an intermediary that knows itself alienated and acquires an alienated knowledge of itself?

*   *   *

[10] See the note on pp. 285–6 of the *Critique*.

The descriptive typology of practice-oriented ensembles has imperceptibly brought us back to the critical experience or to the transcendental analysis of sociality. Return was inevitable. As forms of sociability, series and groups appear to the sociologist as ideal types between which most ensembles are situated. But Sartre transfigures this distinction into an ontological as well as an existential alternative: passivity and action, *exis* and *praxis*, alienation and rebellion. The two ideal types direct the movement of the dialectic from *praxis* to the practico-inert, from the practico-inert to rebellion, to institutions and perhaps (or necessarily?) to the cult of personality.

Does the odyssey of consciousness and the phenomenology of practice-oriented ensembles lead *at the political level* to the communist party or to leftism? At the time when the book was published—in 1960—the transcendental deduction of the cult of personality apparently justified collaboration, *in spite of everything*, with the communist party. Sartre explicitly affirms that the *Critique* belongs to the post-Stalin period, that it would have been impossible before the denunciation of the cult of personality, but now is possible for everyone, because sclerotic Marxism, the voluntarist idealism of the communist party during the Stalinist phase, is critical of itself. By the retrospective discovery that the cult of personality had marked an inevitable phase in the socialist project, the philosopher displayed his virtuosity by placing the seal of necessity upon an absolute power whose horrors he had formerly denied and which he was now exorcising by *post hoc* interpretation.

This reading of the *Critique*, as we have seen, is not the only possible one. To be sure, within the duality of *exis* and *praxis*, the latter prevails over the former and thus, in a sense, party prevails over class. But the party as such does not always and everywhere remain *praxis*. *Praxis* is incarnated in the fighting group, which in turn coincides with the soviets and the revolutionary crowd before it is organized into a party. Compared with the trade union institution, the party apparently remains action, but it too can become debased into an institution. Instead of concentrating on the necessity of the cult of personality, nothing in the *Critique* prevents us from discovering in it the exultation of rebellion, combat, and the tireless resumption of an ever

vain project, but one that would never admit defeat without
renouncing itself and therefore man renouncing its humanity.
In short, the *Critique* lends itself to a leftist reading every bit
as much as a Marxist–Leninist reading.

Which of the two more faithfully translates the thought of
Sartre and conforms more exactly to the text? Such questions
do not evoke categorical replies. In favour of the Marxist–
Leninist interpretation one can bring up the necessity of the
Sovereign, the decisive role of the fighting group as a third
term in the dialectic of working-class *exis* and the trade-union
institution; and there is his stylistic prudence, in order to reserve a place for existentialism on the fringes of Marxism, the
unsurpassable philosophy of our time. But, on the other side,
how can we ignore the difference in tone as the critical experience slides from rebellion to the cult of personality? Humanity
begins with rebellion and the oath; within the group-in-fusion
its pure activity is expressed in a way not yet affected by inertia
or passivity. Perhaps rebellion inevitably is degraded into a
revolution and the group into an institution, but this inevitable
degradation is still alienation or the symbol of alienation.
Man *is* freedom. And it is in rebellion, in the pure act, that
this freedom is unequivocally manifest. Man ceases to be the
enemy of man when he and the other know each other as part-
ners in a common enterprise and when every other becomes
third-man mediator between two others. There is no leader
except he whom everyone spontaneously designates for a single
task, and no institution that establishes a hierarchy and reduces
praxis to function. Epistémon was not wrong to see, in the
phenomenology of the revolutionary crowd, an anticipated description of the 22nd of March movement. In 1968, Sartre
went to interview Cohn-Bendit, the leader who wished not to
be, the one-among-others, the one who, for a few moments or
a few weeks, was a third-man mediator among dozens of,
hundreds of, thousands of students, who followed him because
he expressed aloud joyfully and without reservation what they felt
or dreamed of feeling.

Must we say that Sartre has displayed his treasures of sophis-
try in order to justify[11] Marxism–Leninism, Stalin, and the

[11] Justify in the precise sense that nothing that he condemned morally

concentration camps because he was unable to see another incarnation of the revolutionary will? Has he lacked the patience to wait for leftism, the rebellion of his heart? Imitating Sartre, I would say yes and no. The 'perfect moment', the group-in-fusion, cannot last; it has the purity of lyrical illusion and leaves exalting memories that later on make other rebellions burst forth, rebellions that are also born from the impossibility of living an impossible life. Other rebellions, not the same one, for that has been lost, a victim of its enemies or of the necessity to survive. Socially, the change from organization to institution marks the fall into the practico-inert, the founding of an inert and authoritarian hierarchy and the relegation of most people to a passive *praxis* and an anonymous obedience. Humanly, the tragedy of rebellion begins immediately, at the very minute the apocalypse is achieved. Each of us casts off his freedom so as to gain some stability against it and guarantee his own faithfulness to himself. To simplify things, we have many times written that man or consciousness *is* freedom, but it must be well understood that neither man nor consciousness *are* in the way of things. Freedom either belongs to *instantaneous* consciousness or it constitutes it. What constrains me to agree to the oath is that I alone cannot answer for myself since tomorrow my *praxis* will project itself towards the future as it does today, without being bound by its present decision.

Let there be no mistake: the problem existed for Sartre before the war, the occupation, the Gestapo, and torture had given everybody the sense of consciousness worried about its own freedom. I remember a lecture by Sartre, in 1938, at one of the informal philosophical seminars hosted by Gabriel Marcel, which had precisely the theme of the oath.[12] At the time it appeared to him as a sort of self-mystification. If I wish something today, why need I swear to it? And what will be left of the oath tomorrow if I cease to wish it? In the last analysis, every oath would resemble a drunkard's promise, useless when I abstain and powerless when I am under the influence. No one

---

rather than politically led him to break with the communist party or to deny to it the status of representative of the working class and socialism.

[12] The following week I took up the same subject again and discussed Sartre's analyses.

has either an internal life, since consciousness is essentially consciousness of something, a transcendence of the given towards the future, or a unity through time, since the ego is a neomatic object, the common horizon of successive and indefinitely numbered noeses.[13] The humanism of Sartre, what, after 1945, he himself called humanism, knows neither the spiritual life (in the religious sense) nor the person. Each one is what he does and he does not know today what he will do tomorrow.

Thus, fraternity becomes terrorist not by accident but by necessity. The drunkard cannot, unless in bad faith, swear he will drink no more, nor the gambler that he will never gamble again, nor the activist that he will not betray, but by his oath he can transfer his present will to others and will the punishment that others will rightly inflict upon him since they will be carrying out the decree imposed by his present oath. Rebellion begins with the cry: liberty or death. It continues with the oath: faithfulness or death. It is my brother, my companion, who insures me against an unpredictable future and my very freedom that I will not let myself down.

How to choose between the Marxist–Leninist and the leftist interpretations? As freedom and necessity, dialectic and anti-dialectic, the group-in-fusion and fraternity-terror, the organization and the institution, and finally individual *praxis* and the cult of personality each imply the other, so too do the Marxist–Leninist and leftist interpretations of the *Critique*. Or, at least, choice would demand what the first book does not supply the cumulative dialectic and not just the static conditions of a dialectic that illustrates the myth of Sisyphus. Is it overcoming scarcity (and thus by the development of productive forces) or by the collective ownership of the instruments of production that the class struggle will totalize History completely by giving it at the same time meaning, a direction, and a conclusion?

[13] We shall see below that the existential choice gives a unity to individual destiny.

V

The Golden Age of Historical Consciousness

The *theory of practice-oriented ensembles* is an integral part of what I have called a *Marxism of understanding*. The two parts of Sartre's work together intend to criticize the Marxism–Leninism that communists employed during the Stalinist period.[1] Once again, critique has a double meaning. It is both the refutation of a gross and misrepresentative interpretation of Marxism and the dialectical foundation of Marxist theses on the basis of individual freedom (or, in other words, Sartre wants to bring to light the schemata of intelligibility that make historical materialism possible).

He wishes to integrate all the results of the social sciences with Marxism, which is held to be 'the unsurpassable philosophy of our epoch'. He also wishes to avoid the relativist outcome of the neo-Kantian critics of historical Reason, by discovering a dialectical Reason that would at once be the principle of the intelligibility in history and the advent of Truth by means of History.

* * *

'If philosophy must simultaneously be a totalization of knowledge, a method, a regulative Idea, an offensive weapon, and a community of language, if this *Weltanschauung* is also an instrument that ferments rotten societies, if this particular conception of man or of a group of men becomes the culture and sometimes the nature of a whole class, then it is quite clear that the periods of philosophical creativity are rare. Between the

[1] And that at least some of them are still using today.

seventeenth century and the twentieth, I see three such periods, which I will identify by the well-known names of the men that dominated them: there is the "moment" of Descartes and Locke, that of Kant and Hegel, and finally that of Marx. These three philosophies each in turn become the humus for every particular thought, and the horizon of all culture; they are unsurpassable so long as the historic moment of which they are the expressions has not been surpassed' (*Problem of Method*, p. 7).

This interpretation of philosophy as an expression of an historical moment derives from Hegel, but Sartre formulates it in a broad and, at the extreme, an almost ridiculous way. The Descartes–Locke 'moment' is characterized by a dialogue, as is the Kant–Hegel 'moment'. Marx and Marx alone would represent the unsurpassable philosophy of our epoch. It is an unsurpassable philosophy even though, from 1848, Marx dedicated himself to economic, historical, or sociological study, and left to Engels (who Sartre treats harshly as do most Parisian Marxists) the responsibility for properly philosophical writings.

How does Marxism 'totalize knowledge'? How does it provide a method for the sciences of nature? How can it pass for the commanding idea of Reason? As a theory of revolutionary *praxis*, it is true, Marxism continues to provide questions, concepts, and schemata for the social sciences, and a *Weltanschauung* for certain authentic revolutionaries throughout the world, as well as for a number of intellectuals. It exercises but a modest influence over the United States, which belong, it would seem, to our 'historical moment'. Even in the Soviet Union, Marxism paralyses culture rather than nourishes it. Marxism has never totalized knowledge, not in 1867, when *Capital* was published, any more than a century later. Moreover, Marxism appears to me to be less a philosophy, at any rate in the sense that the word is applied to the works of Descartes or Kant, than a way of philosophizing by negating philosophy (unless the difference between Hegel and Marx is removed, as Kojève[2] has done).

[2] Alexandre Kojève, *Introduction to the Reading of Hegel*, ed., A. Bloom, tr., J. H. Nichols, Jr. (New York: Basic Books, 1969) [Tr. note].

The affirmation of Marxism as the 'unsurpassable philosophy'[3] of our historical moment is accompanied dialectically by the affirmation of the sclerosis of Marxist theory. In fact, Sartre is aiming less at Marxism as employed by Western sociologists than at Marxist–Leninists and at them only in so far as they were expressive of the Stalinist epoch. 'Marxism is stopped. Precisely because this philosophy wants to change the world, because it is and wants to be *practical*, a genuine schism has been brought about, which rejects theory on one side and *praxis* on the other . . . The separation of theory and practice resulted in transforming the latter into an empiricism without principles and the former into a pure and rigid Knowledge . . . Marxism as the philosophic interpretation of man and history necessarily had to reflect the prejudice of planning. This fixed image of idealism and violence did an idealist violence to the facts. For years the Marxist intellectual believed he was serving his party by violating experience, by overlooking embarrassing details, by grossly simplying data and, above all, by conceptualizing an event before having studied it' (*The Problem of Method*, pp. 21–3). Sartre dubs Marxism–Leninism, which, armed with its universal and abstract schemata, knows reality before having studied it, *pseudo-philosophy* and *voluntarist idealism* (*Problem of Method*, p. 28). From it results 'one of the most astonishing characteristics of our time, that history is made without self-awareness.' But Sartre immediately adds: 'No doubt someone will say that it has always been this way. And it was true up to the second half of the last century, that is, until Marx. But what has given Marxism its strength and richness is that it has been the most radical attempt to clarify the historical process in its totality. For the last twenty years, just the opposite has happened: its shadow obscured history because it has ceased to live *with history* and tried by means of bureaucratic conservatism to reduce change to identity' (*Problem of Method*, p. 29).

Marxism, the unsurpassable philosophy of our epoch, monopolized by a bureaucracy wholly preoccupied with planning, has degenerated into a *voluntarist idealism*; it no longer

---

[3] 'Because the circumstances that engendered it have not yet disappeared' (*Problem of Method*, p. 30).

produces anything and obscures our knowledge of our own history. It aimed at allowing man to know the history he makes. In fact, nothing has changed. After Marxism as before it, history is made without being known. The principle of the regeneration of Marxism, such as Sartre suggests and undertakes in the *Critique*, is what I have called a *Marxism of understanding*, or a Marxism based upon understanding (in the Sartrean sense of the term, a sense that, at the epistemological level, does not differ fundamentally from that of Dilthey). 'Whatever discipline considered, its most elementary notions would be *incomprehensible* without the *immediate understanding* of the project that underlies them, of negativity as the basis of the project, of transcendence as existence outside-of-itself in touch with the Other-than-itself and the Other-than-man, of the surpassing as a mediation between a datum that is simply there and its practical signification, and finally, of need as the being-outside-of-itself-in-the-world on the part of a practical organism' (*Problem of Method*, p. 171). Reduced to its essentials, *The Problem of Method* appears to me to contain (1) a renewal of Marxism by integrating it into a theory of *understanding*, (2) the establishment of this theory on the basis of freedom, the project, or the act of surpassing, and yet (3) the retention of the most general propositions that are constitutive of Marxism as it is presently accepted.

What is left of Marxism as 'unsurpassable philosophy'? First of all, the idea, not demonstrated but implicit, that the proletariat represents the rising class to whom the future belongs, and that the bourgeoisie, reduced to the defensive, is and knows itself to be condemned by History. In addition there remains the even less rigorous idea 'that historical materialism provides the only valid interpretation of History' (*The Problem of Method*, p. 21). Sartre summarizes this interpretation, citing Marx, by phrases such as: 'The mode of production of material life generally dominates the development of social, political, and intellectual life' (*The Problem of Method*, p. 34). Or again: 'I have said that we accept without reservation these theses set forth by Engels in his letter to Marx: "Men make their history themselves, but within a given milieu that conditions them." However, this is not the clearest of texts, and it remains open to numerous interpretations. How are we to understand that man *makes* History if, in other respects, History makes him?' (*The Problem of Method*, p. 85).

To be sure, Sartre alludes to the contradiction between the forces and the relations of production; he even accepts without reticence the analyses of *Capital*, whose evidence overwhelms his fine temper and makes commentary unnecessary. But he uses Marxist formulae without either specifying them or even translating them into his own language.[4] One reservation however: quoting the famous text of Marx from Volume III of *Capital*, 'In fact, the reign of freedom actually begins only when labour, which is determined by necessity and expediency, ceases; thus, it is in the nature of things that it lies beyond the sphere of material production properly speaking'.[5] Sartre adds a remark that leaves the reader's mind uncertain: 'As soon as a margin of *real* freedom shall exist for everybody beyond the production of life, Marxism will have lived its span; a philosophy of freedom will take its place. But we have no means, no intellectual instrument, no concrete experience, that allows us to conceive of either this freedom or this philosophy' (*The Problem of Method*, p. 34). Does Sartrism, a philosophy of freedom, find itself in the position of being unable to provide a conception of freedom? If it is only achieved outside material production, what good is the collective ownership of the instruments of production?

Sartre accepts the Marxist schema of historical becoming (forces and relations of production, the class struggle, the proletariat, the ascending class, etc.). He declares that this schema, in the hands of the bureaucrats, ends up as voluntarism in action and as dogmatism in theory, as a metaphysical explanation of events and as an arbitrary interpretation of men and works, wedged by fiat into ensembles, imposed upon reality, and not elaborated in order to understand particular events and the whole. Even more serious, the Marxist–Leninists end up by forgetting the humanity of man or the freedom of *praxis* and, in Engels' formula, they retain only the

[4] These remarks apply to *The Problem of Method*.
[5] *Capital*, vol. III (Moscow: Foreign Languages Publishing House, 1959), p. 799; *Werke*, vol. XXV (Berlin: Dietz Verlag, 1964), p. 828 [Tr. note].

second part, the 'given milieu that conditions them' while forgetting the first, 'men make their own history'. Man, as the act of surpassing and freedom, disappears from the Marxism–Leninism that has crystallized into Stalinism.

Consequently, Sartre reintroduces into his Marxism—authentic Marxism, if you like—the *pluralism* that the neo-Kantians, Dilthey, or Weber discovered for themselves in historical reality as an immediate datum of understanding or as a necessary consequence of the equivocal and indefinite character that human reality offers to the historian or sociologist.

1. *Plurality of significations.* 'Every action and every word have an hierarchic multiplicity of significations. Within this pyramid, the lower and more general signification serves as the supporting framework for the higher and more concrete but, even though this higher one could never get outside the framework, it is impossible to deduce the higher from the lower or to dissolve the higher in the lower . . . The correct procedure is to study these concrete characteristics *on the basis* of the economic movement without ignoring their specificity' (*Problem of Method*, pp. 102–3).

2. *Irreducibility of ideological systems.* 'This example shows how wrong contemporary Marxism is to neglect the particular contents of a cultural system and to reduce it immediately to the universality of a class ideology. A cultural system is an alienated man who wishes to move beyond his alienation,but who gets entangled in alienated words; it is a conscious awareness of finding oneself made to turn aside from an intended path by means of one's own instruments, which the culture transforms into a specific *Weltanschauung*. And at the same time it is a struggle of thought against its own social instruments, an effort to direct them, to draw off their superfluity and compel them to express only the thought itself. The consequence of these contradictions is that an ideological system is an *irreducible*' (*The Problem of Method*, p. 115; emphasis added).

3. *Irreducibility of spheres of action* as well as of socio-political groups in the economic infrastructure. 'In each of these groups, the original movement is made to turn aside from its intended path by necessities of expression and action, by the objective

limitation of the field of instruments (theoretical and practical), by the survival of outdated significations, and by the ambiguity of new significations (very often, moreover, the new ones are expressed through the old). From these considerations, a task is imposed upon us: to recognize the irreducible originality of socio-political groups thus formed, and to define them in their very complexity through their incomplete development and their unintended objectification' (*Problem of Method*, p. 123). *Persons, ideological systems, socio-political groups* and their struggles retain *specificity, originality,* and *irreducibility* in this Marxism of understanding.

One concept ensures the reconciliation (in principle) of the conditioning by relations of production and the plurality of these irreducible significations: the *mediations*. 'Valéry is a petit-bourgeois intellectual, no doubt. But not every petit-bourgeois intellectual is a Valéry. The heuristic inadequacy of contemporary Marxism is contained in these two sentences' (*Problem of Method*, p. 56). To understand a particular existing individual, Valéry or Flaubert, it is necessary to reintroduce into a milieu that has been abstractly defined as bourgeois or capitalist, multiple mediations, including psychoanalysis, so as to interpret, for example, the experience of the child Flaubert, living within *this* bourgeois family, with a mother of a noble family and a father who was the son of a veterinarian (*Problem of Method*, pp. 57–8).

Ultimately, 'existentialism can only affirm the specificity of the historical *event*; it seeks to restore to the event its function and its multiple dimensions' (*Problem of Method*, p. 124). Now, for a century, 'Marxists have had the tendency not to accord it much importance'; the steam engine rather than the French Revolution was the capital event of the eighteenth century. Events have no other function in Marxism than to verify the *a priori* analyses of the situation. By criticizing this prejudice, Sartre rediscovers the traditional problematic of determinism and contingency, of the *broad sweep* of events (to use a current expression) in contrast to a succession of accidents. He deals with this problematic three times in *The Problem of Method*, and offers a solution, or a pseudo-solution, to it.

We know now that critique has brought to light the following points about contemporary Marxism: it keeps nothing of historical totalization that does not fit its own abstract frame of universality, and it rejects under the heading of chance all concrete determinations of human life. It may be that the impact of chance should be reduced to a minimum, but how? 'When we are told: "Napoleon, as an individual, was only an accident. What was necessary was the military dictatorship as the regime that liquidates the Revolution," we are hardly interested, for we have always known that' (*Problem of Method*, pp. 82–3). Was the liquidation of the Revolution by a general *necessary*? The Russian Revolution did not undergo a similar liquidation. Once it has happened the historian calls this outcome inevitable. In advance he will say it is more or less probable. But this probability of a military dictatorship does not answer the exigencies of existentialism or of a Marxism of understanding: 'What we intend to show is that *this* Napoleon was necessary, that the development of the Revolution at the same time forged the necessity of the dictatorship and the whole personality of the one who had to exercise it; it is the historical process as well that provided *General Bonaparte personally* with the preliminary powers and the occasions that allowed him— and him alone—to hasten this liquidation. In short, we are not dealing with an abstract universal, with a situation so badly defined that several Bonapartes were *possible*, but with a concrete totalization where *this* real bourgeoisie made up of real and living men was to liquidate *this* Revolution, and where *this* Revolution created its own liquidator in the person of Bonaparte in-himself and for-himself—that is to say, for these very bourgeois themselves, and in his own eyes' (*The Problem of Method*, p. 83). That the Revolution created its own liquidator, and that Bonaparte bore within him the unique world of the French Revolution is, of course, granted. That in fact it had been the occasion for him *alone* to establish the dictatorship is known to us *after the fact*. Nobody could have foreseen it in 1792. Auguste Comte thought that history would designate Hoche for this function, which was then usurped by Bonaparte. A single shot could have killed Bonaparte at the Pont d'Arcole, ('could have' signifies that the whole of historical conjecture does not exclude such a death in combat). This same conjecture, in its major factors, does not make the dictatorship of Bonaparte inevitable. If the liquidator had been Hoche rather than Napoleon, would the choice of the historical lottery of *this particular liquidator* have made any difference?

Sartre is impatient with this kind of thinking, which is typical of old-fashioned Plekhanov. Or rather, he makes light of it 'because I do not believe that Marxists have made much progress on this question' (*Problem of Method*, p. 131). 'For those men who lived, suffered and fought under the Restoration and who ultimately overthrew the throne, none of them would have been what he was or would have existed if Napoleon had not accomplished his *coup d'état*. What would become of Victor Hugo if his father were not a general in the Empire? And Musset? And Flaubert who, as we suggested, internalized the conflict between scepticism and faith? If, after this, we are told that these changes cannot modify the development of the productive forces and the relations of production during the course of the last century, it is a truism. But if this development is to be made the unique object of human history, we simply fall back into the "economism" that we wished to avoid, and Marxism becomes an "inhumanism"' (*Problem of Method*, p. 132). The proposition that Sartre takes for a truism has not even the merit of a truth. The blood-lettings of the Napoleonic wars and political regimes influenced the development of productive forces. First of all, in the absence of the Napoleonic epic, the experiences lived through by the French of the last century would have been other than what they were. Now in turn, would this epic, in the absence of the particular and unique man, Napoleon Bonaparte, have resembled what it was? This particular and unique man, this child of the Revolution, was not invulnerable to bullets. In passing from the universal and abstract skeleton to the becoming of concrete history, one does not jump from the rational to the irrational. One does, however, renounce necessity (in the sense of determinism) although one does not thereby renounce intelligibility.

Qua method, Sartre's Marxism of understanding appears to me to be closer to Dilthey or Weber than to Marx. To be sure, he acknowledges the economic analyses of *Capital*, but he makes no use of them. On the other hand, he freely uses psychoanalysis and gives himself the objective of an integral understanding of a particular existence, for example, Flaubert. Just as Dilthey, who was a biographer *par excellence*, Sartre, as I said, dreams of a homogeneity between particular existence and universal history. The former must be as totalizable as the latter. 'The locus of our critical experience is nothing other than the fundamental identity of a singular life and human history (or, from a methodological point of view, the "reciprocity of their perspectives"). In truth, the identity of these two totalizing processes is itself proved. But, precisely, experience starts from this hypothesis and each moment of the regression (and, later on, of the progression) puts it directly into question. Precisely if the ontological identity and methodological reciprocity were not discovered each time as a fact and as an intelligible and necessary Truth, the pursuit of this regression would be interrupted at each instant' (pp. 156–7). The ontological identity of a singular life and human history: such is, therefore, the initial hypothesis on the basis of which Sartre intends to establish historical materialism upon a rationality that he is pleased to call dialectical.

Existentialism also wishes to situate man in his class and the conflicts that oppose him to other classes, starting with the mode and relations of production. 'But it can approach this "situation" in terms of *existence*—that is, in terms of understanding. It makes itself the questioned and the question as a questioner; it does not, as Kierkegaard did apropos of Hegel, set up the irrational particularity of the individual in opposition to the universal Knowledge. It wishes to reintroduce the unsurpassable particularity of the human adventure into Knowledge itself and into the universality of concepts' (*Problem of Method*, pp. 175–6).

In short, the understanding of existence calls for a new rationality in order to apprehend multiple significations in their novelty and their totalization. 'The dialectical knowledge of man, according to Hegel and Marx, demands a new rationality. Because nobody has been willing to construct this rationality within experience, I state as a fact that today no one either in the East or in the West writes a sentence or speaks a word about us and our contemporaries that is not a gross error' (*Problem of*

Method, p. 111).[6] Marxism[7] as revised by Sartre is unencumbered by mechanism, positivism, or economism. It ends up not only in an understanding such as the German neo-Kantians meant, but in a new rationality for which the understanding of existence by itself would provide the model.

* * *

It seems that no one has paid much attention to the concept of dialectical Reason, to this new and original type of rationality that would lead to the regeneration of Marxism and ensure a pure meaning to the Marxist vocabulary: the orthodox Marxists are not interested because they pride themselves on science and scientificness, and neither are anti-Marxists, because they are more concerned with contents (the concrete interpretation of history) than with schemata of intelligibility or the formal structure of historical materialism. Both Sartreans and anti-Sartreans have had the same difficulty in understanding dialectical rationality, the understanding of existence by itself.

Let us give an interpretation. Sartre encounters the problematic of German historicism from a Husserlian and Cartesian theory of consciousness.

Praxis, another version of the for-itself, remains the origin of all reflection and the ontological foundation of all experience. *Praxis*, as such, is *dialectical*. Let us provisionally bracket the concept of Reason and simply note that this dialectical characteristic applies simultaneously to the lived reality and to consciousness of it. Whther it is a matter of history–reality or history–knowledge, we are right to call it *dialectical*: knowledge is dialectical because reality is also dialectical. In this sense, as I said, Sartre belongs to the descendants of Vico. We know history, the becoming of man and his works, which are other than nature, because man has made history, but not nature.

---

[6] I quote this phrase within its polemical context because it appears to me to be quite fantastic. He corrects it in a note: 'The false is death; our present ideas are false because they are dead before we are' (*Problem of Method*, p. 111, fn. 1).

[7] *See* Appendix, Note E.

In what does the dialectical nature of lived history and hence the knowledge that we obtain of it consist? As we know, Sartrean consciousness *is* freedom, project, and totalization. Freedom constitutes the essence of consciousness at least to the extent that one has the right to attribute an essence to that which perpetually escapes. To be sure, *praxis* in the *Critique* differs a little from the for-itself of *Being and Nothingness*. But, even though *praxis* tends to approximate life, it retains two dialectical attributes, change and totalization. Acting is never equivalent to an effect, which is determined from without by causes. The field encompassed by the look in order to outline an objective, along with the means available and within a given milieu, is organized by the synthetic power of *praxis*, a power which, however, allows a new organization of the field by the same *praxis* at each moment, and which is never the captive of its own prior action or of another *praxis*.

Praxis totalizes, it does not create totalities. Organic totalities exist; they are living beings of which the whole, the real organism, orders the organic elements. The work of art also exists as a totality, radically distinct from the sum of its parts, wholly present in one form or another in each part, but existing in the imagination, a *noema* of an act of imagination. In contrast, each historical action presents itself as an on-going, never finished totalization. An organization is reduced to an interrupted succession of incomplete totalizations, where every actor's individual act responds to the act of another, who is either a partner or an adversary. An institution even remains reducible in principle to the individual totalizations that make up its skeleton and assure its functioning. Each of us unifies the field in which he carves out his project, which in turn is transformed into an object within the field unified by the other. This phenomenology of consciousness, of totalizing *praxis*, defines the specificity of reality and of historical knowledge.

Where does the radical heterogeneity between the reality that sustains analytical knowledge and that which sustains dialectical knowledge come from? (We are consciously avoiding the word Reason.) The opposition of relations of *externality* to those of *internality* brings us back, it seems to me, to Descartes and the

dichotomy of the extended thing and the juxtaposition of elements in space, on the one hand, and the innovating and meaning–giving totalization of consciousness, on the other. For hundreds and hundreds of pages, I did not find any other origin
for the ontological discrimination between the analytic and the
dialectic, between the for-itself and the in-itself, between organic or human *praxis* and nature.

In fact, the distinction between the two Reasons is but a
result of this ontological discrimination. Between the for-itself
and the in-itself, between freedom and the thing, no intermediary term is even conceivable. The for-itself, having become
praxis, sometimes takes on a biological appearance (need),
sometimes a practical one (labour), and sometimes an agonal
appearance (rebellion and class struggle), but it does not
change ontologically. Negation does not figure explicitly. It
used to signify the flight of consciousness outside itself, perpetually negating itself, vainly trying to realize itself as a thing
or to make itself equal to God. *Praxis* less negates itself than it
negates the world wherein it is inserted and trapped. It tears
itself away from the world rather than from itself, it innovates
and totalizes. The resonance of the analysis changes a little but
the quest for the inaccessible characterizes *praxis* as it does
the for-itself. Each *praxis* totalizes in and by means of its
project, a provisional totalization that inevitably is defeated.
Totalization and detotalization succeed each other indefinitely
without attaining a totality, which would be incompatible with
the freedom of its projects; likewise, the for-itself never rejoins
itself to become an in-itself. If it did, it would thereby cease to
negate and thus cease to project freely towards the future, and
instead simply repose in itself. For-itself as utter negation,
praxis as totalization: these two definitions do not contradict
each other, but they are not, at the moment, equivalent. The
one puts the accent upon ontological negativity and the other
upon ontic positivity.

If, as I believe, Sartre's ontological heterogeneity is based
solely upon the epistemological opposition between analytical
knowledge and dialectical knowledge, how can he admit of the
possibility of a dialectic of nature such as that conceived
by Engels? To tell the truth, he cannot, and he keeps the

possibility open for reasons of political prudence.[8] The formal justification for this prudence is presented in the following terms. The origin of all dialectics and of all meaning is found in consciousness, even if man is an organic being. Thus, it is by turning towards consciousness and not nature that the principle and structure of dialectical relations are to be discovered. But, on another occasion, natural relations could appear dialectical. At such a moment, how can we understand there to be dialectical relations that do not derive from totalization by a *praxis*? One structure is equivalent to that of this totalization: rupture, innovation, presence of the whole in the parts and determination of the parts by the whole, negation of the negation (negation of hunger by food is the negation of an organic equilibrium). This prudential justification accords poorly with Sartrean ontology. If all intelligibility proceeds from consciousness itself, if dialectical relations are alone intelligible as such, natural relations that assume a dialectical form do not necessarily acquire an intrinsic intelligibility. The ontological heterogeneity of the for-itself and the in-itself does not agree easily with the quasi-materialism of certain passages of the *Critique*. The epistemological discrimination of two Reasons cannot overcome this ontological heterogeneity.

Praxis as totalization bears its own evidence within itself as (non-thetic) self-consciousness at the same time as its object, whereas facts, which are blind, have no intrinsic intelligibility. In this sense, dialectical evidence and the intelligibility of *praxis* are opposed to the necessity that natural sciences discover or elaborate. The antithesis (p. 159) of evidence and necessity, which is surely paradoxical,[9] is logically inserted into the Sartrean system: the project of *praxis* itself had its own evidence. The determination of effect by cause and of mathematical relations among variables turn out to be necessary, but, as with facts at the level of the in-itself, they are without internal intelligibility or evidence.

The paradoxical character of this system or vocabulary does

---

[8] Perhaps his prudence is philosophical before it is political, for the status of a phenomenological ontology perhaps appears equivocal when viewed in the light of Marxism.

[9] *See* Appendix, Note F.

not last long. Let us admit the ontological heterogeneity of the for-itself and the in-itself, or *praxis* and materiality. Let us even admit that social realities are in principle reducible to acts of consciousness and that the anti-dialectic within which the dialectic is projected is only to be understood by reference to the dialectic. The immediate intelligibility of my *praxis*, and the intrinsic intelligibility attributed to the *praxis* of the other, *establish* the characteristic that knowledge is *understandable* (what the Anglo-American analysts call teleological explanation), but the evidence of lived experience is not to be confused with a knowledge. The evidence of certain spatial relations is only given to consciousness in a few simple cases; science is developed within and by means of demonstrations that result in evidence without always starting off with any.

Does it happen differently when it is a question of knowing not nature but lived experiences themselves? Yes and no. Whatever the evidence of lived experience, it does not give us knowledge, whether it is of our own lived experience or of the lived experience of others. To be sure, it can be said that we understand nature by the intermediary of variables and relations that we construct or perhaps that the intelligibility of nature remains unintelligible to us. On the other hand, if we understand our own or another's act in terms of its goals, we bring to light, explicitly or implicitly, a relation internal to the conduct or the consciousness of the actor. It is in this sense that Dilthey or Weber half a century ago, or W. Dray or G. von Wright today, interpret historical understanding. None of them has assimilated this understanding to a Reason essentially different from the analytical Reason operative within the natural sciences.

From the understandable or intelligible nature of lived experiences, and thus of historical or human reality, Sartre legitimately deduces certain specific attributes of knowledge of this reality. Sartre's consideration of these questions amounts to a re-examination of fundamental ideas belonging to the tradition of Vico, Hegel, Dilthey, and Weber. As they did, he can establish the foundation for these specific attributes of teleological understanding knowledge on the nature of human reality, on the ontology of consciousness or *praxis*. But how to move from this specificity of understanding and consciousness to a Reason, unless free *praxis* is Reason as such, and even if the *praxis* is that of Hitler?

Let us remain for a moment at the epistemological level. Understanding conduct or modes of thought—of the Bororos,[10] the Puritans, the Stalinists, of Flaubert or of Sartre himself— becomes knowledge, likely if not true, confirmed if not verified, only at the end of an inquiry whose procedures do not necessarily differ from those of other scientific disciplines. Even if the procedures have some originality compared with those of the natural sciences, they do not constitute the equivalent to a Reason that would be essentially other than analytical Reason.

Here and there Sartre endeavours to demonstrate that understanding the economic market or the influence of Spanish gold cannot be done without the aid of dialectical Reason. In fact, he succeeds only in recovering two very ordinary ideas: in the first place, social determinism[11] (or the historical process) operates through the actions of human groups, actions that may be referred to the progressive–regressive method; men react to a disturbing event because of the inherited habits or beliefs that they have and that make them what they are. The human world is constructed by human acts and by things, some of which are natural while others have been humanized by past acts. The action of men is mediated by things, and things only determine developments by the mediation of men and their free *praxis*. There is a double mediation, of men by matter and of matter by men.

In the second place, the whole—the market, the gold supply— determines the decision of each one in the same way as it is determined by the decisions of everyone: nothing in this quite ordinary mechanism goes beyond the limits of analytical Reason.[12]

To what conclusions that may be useful to the social sciences does this critical experience lead? For professional

[10] Cf. Lévi-Strauss, *Tristes Tropiques* (London: Cape 1973), Part 6. Chs. 21–3.

[11] Mediation of things by men and of men by things.

[12] *See* Appendix, Note G.

reasons the sociologist tends to emphasize the transcendence of the social as compared with the individual. The individual enters upon social relations that he has neither chosen nor willed. The social is defined by the constraint to which the individual submits. Whether Sartre is right or wrong to affirm that the social skeleton can be reduced, ontologically, to *praxis*, he is right to remind us that the internalization of the social interests the sociologist less than the externalization of all behaviour. This ceaseless dialectic of consciousness and its milieu is provided by the philosopher–novelist by instants of analysis–images, which are certainly impressionistic but nevertheless convincing.

This same novelist's talent enriches and poeticizes (even if it is sometimes a matter of black poetry) the descriptions of the social at the level of the lived, whether it be of the revolutionary crowd, fraternity–terror, or the extero-conditioning of the series of listeners. Sometimes his political passion, turning into interpretation, reminds us of the danger of arbitrariness, which is inseparable from that of understanding the lived. Theoretically, the existential psychoanalysis of Flaubert is neither more nor less demonstrated than any other psychoanalysis of an historical individual who has never reclined upon a therapist's couch. On the other hand, the understanding of colonialists or bourgeois, of workers or revolutionaries by means of their project, is inexorably twisted into a Manichean vision. The existence of the oppressor is defined by the project to oppress. Internalized scarcity gives each one the will to fight the other. In spite of his calling of universality, man becomes Hobbesian by the curse of scarcity and takes his fellow man for an enemy. Simultaneously with exploitation, if not before it, oppression, and thus the class struggle, coincide with the transcendental début of History. The subtle understanding of the lived is then replaced by reference to the project as grasped by the philosopher-judge of a peoples' court, by the condemnation of some and the acquittal of others. Despite the concentration camps, Stalin is judged by his having the project of a liberator, and every colonialist, in spite of himself, has a project of oppression.[13]

[13] Must we grant a great man the right to the absurd?

Finally, and it is in this way that the *Critique* has been re-juvenated since 1968, Sartre saves the first part of the formula: 'Men make history but they know not the history they make.' Positivist, empirical, microscopic sociology cannot avoid being devoted to the social system or, in other words, it cannot avoid taking the social system as a given. Partial relations are true within a given framework. The changes that the sociologist explicates normally deal with a sub-system or even *one* aspect of *one* sub-system. Putting the emphasis upon *praxis*, rebellion, and totalization at least serves as an antidote.

The sociologist is intensely aware of the weight of institutions that mould individuals, who nevertheless insure that institutions continue to function. By the ontological reduction of all social-ity to *praxis*, Sartre supplies an ideology, if not a philosophy, to establish the basis of a Promethean sociology: man makes himself at each instant by making the society that makes him.

Understanding the lived at the level of the lived, dialectical Reason is nothing more than a teleological explanation of human thought or behaviour. It no longer appears as Reason (in the Hegelian sense of *Vernunft*) in History. Men, it is true, think about electrons and electrons do not think about quantum physics. The Marxist sociologist, however, is not situated with respect to History as quantum physics is with respect to elec-trons. Why does consciousness of a movement that is at each instant innovative and totalizing, at the same time signal the advent of Truth? We would much rather ask if and how the dialectic, according to such a definition, could establish know-ledge of a *single* History? Who, outside of God, could totalize the uncountable multiplicities of individual totalizations?

Granted, the historical past could no longer be other than what it has been. But even so, an event does not become necessary with regard to all that has preceded it simply because it has taken place. Between freedom and necessity there is no *post eventum* reconciliation except by what Bergson called the *retrospective illusion of fatality*. Retrospectively the historian can feel and transmit the sentiment that what has happened could not avoid happening: the free creation of men, *history being made*, would appear, once it had become *history made*, as the unfolding of a necessary process. The novel has precisely as its conclusion the reconciliation in the reader's mind between the freedom of individuals and the decrees of Destiny, which are imposed upon everyone by the intersection of their decisions. Aesthetic reconciliation implies no logical compatibility.[14]

Sartre speaks indiscriminately, it seems to me, of constituting *Reason*, of constituted dialectic, and of constituted *Reason*. Now, the constituting dialectic, in the last instance, is mixed up with individual *praxis*, the origin of reflection and the basis of all historicity. In what sense is the freedom of *praxis* rational? *Qua* free and totalizing, what rationality does my project possess? Even if the totalization of multiple projects presupposes a totalizer, why attribute a rationality to it? The constituting dialectic, *praxis*, presents no characteristics other than the *for-itself*, intelligible if you like, but not rational. But, it must lay the basis for rationality, just as the Cartesian God does.

To be sure, the second volume,[15] at any rate according to the closing pages of the *Critique*, will continue the critical experience towards totalization without a totalizer. The class struggle, which is the necessary result of internalized scarcity, would give a structure and direction to human history—on condition that it is itself overcome. At the level of the lived—and Sartre never leaves this level—there cannot be the equivalent of absolute Knowledge. The final totalization without a totalizer would only appear with the liquidation of the class struggle And in fact, the class struggle makes inevitable the plurality of incompatible perspectives, each class seeing the enemy in the other, and viewing the world in light of an oppression to be continued or destroyed. But the fatality of a static dialectic seems to contradict in advance the necessity of a cumulative dialectic, or even to exclude the possibility.

It is difficult to conceive of a humanity finally victorious over scarcity. But scarcity has not even served to demonstrate that the liberating élan of rebellion and the group-in-fusion necessarily falls back into organization and institution. Seriality and objectivization, or, if you like, the plurality of individuals, and the domination of *praxeis* crystallized into machines over

---

[14] But cf. *Critique*, p. 159 (note).
[15] *See* Appendix, Note H.

praxeis themselves, these two characteristic traits of the social world in tranquillity and of the practico-inert, little by little insinuate themselves into the revolutionary party and into the society that emerges from the revolutionary project.

Sartre would avoid the defeat of the revolution only on condition that he renounce antitheses of the type: 'man is totally free or totally alienated'. More precisely, he would have to recognize in the objectivization of *praxis*, in the existence of each one tied to the existence of others within a milieu of machines, not an alienation but a challenge. Human existence admits of no other condition: neither seriality nor objectifications nor even scarcity will be eliminated from it. Sartrean consciousness in *Being and Nothingness* was condemned as a 'useless passion' by wishing to be God or in-itself. In the *Critique*, it devotes itself to vain rebellions and the relapse into the practico-inert because it wishes to be as sovereign as the Cartesian God. Sartre has attributed an ontological reality to the transcendental ego of Husserl; in his eyes, the socialization of this ego becomes enslavement. Jean-Jacques Rousseau doubted that man could recover his natural freedom within society and civilization. But by what miracle can consciousness make use of its inalienable freedom outside of alienation when the latter results inexorably from seriality and objectification, from others, and from machines?

*   *   *

In *The Savage Mind*, Lévi-Strauss devotes a chapter, in many ways a difficult one, to the *Critique*. I would like to compare the preceding remarks with some of the objections that he formulates against both the theory of History or historical totalization, and against the very notion of dialectical Reason.

Let us begin with the first and easiest theme. The polemic resumes an argument that is in some respects classic: there is no history—in the sense of knowledge of the past ordered according to succession—save for an historian. History as re-told by the historian has been lived that way by nobody. '*Ex hypothesi*, an historical fact is what really took place; but where did anything take place? Each episode in a revolution or a war resolves itself into a multitude of psychic and individual movements.'[16] It is in this sense that I have already spoken of the 'dissolution of the object' or, what amounts to the same thing, the construction of the object: 'the historical fact is no more *given* than any other. It is the historian or the agent of history who constitutes it by abstraction and as though under the threat of an infinite regress' (*Savage Mind*, p. 257).

The historian selects facts in the same way that he constructs them. 'Even though history aspires to signification, it is condemned to choose its regions, its epochs, its groups of men, its individuals within these groups. And it must make them emerge again as discontinuous figures against an historical continuum, which is appropriate to serve as a backdrop' (*Savage Mind*, pp. 257–8). Or again: 'history is therefore never history, but history-for. It is partial, in the sense of being biased, even when it claims not to be, for it inevitably remains partial, that is, incomplete history, which is still a mode of partiality.' The Jacobin and the noble did not live the same French Revolution and they could not write the same things about it. It is enough, then, as Lévi-Strauss does, to add that the totalization of innumerable possible totalizations is worth neither more nor less than each of the partial totalizations in order to conclude that 'the French Revolution as he speaks of it did not exist'. The argument, which is classic for the foundation of historicism (defined by the historicity of knowledge of the past), is asserted with evidence contingent upon but one reservation: *the homogeneity between the experience of history lived by the historical actor and the experience of history as thought through by the historian.*[17] The totalization of the French Revolution by the historian today does not differ essentially from the totalization by aristocrat or Jacobin. That the historian inclines towards one or the other is certain. Does the historian's reconstruction of the Revolution blend itself with a lived experience of the event? Sartre, it seems to me, answers this question affirmatively, and Lévi-Strauss is,

[16] *The Savage Mind* (London: Weidenfeld and Nicolson, 1966), p. 257. Hereafter cited in text.

[17] Natural science also constructs a nature that is neither perceived nor lived by any consciousness. Historical science does not lead towards the reproduction of the lived past; it can arrive at true judgements about it, at a kind of correspondence between the written and the reality.

then, right to assume that this reply is correct. It does, however, cause a problem.

From this first thesis—there is no history as knowledge or reality except for a totalizing consciousness and thus for a consciousness that is itself historical and situated—we move on to a second one: historical knowledge is defined by a certain code or system of coding. The code of historical consciousness consists in chronology (*Savage Mind*, p. 258). There used to be a certain prosaic dry truth in the teaching of dates in the old days. Historical knowledge is defined by the establishment of dates and thus by the order of succession within which the historian arranges the facts he has put together and then selected. But a code defined by dates and thus by the order of succession cannot claim an absolute and unconditional validity. According to the temporal dimension chosen, dates may appear or disappear: the historian of the Revolution counts in days, in months, in years. Thousands of pages will deal with the events that were produced between 1789 and 1815. 'We use a large number of dates to code some periods of history, and fewer for others' (*Savage Mind*, p. 259). Thus, the different choices may appear heterogeneous: the history of the earth or of the human species, which codes in millions or in thousands of millions of years belongs to a different class from the history of the French Revolution, which is coded in days or months. This kind of historical order in turn is differentiated from the history of civilizations, which, in the manner of Spengler or Toynbee, is reckoned or coded according to centuries. There may be neither linear time nor a unique coding system. 'History is a discontinuous ensemble composed of domains of history, each of which is defined by a characteristic frequency and by differential coding of *before* and *after* (*Savage Mind*, pp. 259–60). 'To confine ourselves to a single example, the coding that we use for prehistory is not a preliminary to that which serves us for modern and contemporary history. Each code refers to a system of significations that, at least in theory, is applicable to the virtual totality of human history. The events that are significant for one code do not remain so for another.' (*Savage Mind*, p. 260). Perhaps it would be better to say that they do not necessarily or always remain so. The computer as a form of artificial intelligence seems to me to be significant, both for the history of the human species and for the history of our time.

Finally, according to the code chosen, that is, according to the temporal dimension, the quantity of information and the value of the explication vary inversely: biographical and anecdotal history are rich in information but are explicable only when set within a higher level of history. This higher level sacrifices part of the historical information contained at the lower level, but in return explicates what the other is constrained to report. As a result, a double plurality of histories, as different as those of the aristocrat and the Jacobin, are outlined. But then again, history written at a certain level can, at a higher level, be both repudiated and explicated. The history of the class struggle or racial conflict is not situated at the same level as the political history of the French Revolution: it adds to the intelligibility of the political history or it denies its signification.

No one doubts that the same facts occupy different places according to one's breadth of vision. No one denies that history cuts a whole into pieces and that in this sense it attains no more continuity (except perhaps illusory continuity) than any other knowledge. Everyone admits that events appear significant or not according to his reference—the year, the century, the millennium. On two points there remains room for a further analysis: is it necessary without more ado to put up with a plurality of contradictory histories, written at the same level? Or is the historian forced to take the side, for example, of the noble or the Jacobin?[18] And, in what instance, and up to what point, is the history of a higher level equivalent to an anti-history as regards a lower level?

History-knowledge does not constitute a science as such and it benefits from no prerogative. History defined by the discontinuity of the chronological coding, 'is a method with no distinct object corresponding to it' (*Savage Mind*, p. 262). The transfiguration of history-knowledge, and the reconstitution of a partial past into a supreme truth has no other goal and no other warrant than the transfiguration of History-reality into the advent of Truth. The definition of man by his historicity

[18] Even more: not to take sides must also be to take sides; the arbiter, or someone who would like to be, does not differ from the combatants.

and of Humanity by History represents the last manifestation of transcendental humanism. In fact, Sartre combines in a contradictory system a transcendental philosophy that radically opposes *ego* and *alter*, man and nature, the civilized and the primitive, with the search for a revolutionary solution to the alienation of the ego among others and within the world of things. The *Critique of Dialectical Reason* claims to establish the possibility of Marxism—what Lévi-Strauss translates in the following terms: 'The problem raised by the *Critique of Dialectical Reason* can be brought down to this: under what conditions is the myth of the French Revolution possible?' (*Savage Mind*, p. 254). Possibility of Marxism or possibility of the French Revolution: the two formulae suggest the same idea, the recourse to transcendental analysis in order to confer a philosophical dignity upon the event–advent that would signify man's self-realization. But this golden age of historical consciousness perhaps has already passed. 'A so-called leftist still clutches to a period of contemporary history that bestowed the blessing of a congruence between practical imperatives and interpretative schemata' (*Savage Mind*, p. 254). For my part, I have never ceased to view this 'congruence' as the 'insurance' myth of the leftists. What remains to be determined is the relation between the history that men live, the history historians reconstruct, and the history that philosophers substitute for the historians' reconstruction.

The central argument of this first objection—history, considered as a mode of coding according to the order of succession, enjoys no privilege, either of intelligibility or of explanatory validity—presents no difficulty even if the analysis, which is marginal in Lévi-Strauss' book, is not pushed right through to its conclusion.

The critique of the notion of dialectical Reason by Lévi-Strauss is a little ambiguous because he takes up certain Sartrean concepts without being precise about the meaning he gives them. He admits of the exigency of totalization. But does it go beyond the quite ordinary idea that the ethnographer or sociologist must place each practice and each institution within the whole of society if he is to understand or explain it? The totalization of the culture of an epoch within and by means of a philosophy (assuming that this totalization, of Hegelian inspiration, has any validity whatsoever) seems external and foreign to the rigorous conception that Lévi-Strauss has advanced as being the task of science. He also considers that all knowledge of the other is dialectical, but what does dialectical signify in this instance? Probably Lévi-Strauss is referring to the intelligible teleology, immanent in human conduct, that, within the ontologico-transcendental analysis of Sartre, is translated by the term *praxis* or project. With regard to his concession that it is necessary 'to apply dialectical Reason to the knowledge of societies other than our own' (*Savage Mind*, p. 251), it remains equivocal and perhaps more verbal than genuine, since Lévi-Strauss refuses to recognize the duality of Reasons and seems to assimilate dialectical Reason (as I do myself) to understanding (in the sense of Dilthey) or to the experience of the lived, that is, to immediate experience, or to the totalizing experience that follows analysis.

Despite these difficulties, the major objection is clearly distinguished. There are not two Reasons: 'The opposition between the two reasons is relative, not absolute . . . The term dialectical reason includes as well the perpetual efforts that analytical reason must make in order to reform itself if it claims to account for language, society, and thought; and the distinction of two reasons is based, in our opinion, only on the temporary gap that separates analytical reason and understanding of life' (*Savage Mind*, p. 246).

Perhaps Lévi-Strauss would substitute for the concept of 'dialectical reason' notions that are closer, it seems to me, to what he wishes to indicate, such as 'aggregate understanding'[19] or 'totalizing intuition'. In fact, following his philosophy as a whole, there is only and can only be a single Reason and a single science, even if language, society, and thought throw a challenge to analytical Reason that it never ceases to deal with, and never deals with definitively.

In fact, analytical Reason 'splits up and restores', and this is what constitutes the course and the only course of science. A

---

[19] Unless he means by dialectical Reason the grasping of binary systems of opposition that the phonologist discovers in languages and the ethnologist in myths.

general apprehension takes place at the starting point and at the ending point, which in turn offers a departure point for the next stage. Not only does Reason 'split up and restore' or, in other words, proceed according to Cartesian rules, but it refuses to treat man, *qua* an object of science, differently from ants.[20] The essential differences between *praxis* and *nature*, and between man and animal correspond in the *Critique* to the equally essential distinction between a Reason adapted to knowledge of humanity (dialectical Reason) and a Reason adapted to knowledge of externality (analytical Reason). This duality, which recalls the Bergsonian opposition of matter and life, of intelligence and intuition, is radically rejected by Lévi-Strauss. Thought or consciousness is not self-explanatory at its own level; it does not contain the key to its own intelligibility. All science wishes to be 'reductionist' and seeks schemata of intelligibility, above or beyond lived experience, and beyond what is immediately given.

From one end of the *Critique* to the other, Sartre tries to demonstrate that the socio-historical universe amounts, in principle, to *praxis*, or in other words to lived experience or consciousness. Lévi-Strauss tends in the opposite direction, towards the demonstration that there is a 'human reason that has its own reasons, reasons that man does not know' (*Savage Mind*, p. 252).[21] Language escapes the analytical Reason of the ancient grammarians as well as the constituting Reason of individual *praxis* and the constituted dialectic of structures. It is a dialectic in action (an intelligible system immanent to the object) but not, however, conscious.

In the end, the philosophy of history, or perhaps even historical consciousness, would be achieved, according to Sartre in the totalizing grasp of the whole of human becoming by *a single praxis*. The biography of humanity—the advent of humanity—would appear simultaneously with the consciousness that would embrace it. Lévi-Strauss, on the other hand, has as his final objective the bringing to light of the intelligible schemata of human thought, which are, perhaps, reducible to

[20] Cf. the passage in the *Critique*, p. 183 and the discussion in *The Savage Mind*, pp. 246–7.

[21] Cf. Pascal, *Pensées*, No. 277 [Tr. note].

the laws of physical chemistry. From epistemological antithesis we thus move on to metaphysical antithesis: the ontological specificity of the human realm on the one hand and materialism on the other.

One can wonder why Lévi-Strauss devoted the last chapter of *The Savage Mind* to the *Critique* when nothing obliged him to do so, since at no time does the analysis of *The Savage Mind* cut across the endeavour of the *Critique*. Personally, I see two motives, both of a philosophical order.

Lévi-Strauss seems to have been offended by two passages in the *Critique* where Sartre drove a wedge between primitive and civilized man: in the one he denied that the savage, who, by tracing out a diagram in the sand, shows the investigator the operation of the rules of marriage and the kinship system of his own group, has the power of thought (p. 505). In the other, he employs the expression 'stunted and deformed being' (p. 203) with respect to archaic societies, incapable of an historical project, where the dialectic is expressed and exhausted in repetition.

Perhaps these two passages concerning 'primitives' do not have all the significance that Lévi-Strauss gives to them. Without changing anything important in his thought, Sartre could interpret in another way 'the manual labour governed by a synthesizing thought' of the primitive explaining his kinship system. In the last analysis, he wishes to say that it is the ethnologist who makes up the theory 'of the elementary structures of kinship', while the primitive applies the rules of the structures. As for the 'stunted humanity' of the repetitive collectivities, it precedes the inhuman humanity of the historical collectivities, doomed, so long as scarcity persists, to the dramatic but sterile alternating between rebellion and the practico-inert. To be sure, the definition of the human essence by its *sociality* is opposed to the definition by its *historicity* [22] just as the search for the formal structures of the mind, which are discernible throughout all societies, is opposed to the totalizing dialectic of the project. The dialogue between Lévi-Strauss and Sartre

[22] On p. 102, Sartre does not define man by historicity, but he expects the achievement of humanity from History. The man without history must be a man so as to safeguard the project of universality.

assumes, so to speak, an exemplary signification, each of the interlocutors going right to the end of one of the philosophies of our day. The philosophy of the ethnologist reduces the significance that the historian (or the philosopher) gives to the latest phase, a few thousand years more or less, of the becoming of the human species, while the philosopher prolongs both transcendentalism and progressivism and only recognizes man as fully man within historical societies that are insufficient in themselves but are searching for their own fulfilment.

At the same time the other motive of the dialogue appears. I dare say that Lévi-Strauss does not just wish to take up the defence of the primitive against the civilized, or the repetitive societies against the historical societies. As an epistemologist, he intended to remove some of the undeserved prestige of history-knowledge. By using chronological order, the historical account gives the impression of understanding and sometimes the lyrical illusion of participation. But, as we have seen, there is no history-knowledge of itself. The plurality of historical codings condemns none of them, but it does tend to confer a superior explanatory value upon the intelligible schemata towards which ethnology is tending. As a philosophy of history, the *Critique* becomes an 'ethnographical document of the first order, indispensable if one wishes to understand the mythology of our times'. This is certainly true perhaps for no other reason than that, if Sartre's philosophy excludes the thought of the savage while the ethnology of Lévi-Strauss considers them in some way equivalent,[23] then ethnology must be differentiated from them both. This is a curious reversal from the preceding position where the primitive, laying out the rules of kinship in the sand, in no way differs from the engineer at the blackboard. Let us leave this paradox of *the same and the other* and consider the true formula 'the mythology of our times'. Whatever we may think, Sartre remains an interpreter of the arrogant Western consciousness. *In so far as he wishes to be a Marxist–Leninist*, he attributes a universalist calling to a Germano-Franco-English system of thought. He prolongs the tradition of European conquest even when he denounces the so-called western nations, and even when he conveys the mission of salvation to

[23] That is, both are mythological and hence equivalent [Tr. note].

the wretched of the earth, a mission sacrificed by the proletariats of the wealthy countries to the promises of abundance.

*   *   *

Lévi-Strauss, in a roundabout way, writes that Marxism has constituted the common starting point for his thought and that of Sartre. This remark brings up two questions:

1. Does the distinction of analytical Reason and dialectical Reason make sense within Marxism? Would Marx or Engels have accepted it? Does it appear compatible with their thought?

2. Do, in fact, the philosophies of Sartre and Lévi-Strauss derive from Marxism? Do they represent two possible developments of it?

The answer to the first question demands a long analysis. Let us refer only to two characteristic texts, one of Engels and the other of Marx, so as to reserve judgement on the hypothesis of a discord between their two philosophies (or of Engels' misunderstanding the authentic philosophy of his friend).

As is well known, in the *Anti-Dühring*, Engels set forth the dialectical laws that are valid within nature, and that constitute, so to speak, natural laws (contradiction, negation of the negation, transformation of quantity into quality). Sartre, as we know, takes care not to affirm or deny the dialectic of nature so as not to be clearly opposed to an explicit thesis of Marxism–Leninism. He keeps the dialectic of nature as a possibility but, in fact, even if the laws of nature manifest a dialectical character (namely, that which signifies an intrinsic intelligibility resulting from the structure of the links between its moments or elements), it is only discovered at the end of the exploration, gradually, as the work of analytical Reason, experiment, and argument continues to explicate phenomena.

Deep down, is the possibility of a dialectic of nature, a concession made to Engels and to Marxism–Leninism, in agreement with the inspiration, if not the letter, of the *Critique*? As I have said, I am inclined towards a negative reply. All the ontology of *Being and Nothingness*, the radical heterogeneity of the *for-itself* and the *in-itself*, of *praxis* and *nature*, of *internality*, and *externality*, suggests the common origin of dialectical reality and dialectical Reason. Human reality is revealed only to dialectical Reason because it is itself dialectical. If analytical Reason, at the end of its exploration, discovers the dialectic in nature, then where would the originality of dialectical Reason be? With this hypothesis, why not confine it to the verification of the dialectical character of only certain relations? But then, how could one maintain the gap between the for-itself, for ever in search of its illusive being, and the in-itself, crystallized in a being devoid of sense?

Would Marx have admitted that *Capital* was a work of dialectical Reason? Granted, the conceptual analysis that Marx undertakes in the opening chapters of *Capital* does, if you like, deserve the qualification of dialectical: the analysis presupposes, so to speak, the intelligibility of economic reality on the basis of the most simple notions, labour, exchange value, use value, money. At the same time, it presupposes an intrinsic and intelligible order among concepts, contradictions among them, and the resolution of these contradictions: a commodity has no value unless it answers a need, but the measure of its value depends exclusively on the quantity of mean social labour integrated into it. An increase in productivity, and thus a decrease in the mean social labour necessary for the production of the commodity, reduces its value, which, when the commodity is constituted by labour-power, ends up by gradually diminishing the value of this labour-power as it becomes more effective. Labour-power is worth proportionally less as it produces more in the same time.

This kind of contradiction can be called dialectical; it results however, from a Reason no different in nature than analytical or scientific Reason. Since the value of a commodity depends on the quantity of mean social labour necessary to produce it, the value of labour-power gradually decreases in proportion to the time necessary to produce the commodities indispensable to the worker and his family. That these elementary relations seem, in the eyes of a moralist, to be charged with a sort of bitter irony, that they reveal an 'invisible hand' more harmful than beneficial, is certainly possible. In any event, these relations result from ordinary modes of reasoning.

Even more, the quantitative schemata in the second and third volume of *Capital* belong to what has today become the classic method of model-building. Whether it is a matter of the circulation of capital, of simple or enlarged reproduction, Marx proceeds, without being fully aware of it, the way modern economists do when they make use of mathematics. The influence of the Hegelian dialectic is, in the strict sense, manifest in the conceptual exposition and style of the first volume alone. The demonstrations, whether of exploitation or of the declining rate of profit, owe nothing to the dialectic and even less to dialectical Reason.

Should one wish to distinguish the dialectical aspect of Marxism, one must look for it in another direction: does not the broad movement of history represent a dialectic? The internal contradictions of the capitalist regime are incarnate, so to speak, in a class, the proletariat, which, in its action, is called upon to enforce the decree of reason (*Vernunft*) and overcome its contradictions. The dialectical nature of the broad movement of history may in turn be split up into multiple elements logically tied to each other: history would be presented to the observer in the form of meaningful ensembles, totalizable if not totalities (the capitalist mode of production constitutes such an ensemble). Men or classes, by their reaction to the objective context, would create anew. Meaningful ensembles, modes of production for example, far from succeeding each other according to a law of pure difference, would be connected together by being in contradiction, and historical progression would result from these contradictions. Socialism would preserve the acquisitions of capitalism but, by means of the collective ownership of the means of production, would suppress its contradictions.

That historical data, far from resembling a random collection of facts, are organized by themselves into meaningful ensembles, does not yet imply contradiction among these ensembles nor the calling forth of proletarian *praxis* to suppress the contradictions incarnate within itself. Would Marx himself have seen the expression of an historical dialectic in the intelligibility of the broad movement of history in the way that Engels tends to do in the *Anti-Dühring*? I hesitate to answer this question: the texts do not allow us to be sure that Marx thought differently than his friend on this subject. On the other hand, by keeping to the scientific works of Marx, whether it is the *Grundrisse* or *Capital*, nothing proves that he conceives the dialectic in this way nor that he would have subscribed to *Dimat* or to the dialectical materialism of *Anti-Dühring* that Marxist–Leninists follow.

In any case, neither Marx nor Engels, even if they had clarified the thesis of the dialectic of nature, would have agreed with the thesis of two Reasons, analytical and dialectical, being radically different; materialism prevents them from subscribing to such an epistemological opposition. Marx built up his positive knowledge gradually. He collected available statistics. He would not have established an antinomy between positive knowledge and the criticism of capitalism, even if it remained dialectical, by contrasting reality with his concept and the realization of the concept by human action.

Let us go no farther nor let us claim to settle the matter. Does Sartre's reflection have its starting point in Marx? This is a curious and certainly false way of putting it. Sartre scarcely read Marx in his youth; his basic thought, the radical heterogeneity of the in-itself and the for-itself, was formed very early, upon reading Nietzsche or as a spontaneous expression of his personality, before being expressed in phenomenological language developed in contact with Husserl and Heidegger. It is on the basis of existentialism that Sartre has wished to recover Marxism and give it a transcendental foundation compatible with his own philosophy.

If Marxism has been the starting point of Lévi-Strauss' reflection, he has interpreted it in quite a different way from Sartre's present attempt to assimilate or integrate it into existentialism. Lévi-Strauss has learnt in Marxism to look for meaning beyond or outside the lived. He has himself brought Freud and Marx together and reproached Sartre for having retained only half the teaching of these two masters. Neither Marx nor Freud have in fact remained at the level of the lived. It is necessary to be placed at the point of view of meaning, but immediately given meaning is never the best. 'Superstructures are abortive acts that have "made it" socially' (*Savage Mind*,

p. 254). Whereas Sartre, by granting the ontological and epistemological privilege to *praxis*, is condemned to find the true meaning within consciousnesses (whether it be true or false consciousness), and so ultimately ends up with a legendary history, populated with monsters and victims, colonialists defined by the will of oppression and colonized reduced to the alternative of abject submission or violent denial, a follower of Lévi-Strauss, in the manner of Marx, would seek to bring to light the true meaning of capitalism not in the projects of its actors, but in the intelligible schema of its mode of production. There is only a science of the hidden: Freud and Marx have illustrated Bachelard's proposition in their own ways, and so has Lévi-Strauss. And so has Sartre, after a fashion, but he managed to do so only half-way: even though he denied the unconscious in *Being and Nothingness*, in the *Critique* he allowed of no system of intelligibility that did not, in the last analysis, lead back to the actions of individual *praxeis*. To be sure, these *praxeis* are trapped within the practico-inert, are alienated within seriality and materiality, and, prisoners of their own works, become amenable to analytical Reason. But freedom remains immanent to the *project* of each one, and the advent of human Truth will coincide with the reciprocity of projects, each one free and respectful of the freedom of the other.

Marxism, it seems to me, contains the equivalent to this advent of the Truth of man: the management of the economy by associated producers implies the elimination of the power of man over man and the exploitation of man by man in the same way as does the Sartrean advent of Truth. Even Lévi-Strauss, when he indulges in dreaming about a general interpretation of history, imagines that the class struggle and the slavery (or its more of less subtle modalities) which were contemporaneous with the discovery of hand-writing, will perhaps someday be obliterated after the *technization* of society. The same technology that made inevitable the hierarchy, the privileges of the strong, and the bondage of the vast majority, would gradually, as machines replace hands, and brains make useless and almost anachronistic the opposition between the lofty and the meek, between those who withhold knowledge and those who are content with the execution of innumerable detailed tasks.

But this vision, which his Inaugural Lecture[24] at the Collège de France suggests, remains marginal to his scientific work, whereas the whole of the *Critique* has the objective of granting the dignity of truth to such a vision and of establishing it upon a supposed dialectical Reason.

If we leave aside this all-encompassing vision of the crossroads of humanity, the scientific work of Lévi-Strauss *in a sense* appears more Marxist than the *Critique*, despite the Sartrean declarations of allegiance to Marxism the unsurpassable philosophy of our time.

In *The Elementary Structures of Kinship*,[25] Lévi-Strauss uncovers the system of exchanges of women just as in *Capital* Marx brings to light the system of exchanges of goods. Communication, or exchange of messages, conditions all other exchanges. Even though Lévi-Strauss has not tried to establish the relation of kinship systems (or rules for exchanging women) and modes of production (or rules for exchanging goods), such an enterprise contradicts not a little the spirit of structural anthropology.

To be sure, by going from the structures of kinship to myths, Lévi-Strauss seems to have avoided Marxism; he is not at all concerned with the modes of production, nor even with different systems of exchange, but with the invariants of the human mind, and the forms of intelligibility beyond the diversity of societies and their myths. His is a critique of impure reason and not at all an analysis of the modes of social organization. Despite this incontestable divergence, the enterprise does not exclude, at a lower level, the analysis of the modes of production and kinship systems. If language remains a privileged example for him of a 'human reason that has its own reasons, reasons that man does not know', every language (in the broad sense of the term), every system of communication implicitly contains a reason that science is called upon to decipher. Orthodox Marxists, beyond this deciphering of systems, endeavour to recognize the primacy of relations of production or at least to

[24] Available in English as *The Scope of Anthropology*, Tr., S. O. Paul and R. A. Paul (London: Jonathan Cape, 1967) [Tr. note].

[25] Rev. ed., tr., J. H. Bell, J. R. von Sturner, and R. Needham, editor, (London: Eyre and Spottiswoode, 1969) [Tr. note].

recognize the correlations among systems within each type of society. They are opposed to Lévi-Strauss concerning the interpretation of our own time, for they must maintain the congruence between 'schemata of interpretation and practical imperatives'. To the extent that Marxism is defined first of all by means of a philosophy of contemporary history, the thought of Lévi-Strauss in fact becomes anti-Marxist. To the extent that Marxism, in the same way as Freudianism, uncovers the meaning of what men live, beyond or on this side of what they experience, the connection with Marxism continues to exist. The possible explanation of the structures of the human mind by means of physico-chemical laws, suggested at the end of *The Savage Mind*, results in a radical materialism that the Marxist–Leninists must welcome more readily than the ontological heterogeneity of nature and culture.

*　　*　　*

The Sartre–Lévi-Strauss dialogue, which took place beneath the grand shadow cast by Marx, has most often been interpreted in terms of the synchronic–diachronic and system–history opposition exemplified in the thought of the two men. The decisive opposition seems to me to go deeper: Sartre wished to establish the truth of the Marxist philosophy of history. Lévi-Strauss wishes to establish the scientific truth of his analysis of systems (of kinship and myths). Both of them can apply or make use of the progressive–regressive method at an intermediate level, but the one is oriented towards systems or invariant factors and the other towards the totalization of the human becoming (or totalization through becoming); the one brings out the hidden intelligibility of consciousnesses, the other, beyond schemata of intelligibility, tends towards constituting *praxis*, the ontological origin of social realities; the one aspires to an ethnological critique of reason that would exclude no society from rationality and humanity, the other wishes to open the prospect of a far-off reconciliation of free *praxis* and necessary Truth.

When the *Critique* appeared, the reign of existentialism was completed and the new left had not yet erupted upon the stage of (Parisian) history. Two years later, the publication of *The Savage Mind* coincided with the vogue of structuralism (do we need to say that structuralism as a method or theory has nothing to do with the temperament of the Parisian *intelligentsia*?). Sartre, who in *Nausea* had derided the humanist, who had always defined man by what he did, who did not know the notion of personality, had been rejected by the avant-garde. He continued to take consciousness or *praxis* as his principle of reflection; he did not transfer responsibility for this thought or his action to an id or to a language, or to an impersonal unconscious. The moralism (even if it is an inverted moralism) of Sartrean thought seemed closer to neo-Kantianism or to the phenomenology of yesterday than to presently fashionable doctrines tied to Freudianism or linguistics.

As a *cause célèbre*, the dialogue of the *Critique* and *The Savage Mind* took on a symbolic signification that, at the level of ontology, was justified. Nevertheless, it appears to me to be useful to remember that Lévi-Strauss was refuting a particular philosophy of history or reducing it to a myth. He had never denied knowledge or historical consciousness.

The notion of historical consciousness sometimes presents a strong and sometimes a weak meaning. According to the first, it refers to a certain way of thinking about the place of our society in the becoming of mankind, and a certain attitude concerning the past: respect for tradition, sense of continuity and the well-tried presence of an age-old heritage in our own present. In its weak sense, which is the most general, historical consciousness is understood to mean the consciousness that the men of one generation or culture have of their being as well as of their becoming, or again, more simply, the consciousness they have of time and change. In this second and weak sense, all societies, including primitive societies, have an historical consciousness.

In fact, Lévi-Strauss denies neither the value of historical consciousness nor the historical consciousness of primitives. 'The ethnologist respects history, but he does not accord it a privileged value. He conceives it as an area of study complementary to his own: one of them sets forth the range of human societies in time, the other in space. And the difference is even less great than it might seem, since the historian strives to reconstruct the picture of vanished societies as they were during the times that, for them, corresponded to the present, whereas the ethnologist does his best to reconstruct the historical stages that temporally preceded existing forms' (*Savage Mind*, p. 256). If primitive or distant societies lend themselves poorly to historical accounts properly speaking, it is not so much because they change less or less quickly than because we lack documents.

The historical consciousness of so-called archaic societies results, at least formally, from a choice opposed to that of modern societies. They tend effectively to think of themselves with the aid of a classification system and to eliminate events or to reconstruct the system in spite of changes. 'This constant struggle between history[26] and the system is tragically illustrated by the example of some 900 survivors of about thirty Australian tribes that were haphazardly regrouped in a Government Settlement . . . Even though the social organization was reduced to chaos as a result of the new conditions of life imposed upon the natives and the lay and religious pressures to which they had been subjected, their speculative attitude continued to exist. When it was no longer possible to retain traditional interpretations, others were elaborated from them that were, as the first, inspired by motivations (in Saussure's sense) and by schemata. Social structures that previously were simply juxtaposed in space were made to correspond with each other at the same time as with animal and vegetable classifications appropriate to each tribe . . . There is no doubt that if the process of deterioration had been interrupted, this syncretism could serve as the starting point for a new society, for working out a general system whose every aspect would be found to have been adjusted' (*Savage Mind*, pp. 157–9). The classificatory system with the aid of which these small societies think about themselves must ceaselessly be reconstructed, outside even the exceptional circumstances of regrouping: the individuals of such and such a class having disappeared, the gap must be filled in and the system reconstituted. This last task, which is essentially syn-

---

[26] Obviously 'history' signifies here not knowledge according to the order of succession, but changes and events.

chronic, suffers the ravages of time or history, which represents for them a threat, not a promise.

This predominance of the synchronic over the diachronic does not exclude the meaning of historicity or of pure history. 'The virtue of archives is to put us in contact with pure historicity . . . Archives also . . . constitute events in their radical contingency (since only interpretation, which forms no part of them at all, can ground them in reason). Then again, they give a physical existence to history, for in them alone is the contradiction of a completed past and a present wherein it survives overcome. Archives are the incarnate being of the eventuality.

'By this indirect approach we once again find, in the midst of the savage mind, that pure history that we have already confronted in totemic myths . . . Even if mythical history is false, it does at least manifest in a pure state and in the most accentuated form (even more, one might say, it does so because it is false), the characteristics appropriate to an historical event. On the one hand, these characteristics came from the contingent status of the event, . . . and on the other, from its power of arousing emotions . . . Thus, the classificatory systems allow the integration of history: even and above all, they allow for the integration of what might be thought to defy the system. For we must make no mistake about this: totemic myths, which gravely relate futile incidents and sentimentalize over familiar places, remind us, in fact, of only minor history, the history of the dimmest chroniclers' (*Savage Mind*, pp. 242–3). Such a history was not that of the Burckhardts or Spenglers but that of the Lenôtres and the LaForces.[27]

To the two courses of classificatory thought and thought of events of pure historicity is added, within the historical consciousness of archaic peoples, a third, namely, historical schemata or structures of the becoming of man. 'The legend suggests a double becoming. The one is purely structural; it passes from a two-part system into a three-part system, and then returns to the prior duality. The other is at once structural and historical; it consists in the annulment of the overthrow of the primitive structure, an overthrow that had resulted from historical

[27] Lenôtre and LaForce were anecdotal historians.

events or events conceived as historical such as migration, war, or alliance. Now, the social organizations of the Osage, as it could be observed, in the nineteenth century, in fact integrated both aspects' (*Savage Mind*, p. 69).

I have quoted the texts of Lévi-Strauss at length and compared them with each other in order to make their author say what he perhaps did not wish to say, at least not in these terms: the historical consciousness of archaic societies, despite the predominance that it accords to the system or to classification, ignores neither the pure event nor the structural regulation of becoming; it integrates events or becoming into the system with the aid of myths or legends of origin. At the same time, the kinship between the myths of primitives and the *Critique* is explained. In fact, Sartre invokes the criterion of historical consciousness in order to distinguish 'primitive' from 'civilized' people. Indeed, he offers us not a concrete image of history but an abstract schema of man making history such that it could be manifest within their becoming under the form of a synchronic totality (*Savage Mind*, p. 254). Why should this myth be characteristic of the historical consciousness of modern societies while, according to Lévi-Strauss himself, these societies have chosen to define themselves not by system or by synchrony but by genuine history (which is entirely contrary to the Sartrean myth)? The totemic emptiness within the great civilizations of Europe and Asia results from the fact that they have chosen to explain themselves to themselves by means of history, and this enterprise is incompatible with the one that classifies things and beings by means of finite groups (*Savage Mind*, pp. 232–3).

Civilizations that have taken the path of history perhaps incline towards historical mythologies. Why could a knowledge of the past not free itself from these myths? Why should action within history demand faith in the 'congruence between practical imperatives and schemata of interpretation', as if it were necessary to hope in order to address oneself to the future, or to know it in order to hope? Faith in this congruence, a variation of progressivism, perhaps marks the golden age of historical consciousness. Perhaps Sartre himself bears witness to the completion of this golden age. No macrodialectic, no all-encompassing determinism in the *Critique* guarantees the fulfilment of the universalist project: there remains to man no other assurance but his own freedom. By what sorcery does freedom find no other road open ahead of it but violence?

VI

From Freedom to Violence

Many of my friends are surprised that I carry on a dialogue with an interlocutor who rejects discussion. The insults he periodically heaps upon me certainly do not respect the principle of reciprocity, the highest ethical principle set forth in the *Critique*. Or, at the very least, his abuse manifests a wish for an exclusively antagonistic reciprocity. Their comments do not discourage me: unlike those who make them, I have retained my youthful admiration for the extraordinary fertility of Sartre's mind and for his power of abstract construction, without forgetting his superb indifference to verification and the proper use of reason. As a result of its excess, his rage bothers me little; I accept him as he is, even in his violence and immoderation.

This unequal exchange—invectives against arguments— corresponds in other respects to the logic of our reciprocity. As I have suggested in the above pages and as Sartre has written many times, thought is action, consciousness of action, or even the integrating aspect of action. Strictly speaking, according to Sartre, behind every position taken or every particular commitment, one can discern an existential will, a manner of choosing oneself and situating oneself in the midst of oppressors and the oppressed. Even more, if one turns from the *Critique* to *Being and Nothingness*, it would seem that each of our gestures, each of our judgements expresses the relation to Being by which a particular consciousness has determined its entire destiny. Thus Sartre does not betray his own philosophy, he reveals it (and shows the terrorism in it) when, with respect to my attitude in May 1968, he declared me 'unfit to teach'. The

remainder of the interview, which was a simultaneous denunciation of De Gaulle and myself, belongs merely to the category
of bad literature, and perhaps the triviality of competition,
which turns into the destruction of one's opponent. Here, at
least, he is at one with Marx, a rough antagonist in such sport.
There remains the fact that from the start he has not given me
any benefit of the doubt: just as he wrote that anti-communists
are dogs, he thought that opposition to the May 1968 movement classed me among those whom he cannot, whom he must
not, avoid hating or fighting as one hates or fights evil. To criticize communism one must be on its side; to criticize the
students and Cohn-Bendit one must be on their side.

The theory of understanding as set out in the *Critique* serves
as the basis for this militant interpretation. The result even
reveals the errors (that perhaps psychoanalysis would explain)
that transform a philosophy of human liberation into a philosophy of violence. By considering anti-communists as dogs he
strips them of their humanity. Is it the man or the philosopher
who expresses himself with such verbal aggression, such a
refusal to understand the other in his alterity or to recognize
the possible good will of his opponents? Is it the man or the
philosopher whose only praise comes in obituaries? Has his
philosophy no other goal than to justify this way of being? Or,
does such a life, in part at least, derive from his philosophy? I
shall not discuss it here: I shall stick to the relationship, which
is free of doubt, between the philosophy of terror and terrorism
in action, all of which is in the name of a humanism based
solely upon the presence in everyone of a nothingness, creator
of a total and ungraspable freedom.

Neither memories of youth nor the mystery of the man explain my interest in the *Critique*. The simple truth is that our
starting points, our references, our teachers, and our prob-
lematics are to a large degree the same. In *Being and Nothingness* there are reminders of the *Introduction to the Philosophy of
History*. If, to use his language, the *Introduction* sticks to the
ontic, it nevertheless analyses the structures of human action in
history in a style comparable to that of Sartre in *Being and
Nothingness* and even more, in some respects, to his style in the
Critique. The relativism of perception and historical under-

standing, an interpretation readily given to my thesis, was emphasized by Merleau-Ponty in *Humanism and Terror* in support of his own interpretation of political justice, which, in other respects, I take objection to. Sartre insists that historical understanding must be rooted in a subject who is himself historical; he is drawn to conclusions opposed to mine. I see in it the condemnation of Manicheism and an appeal for the recognition of the other in his alterity. Sartre finds a valid and compulsive reason to be transformed into a judge of the quick and the dead. It is not enough that colonialists have oppressed or exploited; they must be wholly defined by their will to oppression and exploitation.

Does this problematic of history, of knowledge, and of action in history belong to the past? To neglect the present passage of time, our own age, I am told that I risk playing Falstaff and, what is worse, a Falstaff who tackles a monument and a source of national pride. Who can be unaware that some nonsense creeps in here and there in the midst of this 'enormous' book? So why bother to add to it? It would be better to discard the dross and read these hundreds of pages that in the long run are embellished and strewn with analyses that by turns illuminate, annoy, instruct, and fascinate. Maybe so. However, this attitude does not come about without a trace of contempt. Up to now, no serious study has been made of the *Critique* in French even though commentators on the Sartre–Lévi-Strauss debate have not been wanting. Thus, I do not think this 'liberal' dialogue (to understand the other from his point of view even if the reciprocity is antagonistic) is out of character for me, and I even take this dialogue to be a testament of friendship or an expression of what, in my own ethics, is called fidelity. For forty years we have scarcely, if at all, carried on these dialogues face to face, dialogues that Simone de Beauvoir has recounted and that were ended by 'my old chum'. Sartre no longer has any need to test his ideas by having others examine them; probably he will not read my comments nor even try to understand them. Does it matter? I have had genuine pleasure conversing with an interlocutor who is present and absent at the same time.

*　　*　　*

Simone de Beauvoir wrote somewhere that before the Second World War, while she and Sartre were but slightly interested in politics, they expected nothing from partial or progressive reform and put their hope (when they indulged in hope) in a general, sudden, and violent upheaval: in short, in a Revolution (whatever the meaning of that term).[1] Once having chosen the party of the Revolution, Sartre condemned himself paradoxically and inevitably to a dialogue with the Communist Party and Marxism. In France, at least until recent years, there has been no other party dedicated to the Revolution and no other philosophy of the Revolution. And yet, the party of the Revolution had debased this philosophy into Marxism–Leninism. This situation was not without at least some advantages since the incompatibility between existentialism and vulgar materialism justified cooperation but excluded joining them: thus, there could be fraternity without terror. In all these ways, Marxism, at any rate that of Marx, was imposed upon Sartre as *the* philosophy of Revolution to which he must refer from the moment when he left his solitary reflection and took his place, a man among other men, in the fight for freedom.

Despite a current opinion, the philosophy of *Being and Nothingness*, which is incompatible with Marxism–Leninism, did not exclude a prejudice in favour of revolution. On the contrary, it seems to me that the conception of freedom that Sartre developed in *Being and Nothingness* leads dialectically to a philosophy of Revolution.

Freedom such as Sartre analyses in *Being and Nothingness* and even more in *Materialism and Revolution*[2] is always in a *situation*. Even though the situation itself is only defined as such by the project, in certain cases the project may equally run counter to the situation that it has itself defined. 'The situation, the common product of the contingency of the in-itself and of

[1] By temperament, or, if the Sartrean expression noted above is preferred, by an existential choice, I have always preferred reforms to Revolution. Truth to tell, my decision was made not without a lengthy investigation; I read Marx's *Capital*, and the economists in order to justify my choice to myself and so amend it if I had to. I would have liked the truth of Marxism to have shown me which camp to join and which cause to serve.

[2] In *Literary and Philosophical Essays*, tr., A. Michelson (London: Rider, 1955) [Tr. note].

freedom, is an ambiguous phenomenon in which it is impossible for the for-itself to distinguish the contribution of freedom from that of the brute existent . . . Here I am at the foot of this crag, which appears to me as "not scalable". This means that the rock appears to me in the light of a projected scaling— a secondary project that finds its meaning in terms of an initial project, which is my being-in-the-world. Thus, the rock is carved out on the ground of the world by the effect of the initial choice of my freedom. But, on the other hand, what my freedom cannot determine is whether the rock "to be scaled" will or will not lend itself to scaling. This is part of the brute being of the rock. Nevertheless the rock can show its resistance to the scaling only if the rock is integrated by freedom in a "situation" whose general theme is scaling. For the simple traveller who passes over this road and whose free project is a pure aesthetic ordering of the landscape, the crag is not revealed either as scalable or as not-scalable; it is manifested only as beautiful or ugly.

'Thus it is impossible to determine in each particular case what comes from freedom and what comes from the brute being of the for-itself.[3] The given in-itself, as *resistance* or as *aid*, is revealed only in the light of projecting freedom' (*Being and Nothingness*, p. 488). To be sure, the cliff reveals itself to be un-climbable only to somebody who wants to climb it. 'Man en-counters an obstacle only within the field of his freedom' (*Being and Nothingness*, p. 488). One can even say that freedom implies opposition to the extent that one only acts by over-coming obstacles, that one only *does something* by acting upon things. But it remains no less true that freedom, in order never to be an external constraint, and in order to endow the situa-tion with meaning, is only exercised in a situation or, in other words, within a milieu of the in-itself and *materiality* (which limits my ability), and of the *other* by whom I become other than myself, alienated. This milieu of alterity, such as Sartre describes in *Being and Nothingness*, includes three strata: first, the layer of already significant implements (which do not receive their signification from my own project),[4] second,

---

[3] Should this not rather read, 'the brute being of the in-itself'?

[4] Machines, the practico-inert of the *Critique*.

signification that is *already* mine[5] (nationality, race, physical attributes), and finally, the Other, 'as a centre of reference to whom significations return'.

The existence of the Other 'brings a factual limit to my freedom . . . Here I am—a Jew, or an Aryan, handsome or ugly, one-armed, etc.'. This being Jewish, I submit, is imposed upon me by the other. 'Thus something of myself—according to this new dimension—exists in the manner of the *given*; at least *for me*, since this being which I am *is suffered*, it *is* without *being existed* . . . Yet I am unable *in any way* to feel myself as a Jew or as a minor or as a Pariah. It is at this point that I can react against these interdictions by declaring that race, for example, is purely and simply a collective fiction, that only individuals, exist. Thus, here I suddenly encounter the total alienation of my person' (*Being and Nothingness*, p. 524).

The in-itself, things, limit our power. Only others limit our freedom.[6] And even this limitation has only a relative sense: the prohibition in a restaurant 'Jews keep out!' when seen from the outside is not incarnate in '*my* universe, and it takes[7] on its peculiar force of compulsion only within the limits of my own choice and according to whether, under any circumstances, I prefer life to death or whether, on the contrary, I judge that in certain particular cases death is preferable to certain kinds of life, *etc.*'. And, a little further on: 'the only limits which a freedom can encounter are found in freedom. Just as thought according to Spinoza can be limited only by thought, so freedom can be limited only by freedom. Its limitation as internal finitude stems from the *fact* that it cannot not-be freedom— that is, it is condemned to be free; its limitation as external finitude stems from the *fact* that being freedom, it *is* for other freedoms, freedoms which freely apprehend it in the light of their own ends.' (*Being and Nothingness*, p. 525). The *Critique*, in my opinion, adds no other *ontological* limits to my freedom even

[5] The class-*exis* of the *Critique*.
[6] The radical distinction between *power* and *freedom* is hardly Marxist.
[7] The French text of Sartre (*L'Etre et le Néant*, pp. 607–8) says *perd* not *prend*. It seems to me that the sense calls for *prend* [R.A.]. The English text follows the French; we have followed Aron [Tr. note].

though it accentuates the limitations of the powers of *praxeis* within the social world of alienation.

The concepts used in the *Critique* thus appear for the most part in *Being and Nothingness*. If the notion of utensils or instruments no longer holds the same place in the *Critique*, the same idea is expressed in other terms (materiality, machines). The world for the for-itself is a world of tasks to be completed. From that derives the relation of means to an end, a 'connection in isolation, this inert relation within the dynamic' (*Being and Nothingness*, p. 200). It is, however, an original relation since the world only comes into being by way of the for-itself, and it is immediately and inseparably an *instrumental-thing*, a means with respect to a task the for-itself determines by projecting itself towards what is possible. When utility is gone, only the thing, pure externality, to use the scholarly expression, is left. Against this pure thingness or externality is opposed the being-in-the-world of the for-itself, 'which consists in escaping from the world towards a beyond the world, which is a future world' (*Being and Nothingness*, p. 200). The quest for an unknown future in *Being and Nothingness* becomes, without a break or contradiction, the quest for a human or historical future in the *Critique*.

No doubt ontological analyses appear to exclude all optimism. In particular, the game of mirrors or looks encloses us in an apparently insoluble contradiction. 'Thus ceaselessly tossed from being-a-look to being-looked-at, falling from one to the other in alternate revolutions, we are always, no matter what attitude is adopted, in a state of instability in relation to the Other. We pursue the impossible ideal of the simultaneous apprehension of his freedom and of his objectivity. To borrow an expression from Jean Wahl, we are—in relation to the Other—sometimes in a state of *trans-ascendence* (when we experience him as a transcendence that transcends us). But neither of these two states is sufficient in itself, and *we shall never place ourselves concretely on a plane of equality; that is, on the plane where the recognition of the Other's freedom would involve the Other's recognition of our freedom*[8] (*Being and Nothingness*, p. 408). Yet, is not this ontological impossibility equivalent to a practical

[8] Emphasis added.

impossibility? I cannot recognize a subject in the Other without transforming myself into an object for him, nor can I treat him as an object without his escaping me as a subject. The practical conditions for non-antagonistic reciprocity, indicated above, are situated at another level and do not strictly contradict the subject–object alternative. Non-antagonistic reciprocity is eventually developed at the level of *doing* or *acting* rather than at the level of an exclusion of reciprocal and simultaneous recognition affected by the exchange of looks.

Finally, the concept of *understanding*, explicitly identified in the *Critique* as having the meaning given it by the German psychologists and historians, namely, to grasp the meaning of human conduct, appears in *Being and Nothingness* (p. 469) as well. The for-itself, being defined as project, flees towards what is possible and the accomplishment of tasks. Understanding (in the ordinary sense of the term) of the Other in his doing and his acting is evidently achieved by reference to the end that determines it, and this is done by means of his present non-being. Upon one occasion (*Being and Nothingness*, p. 469) the word understanding is to be found within quotation marks.

Sartre has just compared his own theory of the original choice of each individual by himself[9] (the choice of his 'intelligible character', to employ the Kantian concept that so fascinated Sartre in his youth) with the Leibnizian conception. He is trying to clarify the two aspects of this total choice, which are apparently contrary but complementary. On the one hand, 'My ultimate and initial project—for these are but one—is, as we shall see, always the outline of a solution of the problem of being. But this solution is not first conceived and then realized; we *are* this solution. We make it exist by means of our very commitment, and therefore we shall be able to apprehend it only by living it. Thus, we are always wholly present to ourselves; but precisely because we are wholly present, we cannot hope to have an analytical and detailed consciousness of what we are.' The choice of myself is thus at once total and not susceptible to being known by myself, even though 'the world by means of its very articulation refers us to an image of what we are' (*Being and Nothingness*, p. 463). On the other hand, if we

[9] *See* Appendix, Note I.

are our choice, this choice could never be definitive without depriving us of our freedom. In addition, even though 'we are perpetually committed to our choice', we are 'perpetually conscious of the fact that we ourselves can abruptly invert this choice and "reverse steam"', for we project the future by our very being, and we gnaw into it perpetually by our existential freedom . . . Thus, we are perpetually *threatened* by the nihilation of our actual choice and perpetually threatened with choosing ourselves—and consequently with becoming—other than we are' (*Being and Nothingness*, p. 465). This choice is absolute but fragile since it does not enslave the freedom to which we are all condemned. Even so, we are not returning to the Cartesian separation of instants such that my choice at time *t* could not act upon my choice at time *t'*. But the new choice, which reverses the preceding choice, shatters the continuity of time and, at the same time, makes the instant loom up 'carried along by a double nothingness, and, as such, a fracture within the ecstatic unity of our being'. 'Precisely because it is free and perpetually taken up by freedom, my choice is limited by freedom itself, that is to say, it is haunted by the spectre of the instant.'

Sartre then compares this analysis of freedom and existential choice with that of Leibniz so as to recall the existential priority of existence over essence. The deed of Adam commits the whole person of Adam—on this point Sartre is in agreement with Leibniz—but the deed of Adam, according to Leibniz, results in the essence of Adam, and thus, according to Sartre, Adam carries no responsibility for it.[10] If Adam's essence is a datum for him, necessity replaces freedom. Adam is not at all defined by an essence, but by the choice of his goals, by the surge of an ec-static temporalization that has nothing in common with the logical order. Consequently, the order of psychological explanation for Leibniz goes from past to present, whereas according to Sartre interpretation starts from the future (*Being and Nothingness*, p. 469), from an opposition (formulated in a

[10] Sartre does not discuss one of the three characteristics of the free act mentioned by Leibniz, namely, to make up one's mind *rationally* to undertake an action. Sartrean freedom is spontaneity and not a decision taken after a rational deliberation.

modified language in the *Critique*): 'The understanding of an
action on the basis of its original ends as established by the
freedom of the for-itself is not an *intellection*.'[11] In the *Critique*,
he substitutes explanation or deduction for intellection. The
central idea of understanding remains the same. 'The survey
of the total project allows for the "understanding" of the particular structure considered', without the particular structure
being deduced from the ensemble, and without the total choice
determining each particular behaviour or excluding voluntary
decisions in opposition to the fundamental ends that have been
chosen.

The two characteristics that the German psychiatrists and
historians have attributed to understanding, first the interpretation of an action or a behaviour by means of its ends, and
second the interpretation of an idea, an action, or a behaviour
by means of an ensemble and a totality, is noted by Sartre in
Being and Nothingness. There he spontaneously uses the terms
'to understand' or 'understanding' in order to indicate the
interpretation of a behaviour by its goals or by a general
project.

On the other hand, the concepts 'dialectic' and 'dialectical
Reason'[12] do not appear in *Being and Nothingness*. This is an
innovation in vocabulary rather than a fundamental change,
in my view. Dialectic is nothing but another name given to an
aspect of the *for-itself praxis* or to the understanding of *praxis*.
The *for-itself*, in *Being and Nothingness*, was just as dialectical as
praxis in the *Critique*, since dialectic is defined at one extreme
by the project and at the other by *totalization*, and since project
implies *situation*, which itself only appears *totalized* in light of a
project. As for the change from dialectic to dialectical Reason,
it explained by the definition of Reason given at the beginning:
'Nobody, not even the empiricists, have ever taken Reason to
be the simple regulation, whatever it may be, of our thoughts.
In order to be a "rationalism" this regulation must reproduce

---

[11] It must be remembered that, in the *Critique*, *intellection* is a form derived
from *understanding* in the absence of any reference to an individual or
common *praxis*.

[12] However, 'totalization' and 'detotalized totality' do already appear
in the vocabulary of *Being and Nothingness*. For example, cf. pp. 422–3.

or constitute the order of being. Thus, Reason is a certain relationship of knowledge and being. From this point of view, if the relationship of historical totalization and totalizing Truth is able to exist, and if this relationship is a double movement within knowledge and being, it will be legitimate to call this moving relation a Reason' (*Critique*, 'Preface', p. 10). According to this definition, the idea of dialectical Reason adds to the idea of dialectic the single innovation of an essential relation between thought and its object.

The Sartrean attempt, as I have interpreted it, appears to be an ontological transformation of what the German psychiatrists and historians presented as a specific mode of apprehending human reality. To be sure, the theory of *understanding* is derived from an ontology that itself goes back to Vico (man fully knows only what he does) or to Hegel (the dialectic of knowledge copies the dialectic of being, and both copy the dialectic of the Idea). But a Jaspers, a Dilthey, a Max Weber kept understanding as a modality of the knowledge of man by man without assuming or demanding an ontology, and without opposing one Reason to another. Sartre himself goes back from the neo-Kantian or semi-positivist'[13] theory of understanding to an ontology. However, the two projects—on the one hand, to bring to light the specific attributes of understanding in the social sciences or in philosophical anthropology, and, on the other, to bring to light the specific relations between thought and its object—remain distinct.

Not that they are, for all that, radically separable. The specific attributes of knowledge of human things, assuming they can be distinguished, does not depend upon the arbitrary will of the subject; in one way or another, they proceed from the being peculiar to the object. All that is left is that the second project, as Sartre pursues it, does indeed move beyond the exigencies of the first and involve it in probably insurmountable difficulties.[14]

*   *   *

[13] Or even phenomenological.

[14] *The Question of Method* appears as the completion of the first project without the ontological foundations that support the completion of the second.

What consequences for the epistemological theory of understanding follow from the second project, the ontology of
dialectical being, the foundation of dialectical knowledge? We
shall not pursue this question very far, as we are reserving consideration of it for the following volume, and so we confine
ourselves to a few remarks.

Sartre characterizes the dialectic, the issue of the for-itself
and *praxis*, by means of the project, totalization, and the
particularity of experience and the situation. Thus, he tends to
be wary of comparisons, generalizations, concepts, and quanti-
fication. In other words, he tends to suspect all procedures
comparable to those of the natural sciences (and analytical
Reason) that would dissolve or efface the meaning belonging
to *this* Revolution, the particularity of *this* ideology or *this*
culture. However, nothing prevents Sartre, even within the
framework of his own philosophy, from reintegrating the
procedures of analytical Reason into the social sciences.
These procedures become legitimate and necessary to the
extent that the externalization of the internal, the alienation of *praxis*, quasi-objects, or petrified institutions give a
structure to human reality that is close to that of things. It is
enough to set forth the limits to this analytical knowledge,
which is both the issue of the dialectic and subordinated to
it.[15]

At the same time, the Sartrean refusal of causal explanations
within the social sciences results from a 'realistic' conception,
from a metaphysics of causality. Here again it would be enough
to admit a quasi-causality and to tolerate a knowledge that
intends regularities and not, as with understanding, a knowledge that itself interprets totality, particularity, and innovation.

Sartre makes a school-boy, almost caricatural, production
out of analytical Reason and the objects of natural science.
Analysis, combination, deduction, is what he suggests as the
procedures of analytical Reason that eliminate the apprehension of the particular, the novel, and the synthetic [16] ensemble.

---

[15] Cf., for example, *Critique*, p. 489 regarding kinship structures.
[16] Synthetic in the Kantian sense.

Now there is no doubt that physics does not explain the consciousness I have *hic et nunc* of this rainbow above the hills of Lubéron, but it explains the (necessary and/or sufficient) conditions under which a rainbow appears. It is just as true that no psychology or anthropology explains or even understands my unique temporal experience, my qualitatively particular experience of the gamut of colours. Understanding retains something of experiences lived by myself or by others but not everything: *qua* knowledge it allows part of the lived particularity to escape, definitively vanished from the time it has ceased to be present.

Not that objectification, which is peculiar to all knowledge, does not differ according to whether it has for an object the electron or the patient on the psychoanalyst's couch or even the decision of a war leader elaborating a battle plan. The relation of the element to the whole, in one case, and the project, the deliberation, the choice, in the other, denote what is particular about knowledge-as-understanding and perhaps gives it a specific relationship to its object. The ontology of the thing, on the one hand, and the ontology of the for-itself or of *praxis*, on the other, crystallize the epistemological distinction in the form of an antithesis, a reciprocal exclusion that is incompatible with the effective development of knowledge of the world and man.

It will be objected that by reducing the dialectic (which characterizes reality) to be but the expression of the project and the totalization by which *praxis* is defined, we misunderstand two other traits of dialectical reality: contradictions, negation, and the negation of the negation, on the one hand, and the ultimate meaning of totalization—the historical totalization and the totalizing Truth—on the other. We have already said, while discussing the theses of Engels on the dialectic of nature, that Sartre sometimes argues as if dialectical relations demand neither *praxis*, project, nor freedom but are reduced to a movement wherein the different terms contradict each other (or even to a movement wherein they would simply be opposed to each other). Likewise, I said that it was my opinion that this concession to Marxism–Leninism accords badly with his thought. The biological dialectic of want, of need, and of the negation of need by the appropriation of the external world provides an example of a dialectic of organic totalities, not of *praxis*.

If this dialectic does depend on dialectical Reason, we end up with the absurd conclusion that the science that explains this dialectic analytically (whether it is within the framework of an analysis of a system or a cybernetic analysis) lacks its own object. *A fortiori*, a dialectic of nature would either not depend on dialectical Reason and would not even belong to the same category as the human dialectic, or else it would do so and thereby the analytical science of nature would bring it to light and would be sufficient to explain it.

Let us leave the question of the dialectic of nature and ask whether its contradictions hold a central place within the Sartrean dialectic. If contradiction is identical with negation, it follows that the dialectic goes from contradiction to contradiction, or again, that *praxis* negates the situation that it perceives, delimits, and determines by the very act of escaping towards a non-existent future. This negation is absent from primitive societies, which is what reduces, lowers, or encloses them within a repetitive history. But, even by neglecting the distinction between contradictory propositions and incompatible, contrary ideas or concepts, it does not seem to me that the essence of the dialectic implies a logical relation between what is negated (or nihilated) and the always indefinite content of the project. When the Sartrean dialectic reaches the level of history, it turns into combat, the reciprocal negation of classes by each other. Oppressors and oppressed, colonized and colonialists, each of these ensembles is partly a series and partly a group. Each establishes itself by opposition, becomes a series-object by receiving its unity from the look of the other, and forms itself into a group by forging its unity by means of a common will to overcome the *status quo* within and by means of struggle. History, the advent of Truth, which the second volume will have to reconstitute, would put into motion the universals analysed in the first volume, which were discovered by a static and apparently repetitive dialectic—repetitive since the for-itself was necessarily trapped by a contingent necessity within the practico-inert since the group, in order to survive, organized itself, and since the organization gave birth to the institution and sovereignty.

Series and groups [17] are opposed not as contradictory propositions but as ways of individual being within the collective whose characteristics can be said to be contrary. Undoubtedly Sartre plays all the time with the conceptual antitheses of activity–passivity, for-itself and in-itself, *praxis*–inertia, *exis*–*praxis*, internality–externality, series–group, subject–object, for-itself and for-another. Certain of these oppositions, such as the externalization of the internal and the internalization of the external, have a typically Hegelian resonance. The for-itself externalizes itself in materiality, which returns to it the image of its act, graven upon things, and distorted. But these oppositions only constitute a description of the being-in-the-world of a for-itself socialized within a world of objects. *Being and Nothingness* did not include a phenomenological description of these oppositions, but it did call them the dialectic of the for-itself and for-another, which included reciprocal relations as well as opposition. By looking at an other, the for-itself, and therefore each *other*, makes an object, a quasi-in-itself, that, for the for-itself, is continued in a dialectic of collectives, of different ways of being or acting with others.

I would also hesitate to write, as Lawrence Rosen did in his excellent article, that 'only when events pose a contradiction is history made'.[18] There is history from the time that the for-itself, within the world of plurality and materiality, constitutes a perpetual possibility of negation, rupture, and creation. What is opposed to history is repetition. It is not necessary 'to define man by historicity—since there are societies without history— but by the permanent possibility of living *historically* the breakdowns that sometimes upset societies of repetition. This definition is necessarily *a posteriori*; that is, it arises in the midst of an historical society, and it is itself the result of social transformations. But it may be applied retrospectively to societies without history in the same way as history itself returns upon them in order to transform them, first of all externally, and then within and by means of the internalization of externality'

[17] *See* Appendix, Note J.
[18] *History and Theory*, X (1971), 283.

(*Problem of Method*, p. 167, fn. 1). History is not born from contradiction but from the permanent possibility of negation and
overcoming. This negation results, by its contingent necessity,
from being-in-the-world and consciousness condemned to
freedom, freely enslaved and slavishly free. The movement of
negation by the for-itself is thus manifest by a series of oppositions and contrary terms that serve to designate, to describe,
and to understand the alienation of freedom and freedom
within alienation, the contingency of necessity and the necessity of contingency, the externalization of the internal and the
internalization of the external, and the circularity of *praxeis*.
The movement of the for-itself is expressed and revealed in the
reciprocal action of contrary terms. In this sense, contrariness,
if not contradiction, is inserted into the very heart of the
dialectic. Even so, dialectic still has its origin and unique condition in *praxis*, alterity, materiality, and perhaps, so as to lay
the foundation for the violence of history, in scarcity.

No progression, no forward movement results at this point
in the analysis (or of the critical experience) from this dialectic
of contraries (or, of the for-itself, alterity, materiality, and
scarcity). If the reader has another impression, it is because of
the use of the term totalization, which in fact displays a multiplicity of meanings.

Each consciousness totalizes the field of its perception or
action, and each *praxis* totalizes, from *its own point of view*, the
ensembles to which it belongs. The structure of an organization,
whether of kinship or official relations, is made from the petrified structure of relations among individuals, from the inertia
that is inserted into consciousnesses, but not without each consciousness freely assuming its alienation or its functions and
totalizing the ensemble *in its own way*, an ensemble ceaselessly
totalized and detotalized, a non-organic totality that each
consciousness totalizes but without these multiple totalizations
constitute an inert and definitive totality. The totalization by
the for-itself or *praxis* thus, in non-Sartrean language, amounts
to a global apprehension. But the very plurality of these
global apprehensions is enough to show and demonstrate the
partial nature of each one of them. The totalization of History,
from this point of view, could only be *one* totalization of *one*

history. By definition, the historian does not remember everything, the wails of the victims are lost in oblivion along with the pride of the victors; no one will retain the unique, ungraspable lived experience, richer than all concepts, more precious than all triumphs, my joyful days of childhood, my grief at the moment when one dear to me dies. And why do these heart-rending experiences deserve to be saved? No synthesis will ever succeed in uniting the particularity of the individual person with universal History.

When Sartre defines Marxism as the 'totalization of knowledge' are we still dealing with the same totalization? It is not a matter of the whole or of the totality of knowledge. No consciousness dominates and integrates the complete knowledge that the men of his times have acquired. What the Marxist philosophy must supply, according to this formulation, is the system of concepts or the method or mode of thought that would allow one consciousness to grasp major significations and the unity of knowledge peculiar to the epoch. Given not simply the immensity of knowledge but its dispersion, is such a totalization possible? In any event, the fact is that Marxists do not accomplish this totalization. By and large, non-Marxists, and Anglo-Americans in particular, understand by philosophy the analysis of scientific or ordinary language, sometimes granting to reflection upon human existence a mission of wisdom. Hegelianized Marxism, of which Sartre's existentialist Marxism represents a personal modality, occupies a place in the contemporary intellectual scene that is enhanced somewhat in favourable circumstances—I should say, when events (externality) dispose favourably towards Marxism intellectuals who draw back from adherence to Marxism–Leninism.

Does the totalization of History approximate the first or the second sense? It is situated, it seems to me, between the two because it adds to the first sense (i.e., the global apprehension by a *single* consciousness, which is thus an embracing but partial apprehension) the experience of a recovery of the past, which was analysed in *Being and Nothingness*. The meaning of the past always comes to it from the present, from my present, which is to say from the future since only the future, my project, quali-

fies my present being. In fact, Sartre establishes a sort of homogeneity, an essential kinship, between self-knowledge and
historical knowledge by means of the intermediary of my past,
of others, and our common past, inscribed in the 'objective
spirit' that is in me as I am in it. 'I alone, in fact, can decide
at each moment the *bearing* of the past. I do not decide it by
debating it, by deliberating over it, and in each instance evaluat-
ing the importance of this or that prior event; I do it by projecting myself towards my own ends. I preserve my own past
with me, and I *decide* its meaning by action.' Or again: 'the
order of my choices of the future is going to determine an order
of my past . . . A living past, a half-dead past, survivals, ambiguities, discrepancies: the ensemble of these layers of pastness
is organized by the unity of my project' (*Being and Nothingness*,
pp. 498 ff).

In an at least analogous way, the choice by each individual
of his own past represents or prefigures historical choice. 'If
human societies are historical, that does not simply prove that
they have a past, but that they *recover* it in the guise of a *monument.*' If one grants again the homogeneity between an active
recovery, lived from his past by each individual, and the recovery of the past by historical knowledge, the result is that the
signification of the past remains in suspension while history
itself continues. 'Thus, human history would have to be *finished*
before a particular event, for example, the storming of the
Bastille, could receive a definitive *meaning*. Nobody denies, of
course, that the Bastille was stormed in 1789: the immutable
fact is there. But must we see in this event an inconsequential
riot, a popular outburst against a half-dismantled fortress, or
an event that the Convention,[19] anxious to create a famous
past for itself, was able to transform into a glorious deed? . . .
He who would like to decide the question today, would forget
that the historian is himself *historical*, that is, the historian his-
toricizes himself by illuminating "history" in the light of his own
projects and those of society. Thus, we must say that the meaning of the social past is perpetually "in suspense"' (*Being and
Nothingness*, p. 501). Of course, death transforms the lived into
destiny. What has been can no longer not have been. It becomes

[19] Why the Convention?

a brute, immutable fact: the Bastille was stormed on 14 July 1789; Jean Sans Terre died there. But Richelieu, Louis XV, and my grandfather, all transcended transcendences and objects for consciousnesses, have not, for all that, acquired a definitive meaning. They have lost their freedom, the capacity to form projects, and they can no longer resist the signification that subjectivities will give to them, but these subjectivities themselves protect their freedom. In addition, after my own death, my life having become destiny remains in suspense and in suspension as well, for the reply to the question: 'Definitively, what will be the historical destiny of Robespierre?' depends upon the reply to this previous question: 'Does history have a meaning and a direction?' That is to say, must it be completed or merely *terminated*? The question has not been resolved—perhaps it is insoluble—since all the replies that are made to it (including the idealist reply, 'the history of Egypt is the history of Egyptology')[20] are themselves historical.

The understanding of the past by reference to a willed future, the historicity of societies (thanks to the incessant re-covery of the past by the present, stretched towards the future, and of the dead by the living), the transfiguration of the significance of brute facts in light of another lived and willed present, and finally the effort of the historian to safeguard the dimension of choice and project in the past, and thus not to misunderstand that our own past has been the future of actors who intentionally or unintentionally made their own future, which has become our past—this description, which is common to both *Being and Nothingness* and to my *Introduction to the Philosophy of History*, justifies one of the two meanings of dialectical *Reason* and a certain relationship of knowledge and being (namely, a sort of essence of historical being).

Then again, the impossibility of a definitive signification, the very impossibility of a totalization that might be other than situated and *one-sided* seems to result from the same analysis. To accede to the *understanding* of the German psychiatrists and historians, which, keeping both project and totalization, does

[20] This formula, I believe, has been employed by Léon Brunschvicg. It is also quoted on p. 34 of my *Introduction to the Philosophy of History*.

not *explain* mechanically nor determine the present on the basis of the past, but proceeds by the double regressive–progressive route to *dialectical Reason*, it is necessary to add the totalizing Truth to the historical totalization. Or, to use an expression employed in other circumstances, it is necessary that the intelligibility of history results in the totalization of a *single History*. Now, the movement of knowledge implies movement within being and vice versa; knowledge of a *single* History is possible only on condition that History is unified in its becoming, that it has a meaning that is, if not definitive—if it were definitive freedom would disappear—at least provisionally definitive or, to say with Marx, that at least prehistory is completed. As the class struggle, interpreted in light of internalized scarcity and considered as irreducible and inexpiable opposition of oppressors and oppressed, constitutes the motor, the mainspring, the praxeological principle of historical movement, it seems to me that the end of the class struggle and of oppression, even more than the end of exploitation, will complete prehistory and therefore authorize us to speak not only of dialectic but of dialectical Reason.

*   *   *

Perhaps this analysis of the movement from understanding to dialectic and from dialectic to dialectical Reason throws a new light on the dialogue between Lévi-Strauss and Sartre, on the one hand, and upon certain *philosophical* motives of *political* disagreements between Sartre and me, on the other.

Certain philosophical and epistemological positions held by Lévi-Strauss and Sartre are and will remain irreducible. Each society, however limited it may be, even if it consists of but a few dozen men and women deprived of everything, discovers no other meaning to existence and the world save within its own particular collectivity. 'In its own eyes, each of the dozens or hundreds of thousands of societies that have succeeded one another since man first made his appearance, has laid claim to an ethical certainty—similar to that which we ourselves can invoke—in order to proclaim, whether it has been reduced to a small nomad band or to a hamlet lost in the heart of the forest, that all the meaning and dignity of which human life is capable is concentrated in it' (*Savage Mind*, p. 294). To the extent that dialectical Reason is searching for a totalizing Truth of History, resuming an Hegelian ambition with the aid of partially Marxist concepts, it implicitly reduces the value of thousands and thousands of societies and millions and millions of men who would not survive within this totalizing Truth save in terms of the means, antecedents or conditions of this advent. Between the *postulate of equal dignity for all societies*, however unequal they have been in size, power, success, and duration, and *dialectical Reason*, which accedes to a totalizing Truth by following the movement of totalization in action, there does in fact exist a contradiction that does not come from misunderstanding but from irreducible and incompatible existential choices.

A second contradiction, which pertains to both reality *par excellence* and to the orientation of knowledge that seeks to be scientific, results from this first one. The universals that Sartre analyses and describes phenomenologically, if translated into another language, could be, strictly speaking, accepted by Lévi-Strauss. He could accept them, at least, to the extent that Sartre's esoteric vocabulary would be content to translate the presence of collectives in individuals and of individuals in collectives at the same time as the diverse modalities of this reciprocal insertion. But Lévi-Strauss is hardly interested in these descriptions to which Sartre attaches such great importance. They tend to show the intelligibility of the *whole* of historico-social reality at the same time as the permanence of freedom within the most extreme forms of alienation. But this typically Sartrean problem, which is tied to the ontology of the for-itself, is foreign to Lévi-Strauss. Even more, Sartre is inclined to give a privileged status to historical knowledge as the dialectic rather than as knowledge of institutions, structures and systems of behaviour heading towards the inertia that has provisionally seized the élan of *praxis*. In the end, when the political man carries away the philosopher, Sartre accuses all those who place the accent upon the petrified structure of a society or a collective of serving conservatism by forgetting— which means by denying—the *praxis* by which every society comes into being and maintains itself, by which History, thanks to the negation of the inert object that the empirical sociologist confuses with society, also progresses.

The dialogue does not necessarily fall to this level of vulgar polemic. Lévi-Strauss does not neglect lived experience nor the global apprehension of data by consciousness either at the beginning or end of scientific research. Neither does Sartre neglect the regularities of behaviour, duties and rights, modes of kinship, systems of behaviour, and the order imposed upon consciousnesses without which there would be a welter of actions, dispersed in a plurality of collectives, themselves successively series and groups, and not a totalizable ensemble. That these collectives do not eliminate *praxis*, the project, or the for-itself, as Sartre untiringly tries to show, does not appear to me to justify so much effort and so many pages. It is not just that every institution (in the Durkheimian not the Sartrean sense), such as customs, rites, beliefs, and modes of kinship and labour, is *arbitrary* and, in this sense if you like, that every institution emanates from freedom (which is not to say that one could attribute a personalized freedom to them). But, even more than that, they differ from natural determinism in that they are not prevented from their own violation so that, if you like, each *praxis* maintains in the very depths of its alienation and amid the thickest part of the social glue, the capacity, at least in theory (or ontology), to tear itself away from its inertia. This power is just as in *Being and Nothingness*, where no existential choice made with respect to being would definitively enclose consciousness, where consciousness always remained master of itself and of its possible conversion.

Even if Lévi-Strauss does not exclude lived experience, and even if Sartre does not exclude structures (in a vague sense of the word), two disagreements exist at a deeper level. Which of the two Reasons can account for the other? Which brings with it a valid and scientific knowledge? And secondly, where is the being that knowledge must reach in order to explicate human reality, and thus societies and history, located?[21]

Dialectical Reason, as we have seen, tends to be mixed with consciousness itself in its movement towards the future, in its

[21] *See* Appendix, Note K.

negation of the given and its pro-ject of itself towards a non-being that has to be. The moment of negation, the decisive moment of the dialectic according to the present interpretation, is thus found internal to the for-itself and *praxis*. Negation is inseparable from consciousness, which is temporalized and made by making itself; it is by means of consciousness that the in-itself comes into being and knowledge. The result is, in Sartrean thought, a priority of the for-itself over the in-itself, and thus of dialectical Reason over analytical Reason. The global apprehension of the given by perception presents us with relations of externality, which lend themselves to dismantling and restoration, and to an analysis and deduction, only when the project comes to rest, by the detotalization of the totalization and the renunciation of understanding in favour of explanation.

This priority of life over knowledge does not yet imply that dialectical Reason as a mode of knowledge could give an account of analytical Reason. From the very first, the primacy of the former over the latter appeared in its purity and evidence only at the ontological level. The critical experience shows us a socialized and trapped *praxis*, apparently a prisoner of rights, duties, and crystallized institutions, anxious about its own interests and subordinate to a sovereign group, at once isolated from others and lost within ensembles. And yet, in spite of everything, Sartre finds *praxis* again master of itself beneath the superimposed layers of materiality and seriality that consciousnesses internalize but never entirely absorb.

We agree that this phenomenological description of the structures of consciousness as well as collectives depend upon dialectic Reason. But it is as yet only a question of a philosophical knowledge or an ontological truth. Let us admit again that the relation of the historian to the past, to which he has no existential relation, maintains a kinship in depth with the lived relation of individual consciousness to its own past. What remains of this relation is nothing less than that the historian must, through the evidence, that is, through words and deeds, patiently reconstitute the existence of another or of collectives, series, or groups. Something of the original dialectic of consciousness continues to exist in the understanding of oneself,

of others, or of historical becoming: the reciprocal inter-
relationship between the individual elements and the whole
(the former are meaningful only within the latter, and the
latter cannot be understood except by an indefinite analysis
of the former). At certain moments of the narrative, it is imperative that the historian attempt to place himself at the
moment of decision. He must consider the possibilities as
genuinely possible outcomes whose possible being a *praxis*
turned into realities. The critic of strategy does not understand
acts or decisions save by confronting them with those that the
actor or the strategist has declared definitely not to exist. The
subject of understanding, whether he considers an individual
existence or epoch, sometimes harbours the inevitable and impossible ambition of living out an existence that he reconstitutes. Or rather, he has the illusion, which he gives to himself and to others, that he lives and partakes of another existence. Yet, must this understanding–knowledge be knowledge
and, therefore, could it be true? In other words, even if the
dialectical nature of reality is transferred to the knowledge we
gain of it, we still have to establish the *truth* of this knowledge.
Existential psychoanalysis, such as Sartre undertakes, resorts to
steps comparable to those of every biography and psychoanalysis, even though these latter do not use properly Sartrean
concepts such as passivity, activity, active passivity and passive
activity. His is an understanding marked by the original dialectic of consciousness, but it still demands ordinary research
procedures and proofs in order to avoid the arbitrariness of
intuition or impressionism. In this sense, only analytical
Reason confirms the truth of an understanding–interpretation.

If psychoanalytic understanding does use universals (in fact,
they are the abstract universals of the ontology of *Being and
Nothingness* or the *Critique*), sociology does not always tend
towards understanding. Even when it wishes to retain certain
aspects of dialectical reality, it makes use of all kinds of procedures, including those charcteraistic of natural science. It
constructs its object, it elaborates models, (the perfect market
of liberalism, conflict models that lead to extreme behaviour,

organigrams of organizations, and so on); it substitutes quanti-
fiable opinions for lived experiences, and searches for correlations or causal relations among variables. If certain passages
were eliminated, it is of course true in a sense that all the human
or social sciences could discover their object in *certain aspects* of
the social reality described by the *Critique* (without any use
of dialectical Reason for the analysis of the market or the
impact of the gold of the New World). The central proposition, that the action of men is mediated by things and that
things are mediated by men, is sufficient to justify the reference
to lived experiences and to collective or individual choices, even
when the historian intends or follows a process. In the same
way, it authorizes us to neglect the lived experiences of individuals when the sociologist is concerned with the mechanisms
by which the 'invisible hand' produces certain results that are
surprising for the actors or when he is concerned with the internal structure of a language, of a kinship system or a political
regime. Even if the ensemble of prohibitions and obligations is
strict and imperative there is scarcely a society where one does
not find many cases of cuckoldry or incest. These examples
illustrate one of the meanings that Sartre attributes to the permanence of freedom within alienation. On the other hand,
neither a system of rules nor a phonological or semantic system
of a language (even though every system implies a for-itself so
that such systems may be used) refers to a constituting *praxis*
nor even to a constituted *praxis*. A language or a kinship system
constitutes a totality whose structure can be understood by the
linguist or ethnologist only by the typical steps of analytical
Reason, and these steps mean dismantling and restoration. This
is true even if the final explanation brings to light an ensemble
of terms in binary opposition, or in other words, a structure
inert to the object and unknown to the subject, a structure that
reproduces certain traits of the dialectic.

The social sciences also study social objects that either do not
present a dialectical structure in the Sartrean sense (processes,
mechanisms, the invisible hand etc.), or they present a hidden
dialectic that, contrary to the structures uncovered by the
labours of psychoanalysis, are discovered by a strictly analytical
investigation.

At the same time, the double Sartrean claim, namely, that only dialectical Reason allows for the understanding of human history, and that it is equivalent in the *epistemological* order to a Reason that is radically heterogeneous compared to the analytical Reason of the natural and positivist sciences, falls apart. Nothing prevents us from reserving a part of the understanding to a dialectical Reason when it is important not to eliminate from a known object certain characteristically dialectical traits, not to forget that men have lived our past as their own future, and that they have made it by making themselves. Finally, the dialectical order is important when we want less to explain a system of wife exchange, gifts or commodities, than to understand how Others have been able to find meaning and salvation in an existence that to ourselves seems nonsense and perdition.

Lévi-Strauss reproaches Sartre for cutting himself off from other societies, for enclosing himself in the *cogito* and not leaving it. The reproach is partly justified by the way that Sartre, in search of the foundation-of-the-possibility-and-the-truth-of-Marxism, slides from his *praxis* to universal History by resorting to abstract universals borrowed from the mode of western thinking.[22] It is a reproach that does not touch the concept of understanding of the German psychiatrists and historians, an understanding that, on the contrary, has been given the objective of acceding to the Other, of being capable of grasping the diversity of ways of thinking, sensing, and action. Granted, understanding-empathy (*Einfühlung*) courts the risk, under the pretext of escaping the ego in order to encounter the other, of simply finding itself again in the other. The understanding of the Other in his alterity, that understanding of the ethnologist who, gaining the greatest recompense for his own loss of a natural feeling of belonging to a country, lives simultaneously the existence of the Bororos and that of his own society, or at least he feels he can understand how to be both Bororo and French in 1973. Such understanding is always threatened with being blocked before an ungraspable alterity or defeated by the illegitimate assimilation of the other to itself. And yet, it con-

---

[22] Even though Lévi-Strauss discerns a kinship with the Melanesian mode of thinking.

stitutes the initial and final step of the ethnographer and the historian.

* * *

The consequences of the ontological transformation of understanding into dialectical Reason that we have so far commented upon do not yet imply that the taste for Revolution and a lack of it for reform have become a philosophical truth or that the strange alliance between Reason and violence, whereby the other—the conservative, the reformist, anyone who says 'no' to the revolutionary apocalypse—takes on the grim traits of the anti-man, is sealed.

I have never ignored the specific characteristics of the historicity of the knowing and acting man, such as Sartre described them at the ontological level in *Being and Nothingness*. History is in man as man is in history; he makes it by making himself; he is liberated from it by willing himself a future in the light of which he gives himself another past. On some points, and moreover on fundamentals, Sartre and I have discussed interminably, as Simone de Beauvoir has said, without ever convincing each other or reaching agreement.[23] Sartre used to maintain his conception of freedom and the choice of his being by each individual only by denying all psychological heredity. The for-itself began as empty freedom. I used to reply to him, 'You have never looked at a baby'. Freedom, in his view, existed, operated, and was realized in the forward flight of the project. Even though it is delayed and, therefore, denies the instantaneousness of Cartesian freedom, freedom creates neither the person nor permanence but remains for ever open towards new futures. To the extent that motives, the confrontation of pro and con, emerge from the project rather than determine it, it is spontaneity much more than choice. According to

[23] Concerning psychoanalysis and the unconscious, he has progressively been persuaded. I used to tell him: 'If your ontology prevents you from accepting the notion of the unconscious, all right: find another concept. But, you can neither ignore nor reject the knowledge, experience and modes of interpretation of psychoanalysis.' The concept of bad faith allows him to integrate part of psychoanalysis.

Simone de Beauvoir, Sartre refuses to admit 'that he has any identity whatsoever with his own past'.[24] I have quite another experience that I too call freedom. Each of us is born with his chromosome heritage and into his family milieu that is already half determined or is being half determined before we reach a thetic self-consciousness. I put the effort of liberation not in the spontaneity of the for-itself but in the reflective decision, taken on the basis of a me-object who is and is not *I*, and of whom I am not the unconditional master. Whence the dialectic of freedom and fidelity, whence the miserable succession of misfortune that time does not heal, whence the return to a guilty conscience and the unhappy memories of lost opportunities, of mistakes made, of words that ought to have been said and were not, of judgements that I ought to have published and that I reserved for friendly conversations? I have never sensed myself to be 'condemned to freedom' rather than condemned to an always incomplete liberation, as external constraints limit our power and internal ones our efforts of detachment. Just as the identification of the nothingness—distance from self to self-consciousness (to be what one is not and not to be what one is) with non-being, as it is defined in the philosophical tradition (but which has always appeared to me to be a word-game), so too the absoluteness of freedom presupposes a consciousness without biological determination, a freedom—spontaneity that gives itself reasons but does not obey them.

Is the Revolution a social or collective transposition of Sartrean freedom? In a sense, an affinity exists between the two: both negate the given towards an unknown future. Both are defined by negation and project, the rejection of what is and the will to accomplish a task that appears in the hollow of constituting *praxis* or the group. Even more, if the for-itself afterwards finds arguments to rationalize an already made choice, why would the group have to know where it is going before setting off? Why would a class or a party have to know about or imagine the regime that it projects to build before

---

[24] The text is reproduced in Michel Contat and Michel Rybalka, *Les Écrits de Sartre*, p. 419. It is from an interview given to Madeleine Gobeil that appeared in the American edition of *Vogue*, No. 146 (July 1965), pp. 72–3.

throwing down the one that exists? Thus, I see a similarity between the absolutism of freedom and the absolutism of the Revolution, while reform assumes the acceptance of part of what is and the limitation of change.

This interpretation allows a fault in the theory of dialectic Reason to continue to exist. Why and how can the projects, which are entirely free, dispersed and discontinuous, comprise a *single* History that is itself the condition of dialectical Reason? (The intelligibility of *history* amounts to the Weberian notion of intelligibility and assures neither historical totalization nor totalizing Truth.) In other words, so that freedoms, either because of or in spite of their absolute nature, can overcome each other to achieve a totalizing Truth, they must not express themselves or act in any way whatsoever. The constituted dialectic must at least allow for partial totalizations that themselves are ultimately integrated into a totalizing Truth. By what subterfuge will the negation of the social given by the action-group become rational, *per se*? The answer, which appears so paradoxical at first, admits of hardly any doubt: by the intermediary of violence. The first proposition is that *praxis* can only be totally free or totally alienated. The sole reasonable reply to alienation is rebellion, the refusal of alienation, and the quest for alienated but not lost freedom. Or again, rebellion arises from the impossibility of living an impossible existence. There again, the intrinsic rationality of the dialectic holds for the negation of the given; now, as the given is mixed with the social reality whose structure is indicated by the will to negate, the negation ends up, by means of a series of equivalencies, in a rebellion that only succeeds within and by means of the Revolution. The defeated rebellion in fact entails a fall back into seriality, the practico-inert or, concretely, into the impossible life that the group wished to surmount.

The link between Reason and violence is also outlined by another route. From the moment when the *Critique* ended up on the threshold of totalizing or cumulative history, the class struggle, with its priority of oppression over exploitation and of the will to oppress over a deduction from the surplus by the privileged, has been described, elaborated, and demonstrated to be the motor of history. It is by means of the class struggle, by the antagonism of groups where everyone wishes the death of the other, that the dialectical movement, whose completion is marked by the advent of totalizing Truth, progresses. To be sure, the contingency of scarcity is what makes men enemies for each other. History remains no less the history of men as it has unfolded up to the present when it is defined essentially by struggle and violence. And it will be defined by violence up to the end of pre-history, up to the day that Marxism will cease to express our history, for as yet, no one is able to conceive of the philosophy of freedom, of a free society without classes and without exploitation, founded on the reciprocity of *praxeis*, even if worked-upon matter and the Other allow an element of alienation to continue to exist.

In other words, in the world of scarcity and classes, the dialectic, which is to say, negation, is identified in the final analysis with struggle and thus with violence. Historical *praxis*, the origin of the dialectic, does not deserve the qualification of being rational save to the extent that the totalizing Truth is achieved by means of it. This Truth, in turn, is not achieved save by the class struggle or by the struggle of oppressors and oppressed, and thus by violence. Dialectical Reason is violence, and Violence is the Truth of Marxism until the day when another philosophy, entirely unthinkable today, a philosophy of freedom achieved, and not of freedom being achieved by violence, will put an end to the moment of Marxism. Then Marxism will be *completed* and not just *ended*.

The preface to Frantz Fanon's, book *The Wretched of the Earth*, expresses in an extreme form and in a philosophical language the humanization of man by violence. The theme had already been dealt with in the closing scene of *The Devil and the Good Lord*. 'We find our humanity on this side of death and despair; the rebel finds it beyond torture and death. We have been sowers in the wind; he is the whirlwind. The child of violence, at every moment he draws from it his humanity. We were men at his expense, he makes himself a man at ours: a different man, a man of higher quality . . . High-minded people, liberals or just soft-hearted folk,—the neo-colonialists— protest that they are shocked by European inconsistency. But they are either mistaken or in bad faith, for with us there is nothing more consistent than a racist humanism, since the European has only been able to become a man by creating slaves and monsters. While there was a native population somewhere this imposture was not shown up . . . Today, the native population reveals its own truth. And at the same time our exclusive club reveals its weakness. Namely, that it is neither more nor less than a minority. Worse than that, since others become men in name against us, it seems that we are the enemies of mankind. The elite shows itself in its true nature: a gang.'[25] And a little farther on, we read, in a language that recalls that of the *Critique*: 'For the folk across the Mediterranean, new men, freed men, no one has the power nor the right to give anything to anybody. For each of them has every right over us, and the right to everything. And one day, when our human kind becomes full-grown, it will not define itself as the sum total of the whole world's inhabitants, but as the infinite unity of their reciprocities.' One more step to take: the colonialist, driven out by the revolt of the colonized, is in turn about to internalize the violence that threatens him, and become a native. 'Violence, proclaimed by some, disowned by others, turns in a vacuum. One day it bursts out at Metz, the next at Bordeaux. It's here, there, everywhere, like in a game of hunt the slipper. It's our turn to tread the path, step by step, which leads down to native level. But to become natives altogether, our soul must be occupied by formerly colonized people, and we must starve of hunger. This won't happen. For it's a discredited colonialism that's taking hold on us. This is the senile, arrogant master who will straddle us . . . Eight years of silence. What degradation! And your silence is of no avail. Today the blinding sun of torture is at its zenith. It lights up the whole country. Under that merciless glare, there is not a laugh that does not ring false, not a face that is not painted to hide fear or anger . . . In other days, France was the name of a country. We should take care that it does not become the name of a nervous disease.'[26] The internalization of the violence of the colonized by the colonialist does not *complete* the

[25] 'Preface' to Frantz Fanon, *The Wretched of the Earth*, tr., C. Farrington (London: MacGibbon and Kee, 1965), pp. 20, 22.
[26] *Ibid.*, pp. 24–5.

dialectic. Internalized violence will, in turn explode, in the violence of the colonialists, which is to say, the French, who will engage in violence against each other. The last moment of the dialectic will, in a certain way, justify the moments that will have preceded it: man will emerge renewed. Perhaps, it must be said, he will die from this dialectic of violence, or from this dialectical violence that is the advent of man. 'Will we recover? Yes, for violence, like Achilles' lance, can heal the wounds that it has inflicted. Today, we are bound hand and foot, humiliated, and sick with fear. We cannot fall lower . . . Every day we retreat in front of the battle, but you may be sure that we shall not avoid it. The killers need it . . . This is the last moment of the dialectic. You condemn this war but do not yet declare yourselves on the side of the Algerian fighters. Never fear, you can count on the colonialists and their mercenaries. They'll make you take the plunge. Then, perhaps, when your back is to the wall, you will let loose at last that new violence which is raised up in you by old oft-repeated crimes. But, as they say, that's another story. The history of mankind. The time is drawing near, I am sure, when we shall join the ranks of those who make it.'[27]

I trust the reader will forgive the length of these quotations. The text is not lacking in a certain eloquence, despite the mixture of rhetorical styles and its sometimes grotesque rhetorical excesses. 'It is enough today for two Frenchmen to meet together for there to be a dead man between them.'[28] Who has kept such a memory of 1961? The civil war that was proclaimed and the promise of re-birth have not taken place. The French have had neither to fight nor to die in camps. They have recovered from their Algerian neurosis not by unleashing the violence they had internalized but, quite the contrary, by coming to terms with what external violence legitimately demanded.

I have chosen this example of a political position taken by Sartre concerning on-going events because I adopted the same one: I recognized the legitimacy of the fighting undertaken by the 'Algerian rebels', without denying that perhaps at beginning

[27] *Ibid.*, pp. 25–6.
[28] *Ibid.*, p. 25.

they represented but a minority of a colonized people. In the world and in the France of 1955 (the date of the elections that put Guy Mollet in office), Algeria's attaining independence appeared to me inevitable and, at the same time, it appeared to conform to 'political justice' as the term was then largely understood by those who, for want of a better word, can be called the representatives of the 'French conscience'. And finally, it appeared to be compatible with the interest and future of the country once it had overcome its ordeal. However, even though Sartre and I were in agreement about the independence of Algeria, we had not really been able to hear or understand each other: the dialectic of violence and the ironic reference to tender souls and liberals (even though liberalism has nothing to do with the Algerian business), these two aspects, the one fundamental, the other marginal, reveal and illustrate both political divergence and philosophical opposition. Let us say first of all, so as not to return to it, that the violence of these remarks puts me off even when they are not accompanied by action in the same style. Francis Jeanson acted in accordance with the Sartrean dialectic by organizing a support network for the F.L.N., the Algerian Liberation Movement. The evidence that Sartre was able to give at the trial of the Jeanson organization corresponded to the logic of his thought. Personally, at that time, during 1960 and 1961, I was writing against both the O.A.S. and against civil war.[29] Not that I was unconditionally opposed to violence, as Sartre affected to believe. On the contrary, I know (and who does not?) that human history advances blindly upon the ruins of civilizations and over the dead bodies of the innocent. States are built by violence and are maintained by force that has become an institution, a camouflage of violence that is henceforth unperceived even by those who suffer it. Justice deserts the victor's camp, as though the dialectic reversed roles but without leading to reciprocity and recognition in equality. I do not even think that compromise is always better than fighting, nor that Algerian independence could have been attained

[29] At that time Merleau-Ponty found himself on the same side as I was; he wrote to tell me so, towards the end of 1960, when he was preparing a statement in reply to that of the '121'.

other than by violence. What I hate is not the choice, *hic et nunc*, at a particular conjunction of circumstances, in favour of violence and against negotiation,[30] but a philosophy of violence in and for itself, not as means that is sometimes necessary for a rational politics,[31] but a philosophy that lays claim to an on-tological foundation and psychological function or effectiveness.

'Violence, like Achilles' lance can heal the wounds it has inflicted.' Maybe. Two friends, suddenly angry with each other, find themselves exhausted and friends again after a good scuffle. Perhaps it would be better to get rid of 'morbid humours' and accumulated resentment by real anger and cries of fury rather than suppress a strongly held aggression towards another or express it passively by seething with anger and by having to will to oneself and to the world not 'to act out' one's violence. Yes, suppressed violence sometimes corrupts the blood. But has not the violence unleashed in the French Revolution, the June Days, the Commune, also corrupted the national conscience? I never manage to read without some uneasiness the passage in the *Recollections*[32] of Alexis de Tocque-ville where, from February 1848 on, he estimates that violence will inevitably be used against the Paris crowd, and how he resigns himself to it in advance. At least he did not see a mo-ment in the dialectic of Reason in this battle. He regretted that the old and proud nobility had been violently eliminated rather than preserved in a new role while being deprived of their privileges. From the Third Republic on, French intellectuals transfigured the French Revolution as if it had not cost twenty years of foreign wars and a repetitive civil war as a counterpart to its acquisitions. And even these were hardly consolidated after a century. In each of the circumstances when France seemed to be threatened with a new episode in this civil war— the Popular Front, the Liberation, the Algerian crisis, and the O.A.S., the events of 1968—I think would have been better to have tried to reduce the volume of violence. Not by liberalism,

[30] I had a conversation with Frantz Fanon in Tunisia during the Algerian war. He lived out violence quite differently than did Sartre.

[31] Clausewitz or Lenin conceived of violence in this way.

[32] Tr., G. Lawrence, ed., J. P. Mayer and A. P. Kerr (London: Mac-donald, 1970) [Tr. note].

unless it means the rejection of Manicheism and refusing to exclude the vanquished from the law, unless it means the will, never fully achieved, to see the world with the eyes of the other. Understood this way, it hardly accords with tender souls. And as for the dialectic of violence practised in the study, pen in hand, rather than underground in the shadow of possible torture, I prefer not to judge so long as I have trouble in understanding it. I should also say that I have trouble imagining from within the lived experience of the one who develops it in words.

Is it not a question of a taste for Revolution, which Simone de Beauvoir attributes to Sartre even before he emerged from the cave of speculation towards the tumult of politics? Of course, an interpretation of the *Critique* as a whole on the basis of his personal temperament would not demand an excess of subtlety from the commentator. But what is essential would be allowed to escape: the structures of freedom in both *Being and Nothingness* and the *Critique*. Some commentators have upheld the thesis, wrong in my view, of a rupture between the two books. Certainly the tone changes from the one to the other, and the *Critique* seems to describe the enslavement of *praxis* with the same ingenuity employed in *Being and Nothingness* to demonstrate the absoluteness of freedom. An attentive reading of the *Critique* tends in fact towards the same demonstration as in *Being and Nothingness*: freedom survives despite the enslavement within the practico-inert.

Freedom is limited only by itself and the freedom of others, we read in *Being and Nothingness*. But this absolute of *freedom*[33] does not contradict the limitation of our power. The rock we cannot climb does not determine our impotence; it is not 'unclimbable' in itself. It is not an external obstacle into which the for-itself collides, but becomes an obstacle by the project of the climber. But then again, Sartrean freedom is meant to be radically foreign to Stoic freedom: internal freedom, freedom of thought despite external constraints, freedom of suffering with indifference what does not depend upon us. Sartrean freedom *exists* as doing and acting. The absolute of freedom did not,

[33] *See* Appendix, Note L.

without something of a paradox, tolerate the obstacles it used to create for itself or that the Other created for it. The concept of the absolute is justified in spite of everything by the existential choice of each consciousness by itself with respect to being, an existential choice that was reproduced within the continuity of time, where it was historicized, and that left the possibility of conversion (or of another choice) intact. It was also justified by the responsibility that it established: to speak under torture or to give in to fatigue is still to choose oneself freely since others did not speak, others resisted torture, since it is I who chose to speak or sit down beside the road.

The *Critique* is not deduced from *Being and Nothingness*. Over the years, Sartre has wished to elaborate an ethics on the basis of his ontology. He has elaborated a philosophy of history or the abstract universals of a possible philosophy of history. His political commitments have oriented him in this direction. But it was enough for him to describe phenomenologically the fundamental structures of the situation totalized by the look and the relationships with the Other and with collectives, and to substitute *praxis* for the for-itself, in order to suggest to the superficial reader the false idea of a radical conversion. According to the reading we have made of it, the *Critique* is intent upon maintaining the ontological and epistemological primacy of *praxis* or constituting dialectic and thus of the dialectic of the individual consciousness. Social man, who submits to *exigencies*, who affirms *values*, who is attached to *interests*, who is in a class or is imbued with it, an atom of a series or an actor of a group, derives ontologically from *praxis*. None of the collectives, series, or groups overcomes this derivation as such. How can one resolve this apparent contradiction between the absoluteness of freedom and the practico-inert, the inevitable inscription of *praxis* upon matter, the secret understanding of the meaning of our action by the other, this dialectic of materiality and serial-ity? Either this dialectic is as permanent as the dialectic of the for-itself and the for-another, of the for-itself-subject that be-comes an object for the look of the other, or *praxis* can only be totally free or totally alienated. Certain texts and a note that I have quoted above,[34] agree with the first alternative. But

[34] See above, pp. 101, 113–14 (*Critique*, pp. 285 and 349, note).

ultimately, from all his non-passive passion, Sartre choses the second alternative, even if certain structures of alienation, which are inseparable from materiality and seriality, do not disappear with the disappearance of classes, capitalism, and oppression. History, such as we live it, affected by scarcity, has the class struggle as its motor and meaning. It is identified with the dialectic of violence. Thus Sartre rejects liberalism (at least, what he means by this term) and reform not after an examination of its particular oulook, but in principle. His choice of violence and Revolution is philosophical at the same time as it is political.

For a long time I have reproached Sartre for endowing with philosophical dignity his political opinions, his verbal taste for Revolution, his indulgence for crimes committed in the name of good ideas (revolutionary ideas), his severity for crimes committed in the name of bad ones, and in short, for laying the philosophical foundations for the conscious and voluntary choice of the attitude of 'double standard'. I have been both right and wrong: I was criticizing the implications of his philosophy on the basis of the implications of my own. In contrast to the fascist philosophies of violence, Sartre's philosophy has humanity as its horizon, not as a whole, as a sum-total of the inhabitants of the planet, but as 'the infinite unity of their reciprocities', as a universalist whole and, in its aspirations and values, is therefore strongly opposed to fascism. Even so, we still must know whether a philosophy that carries such implicacations as the *systematic* choice of violence or Revolution deserves to be taken for a dialectic of man.

Why do we end up even thinking that Sartre's conclusions may even be related to fascism? I see two main reasons: the absolutist conception of freedom (or negation), and the consequent refusal to accept the inevitable socialization of *praxeis*. And second, the refusal to compare real or possible regimes with each other so as to choose, according to time and place, such and such a path towards liberation. The subject, whether it be individual or collective, is made into such and such a subject by doing. It is not an empty freedom but a way of being, thinking, and willing. It is never a thing and is always capable of starting itself up again and breaking away from its own past, but it is never capable, as Sartre claims according to Simone de Beauvoir, of denying its identity with its own past, and starting off anew for a new future.[35] We are all heirs of others and of ourselves, and if there is no inheritance save for a free being who can call things into question again, it only makes sense to do so as regards a heritage. No one, whether individual or collective, is suddenly and completely freed. The Kantian conversion by which a man breaks with radical evil belongs to the religious realm; translated into profane terms, it turns into illusion or myth for the individual and into a principle of violence in history. Let us go a step further. Let us postulate that each one chooses the party of the oppressors or of the oppressed and that, rather than choose between a Soviet-type regime and a capitalist–democratic regime, there are only two camps, the one of hangmen and the other of their victims. And here am I, with all anti-communists, transformed into a dog. It is true that in 1969 Sartre could write a text, a very fine one, moreover, entitled 'Socialism Come in from the Cold' without the risk of falling into the canine realm. Tolerable anti-communism varies according to Parisian caprice and the expectations of youth.

*   *   *

Let us take leave of these ill-tempered quarrels. According to Lionel Abel[36] and Maurice Cranston,[37] the *Critique* finds its public and will have its influence in the third world, because Sartre is attached to, interested in, and joined (by his thought) with groups not yet bureaucratized, even if they are organized and, by this fact, can offer individuals an access to historical action. Perhaps leftists in industrial societies, whether by reading it or not, have applied the lesson that the *Critique* seems to offer. If dialogue with the *Critique* gives rise only to the philosophical formulae of the *Ideas that Have Shaken France*, the fore-

---

[35] *See* Appendix, Note M.

[36] 'Sartre and Lévi-Strauss,' *Commonweal*, 39:13 (27 June 1966), pp. 346–68, and republished in E. N. Hayes and T. Hayes, eds., *Lévi-Strauss, The Anthropologist as Hero* (Cambridge, Mass.: M.I.T. Press, 1970), pp. 235–46.

[37] 'Sartre and Violence', *Encounter*, 29 (July 1967), pp. 18–24.

going pages, even though they are less numerous than those of the *Critique* itself, would not deserve to have been written.

Now, even though it is not appropriate for the author to speak on such a question, it does not appear to me to be immodest to affirm that the problems we have dealt with here continue to exist, problems that, as yet, Sartre has treated in a philosophical vocabulary that has become unfashionable, an Hegelian and phenomenological vocabulary rather than a Nietzschean and structuralist one. These problems exist even though certain English and American analysts willingly believe them to have been resolved.

Implicitly, such quite ordinary propositions as 'man makes history but he is made by it', 'man makes history but he knows not the history he makes', 'man makes history on the basis of given conditions', contain within them the dialectic of the internal and the external, of sociality and historicity, of the immediately given understanding of being in a situation and the necessary objectification of human reality so as to explicate it, or even, after a long detour of exploration, to return to an enriched and mediated understanding of the initially given outlook. The ontological transformation of understanding draws Sartre towards a radical and, as such, untenable opposition of two Reasons. Not only does he succeed in misunderstanding the kinship of procedures of investigation of both men and things, but he accepts only with some reticence what the phenomenology of alienation would allow him to accept—the models, systems, constants, and generalizations in the absence of which the historian's, or the economist's, or the ethnologist's understanding would not differ from the understanding of the political man, nor would the commentator differ from the original author, or the ethnographer from the primitive. The Sartrean and ontological version of understanding would condemn the historian or ethnographer, as Sartre reproaches Lévi-Strauss, to see only himself in the other or to see only the other with respect to himself, and consequently to destroy what constitutes for the historian or the ethnographer their task and reward *par excellence*, which is to succeed in keeping their distance from their own ego, or, in other words, to recognize alterity.

In the the same way, totalizing Truth reduced to the class struggle, with its vague perspective of non-antagonistic reciprocity, caricatures the classical philosophies of history. Must we overcome scarcity? And can we do so without prohibiting the birth of those whose number would reproduce scarcity indefinitely? And thus, can it be done without killing them? How to obey the rules of such a reciprocity within a regime of equality? Is a fully egalitarian reciprocity compatible with the objectification by each of the subjectivity of the other and with the necessities of organization, with the fatality of the institution and with the bursting forth of the Sovereign? Can action in history avoid being degraded into violence from the time that it is determined solely in terms of the alternative of oppressors and oppressed, dominators and dominated, without even knowing if every society does not contain a similar dichotomy in one degree or another? Or if the actual power of man is not exercised only in terms of the degee and mode of domination or oppression?

At the end of the *Critique*, the analysis of historical consciousness in thought and action, far from being completed, remains a task or a project. It is an epistemological task since the human sciences do not always deal with man as an ant and since they would lose all contact with the way men communicate with each other if they eliminated from their object humanity, consciousness, and freedom. It is a necessary project if man, you the reader and me the writer, is embarked on a collective adventure in which he actively participates, and does so even when he abstains from acting. Whether it is the prodigious pride of the Sartrean subject or the strange modesty of the philosopher who denies his *I* and refuses to attribute his work, personal as it is, to it, what difference does it make? We know well that we have lived and that we still live in an epoch full of sound and fury. What does it mean? Does it mean anything? Futurologists will not tell us. How to answer without asking oneself about the plurality of historical worlds and the scope of human possibility? After such questioning each of us will in the end answer on his own responsibility, conscious of his insignificance in the midst of three and a half thousand millions of his fellow beings, conscious as well that, for him, everything depends on it. Each of us is himself judged by being committed, and my commitment threatens me, whatever follows from it, with perdition, unless I am the Prince who gambles the salvation of his soul against the salvation of the City and for whom success is justification.

Action in the history of the subject, the citizen, the Prince, the party: from philosophy of history to political philosophy. Only those who have renounced life in the community, where, by chance, they were born and whose destiny they will to assume, would hold such a problematic to be anachronistic.

VII

Concluding Remarks

In the Preface to this book, I suggested that the *Critique* resembles an unclassifiable baroque monument, foreign to every school, outside every philosophical movement, and that it was the expression of an original and powerful personality. In spite of everything, perhaps at the end of this exposition and these critical remarks, the reader has discovered that the problems to which Sartre tries to offer his solution are more classic than his mode of presentation would lead one to think. In these final pages I would like to make such problems explicit and, as a transition to my second volume, I would make use of certain concepts of Anglo-American analytical philosophy, which, on any philosophical continuum, are situated at the extreme end, quite opposite to the existentialist philosophy of the *Critique*.

In analytical language, the *Critique* tends towards the following objective: *to establish ontologically the foundations of methodological individualism.* Of course, neither Sir Karl Popper nor F. Hayek, assuming they had read the book, would find their familiar universe in it. It is still true that both deny, either explicitly or implicitly, the ontological reality of collectives. Now, Sartre also intends to reduce all human, socio-historical reality to individual *praxis*, which, according to him, is the sole ontological reality or, at the very least, is the ontological origin of practice-oriented ensembles or of the anti-dialectic wherein individual *praxis* is alienated and seems to disappear.

All historico-social reality being, in principle, ontologically reducible to individual *praxis*, and *praxis* being defined by the project, *understanding* becomes the normal, if not the unique, mode of anthropological knowledge. The Sartrean theory of *understanding* is derived from the German psychiatrists and historians whom, directly or indirectly, he has succeeded in studying. But the theory of *understanding*, thoroughly familiar to neo-Kantians at the end of the last century, has been taken up again by a number of analysts; it is presented by them in, so to speak, a positivist or prosaic form. Is not to understand an action in daily life first of all to grasp its intended end? Will not even the historian who asks *why* Hitler attacked the Soviet Union in June 1941, be drawn inevitably to reconstitute the deliberation of the Führer, the *objective* that he hoped to gain, by the *means* chosen with respect to a given set of *circumstances*? William Dray and Georg Henrik von Wright,[1] by showing or demonstrating by argument in an analytic style the necessity or validity of *understanding* as an interpretation or explication of action by its ends, at the same time have brought to light certain specific traits of the historical sciences or of history alone. Certainly neither the analysts of Dray's nor G. H. von Wright's school present their thesis in ontological language. Perhaps they would refuse to give it an ontological signification or perhaps they would think an ontological controversy beside the point. Provisionally, I limit myself to two incontestable propositions: Sartre establishes his methodological individualism onto-logically, and he deduces the decisive role of teleological explan-ation from it, that is, explanation by means of ends, in the social sciences, a teleological explanation that the analysts (who, for the most part, know about German historicism only through the intermediaries of Croce and Collingwood) rediscover by their own methods.

These who hold to methodological individualism, such as Sir Karl Popper, refute the theory that may symmetrically be termed *methodological holism* and whose exemplary instance, in their view, is Marxism. They would accept more easily the reality of *societal facts*, social facts, or ensembles that are episte-mologically or ontologically irreducible to individual facts even if the irreducibility of social ensembles seems to contain within

---

[1] William Dray, *Laws and Explanation in History* (Oxford: Oxford University Press, 1957), and G. H. von Wright, *Explanation and Understanding* (London: Routledge and Kegan Paul, 1971).

it the seed of the errors of historicism. That is to say, according to a peculiar definition of the word, historicism is an interpretation of history as an irresistible movement of a totality to whose general determinism powerless individuals submit. In fact, as other analysts have clearly demonstrated, the choice of *collectivism*, or in other words, of the irreducibility of collectives to individuals, does not logically imply any adherence to historicism as understood by Sir Karl Popper. The methodological quarrel of individualism and collectivism is not to be confused with the philosophical problematic of laws or of historical determinism.

By a curious paradox, if the methodological individualism of the analysts tends towards an historical philosophy of human freedom, to a political doctrine of reform, and to an action inspired by that of the engineer, the ontological individualism of Sartre must establish a peculiar Marxism, a dialectical interpretation of historical totalization. The reconciliation of *ontological individualism* and *dialectical totalization* is not just another name for the same task, the reconciliation of *existentialism* and *Marxism*, a reconciliation that demands a reinterpretation less of existentialism than of Marxism.

1. Individualism, whether it is methodological or ontological, must rediscover the social or collective facts that constitute the object of the so-called social sciences. In fact, Sartre does rediscover them but, in accord with his own inspiration, only as the result of an ontological process. *Praxis* is alienated and cannot avoid being alienated, since it exercises its freedom (or, if one prefers, it *exists* its freedom) by incarnating itself in matter and by objectifying itself in its works beneath the gaze of the other. Let us, provisionally, abstract from these two contrary movements of *alienation* and *revolt*, which above all have political significance, and consider the concepts by which the dialectical experience, the universals of the social condition of consciousness (or of socialized consciousness), may be transmitted. It appears that ontological individualism excludes none of the *collective facts* or *social ensembles* (or *societal facts*) constituted or intended by the social sciences. These include (1) *class-being*, which is present in the consciousness of each member of a class, (2) rules of *organization* and *institutions*, collectives sometimes

close to *exis*, and sometimes close to *praxis* (to passivity and activity), (3) hetero- (or extero-) conditioning, (4) the crowd dispersed and the crowd in action, (5) *praxis* concentrated in a *sovereign group* and, ultimately, in an *Individual* (cult of personality), and (6) *praxis-process*, a substitution within the framework of ontological individualism of an historical and general movement, which determines individuals rather than is determined by them, and which unfolds according to its total being, not according to an individual or common *praxis*. In other words, ontological individualism, by means of the intermediaries of the anti-dialectic (the practico-inert) and the constituted dialectic of series and groups and their own dialectics, could fulfil the exigencies of the Anglo-American analysts for methodological collectivism.

Sartre is hardly concerned with satisfying these exigencies. Quite the opposite; he has his own ontological concern, which is to save freedom, and his own epistemological concern which is to safeguard the intelligiblity of what is not to be understood on the basis of the teleology of individual consciousness.

The sociologist puts up with this saving of freedom. Sartre assures us it is saved in two ways. Let us, he says, admit the fatality of alienation within the practico-inert. What remains is for each one to determine himself freely on the basis of his class-being, the bourgeois denying the free being of the worker or refusing to recognize the worker's own esteem, the worker denying the negation of his free being by the bourgeois or, just the opposite, choosing to be humiliated and offended, to suffer under the paternalist power of the employer and see himself turned into a scab, an employer's collaborator, enrolled in the imaginary union created by the class enemy. But on the other hand, *praxeis* trapped within the practico-inert always retain the capacity for rebellion, for beginning humanity, or for beginning it again. Now, the sociologist is also interested in the way that the different members of a class live out their situation and interiorize it (or, if one prefers, how they live their class-being), reacting to their situation. Furthermore, he does not exclude the freedom of individuals regarding institutions: in fact, there must be freedom concerning them because, whether individual acts violate or respect the rules of institutions, the institution has no other reality in the eyes of the individualistic methodologist.

The second point, to safeguard epistemologically the intelligibility of reality that is not understood on the basis of the constituting dialectic, to save the reality of individual *praxis*, poses problems of a quite different complexity. In fact, it would be important to distinguish between *de jure* intelligibility (another name for ontological reducibility) and *de facto* intelligibility resulting from a knowledge brought about methodologically. No one, not even Sartre, holds that the explanation of social phenomena is always and everywhere found in the intentions of actors. And even more, no one holds that the social sciences could radically neglect the subjectivity of actors and explain social phenomena in a strictly objectivist way by abstracting from the experiences lived by socialized consciousnesses. What maintains and distinguishes various scientific attitudes and philosophical schools is which side they begin with.

If man is studied as ants are studied, if man's humanity is studied by neglecting the intentionality of the actors, or, quite the opposite, by concentrating one's attention upon it, the antithesis continues to exist. But Lévi-Strauss in his polemic against Sartre, and Sartre in the *Critique*, push their theses to the limit. The former dreams of a science or man comparable in its structure to a science of insects or microbiology. At the end of *The Savage Mind* he upholds, at least hypothetically, a materialism that establishes the possibility of such a science. It is enough, however, to go back to an article that deals with the relations between anthropology and history[2] and to his Inaugural Lecture at the Collège de France[3] in order to appreciate the place left, provisionally or not, for the human knowledge of man or, in other words, for the understanding of others in their intentionality. In the article just cited, Lévi-Strauss writes that history specifically refers to the lived, to the consciousness that the actors have of themselves, the rules they obey, and the

[2] In *Structural Anthropology*, Tr., C. Jacobson and B. G. Schoepf (London: Allen Lane, 1968), pp. 1–27.

[3] Available in English as *The Scope of Anthropology*, Tr., S. O. Paul and R. A. Paul (London: Jonathan Cape, 1967) [Tr. note].

customs they practise. But it does not, for all that, renounce a grasping of anything beyond the lived, the meaning hidden in the social unconscious or achieved by actors without their having thought it out in advance.

On his side, Sartre excludes neither the structures of languages nor the forms of kinship. Language in his conceptual system becomes a modality of the practico-inert, but, from this very fact, it becomes more an instrument for than a constraint upon freedom. Besides, there is no need to be a disciple of Chomsky and possess the secrets of generative grammar to uphold the freedom (competence) of every speaker and every consciousness to compose an indefinite number of enunciations with a limited stock of phonemes and morphemes, according to a limited number of syntactical rules. In this sense, the structures of language all remain as reconcilable with the freedom of *praxis*, as Sartre understands it, as do the elementary structures of kinship. In the case of language, even more than kinship relations, scientific knowledge progresses by the analysis of different phonetic, semantic, and syntactic aspects of language, not by the participatory understanding of the speakers, which does not exclude understanding the appropriate way of speaking of an individual or a group.

Apart from misunderstandings and needless extremism on both sides, opposition continues to exist deep down. Epistemologically, there is a place for structural analysis and for understanding (for analytical Reason and for dialectical Reason) according to one's orientation and curiosity, and according to the characteristics of the intended object. In the next volume, we will re-encounter the authentic problems that phenomenologists and analysts pose in distinct vocabularies rather than in fundamentally different terms. What remains true is that Sartre, as a result of his ontology, gives primacy to teleological understanding, while Lévi-Strauss reserves it for analysis. The ontological primacy of *praxis* leads to the primacy of understanding or dialectical Reason; the epistemological and perhaps even the ontological primacy of *structures* has the consequence not of excluding understanding of the lived at either the starting point or the conclusion, but of putting the analysis of structures at the centre of scientific activity, because the meaning of the lived is not graspable at the level of the lived, 'but in a human reason . . . that man does not know', in the structures of institutions and in language that account for the meanings that consciousnesses live or intend without revealing the genuine meaning.

2. Even if Sartre can give a place to analytical science, though not the whole place, which is what the structuralists claim for it, his elucidation of collectives is unequal to the task of reconciling ontological individualism and, in the sense that this expression is currently interpreted, a dialectical philosophy of history. Sartre succeeds or thinks he succeeds in doing so by distinguishing between totality and totalization and by identifying, so to speak, totalization with the activity of individual consciousness.

As consciousness is actually totalizing, it grasps the gardener and the road-worker in a single glance and unifies the situation by means of its relation to a future towards which it projects itself. At the same time, totalization is radically different from totality. A collective reality never constitutes an organism. It lends itself to totalization by multiple consciousnesses, but it never becomes organically united, a being in-itself. The concept of totalization safeguards the primacy, the ontological mono-poly of individual *praxis*. Does it allow for a dialectical philosophy of history, in other words, for a totalization of becoming?

I see two fundamental difficulties. The relations among the elements of the totalization do not have a determinate nature, much less a rational one (whether rational refers to judgement or to *Vernunft*). The practical negation of the given by the project has nothing in common with the contradiction between two propositions or the contrariety between two concepts. How does the totalization by consciousness contain any logic whatever, when the essence of freedom, from which the project emanates, is to have no essence? In other words, when the essence of freedom is to innovate, to create, to make what is not come into being? To be sure, consciousness in Hegel's *Pheno-menology* is also creative; it created itself by itself through the diversity of its successive incarnations. The movement from one period to another contains within it a rational plot, which follows from the intelligible relations between the concept of one period and that of the following one. Even without ending in absolute knowledge, history would be dialectic, as the becoming of societies would represent the becoming of ideas. I do not see how it could be the same in the Sartrean dialectic, which excludes every anticipated determination, every constraint, every limitation, and which has individual *praxis*, anterior to and superior to all laws and all truths, as its ultimate resort.

So that human history may acquire a unity despite the absolute of human freedom that would destroy it, it must end up in a truth that, retrospectively, confers upon it a *single* meaning. To confine ourselves to the closing pages of the *Critique*, it is the class struggle, under the double form of internal and external bourgeois-and-proletarians, colonizers-and-colonized, that marks the threshold of history and that will allow the universals elaborated by the theory of practice-oriented ensembles to be brought together again and set into motion.[4] Be that as it may, *either* this class struggle is eternal, as two of the Sartrean analyses suggest: first, the analysis of materiality, the inevitable inscription of my act upon matter, and second, the inevitable objectification of my *praxis* by the look of the other and of my words by the interpretation that he will give them. Under this first hypothesis, the class struggle becomes an invariant of complex human societies, not the motive power for the unification of human becoming. *Or*, the Revolution of today and of tomorrow will put an end to the struggle of oppressors and oppressed. And it will make an end of it in a double sense: it will complete it, and it will subsequently appear as that towards which the past was heading. Nothing in the first volume of the *Critique* permits us to uphold the second alternative save as a possibility or a hope. Nothing permits us to give a definite content to this hope, since today we cannot even conceive what a philosophy of freedom beyond Marxism and alienation would be.

Sartre's Marxism can pass for a development of the philosophical fragments of the young Marx, who devoted his intellectual life to filling in the socio-historical contents of the schema of a consciousness that is liberated from its alienation by

---

[4] Sartre's second volume therefore will be less a philosophy of universal History than one of modern History.

overcoming capitalism. A century after the publication of *Capital*, Sartre has nothing to say about the socio-economic structure of our epoch. Even though he observes the reconstitution of the sovereign group in Stalinist socialism, he maintains the unconditional imperative of anti-capitalist rebellion by half-heartedly calling upon the analyses of Marx and insistently calling attention to the evident facts of oppression or exploitation.

Over and above such difficulties, does the substitution of totalization by individual consciousness for totality remain compatible with a dialectical philosophy of history in the sense of Hegel or Marx? Before we begin, let us note that the definition of the advent of Truth by means of the end of oppression (or the class struggle) seems to be of Kantian inspiration. What is involved is a regulatory principle, an idea of Reason and not a concrete universal. But perhaps that is not essential. Does the concept of totalization retain the same meaning when it designates (1) a global vision of individual *praxis*, (2) the unification of knowledge by Marxism, and (3) the recovery of the human past by a consciousness? The dialectical experience ends, in the closing pages of the *Critique*, by raising the question of the possibility of a totalization without a totalizer. It is a question for which an affirmative reply does not seem impossible if the understanding of the historian is not identified with that of the historical actor, or in other words, that the understanding of the committed *praxis* is not identified with that of the detached *praxis*. So the historian does not see the problems surrounding the youthfulness of Louis XIV upon his ascent to the throne either in the way that members of the Fronde saw them or how the partisans of Mazarin did: he understands the attitudes of both groups, their conflicts and the result of their conflicts. Assuming that one would like to maintain the subject of one's retrospective understanding rooted in history, the incompleteness of the future justifies the provisional nature of one's interpretation, rather than the interpreter's lack of ability, whether he be close to the situation or removed from it, or his inability to raise himself above the incompatible projects of the actors.

What makes it difficult to pass from ontological individualism to a dialectic of general history is the concept of totalization and the transformations it undergoes throughout the *Critique*. Precisely to the extent that the historical ensemble, the practico-inert, or institutional collectives are totalized without being totalities, each consciousness has a perspective, a general one if you like, but also a partial one, just one perspective among others. By definition, no single one can be true since each is the truth of a consciousness and since there is no observer beyond the multiplicity of observers situated at the level of human reality. Logically, totalization therefore appears strictly contradictory to a philosophy of history that claims to embrace the whole of human history, not in the sense that nothing could be omitted from what has affected a consciousness at some time past, but in the sense that understanding would retain and synthesize everything in human becoming that deserves to be preserved or deserves to be raised to the dignity of history. Hegel's philosophy of history is total in the sense that it neglects none of these concepts, none of the incarnations of consciousness, none of the epochs indispensable to understanding the truth of humanity through time. This totalization belongs to *one* consciousness, but to a consciousness that is not committed, to the consciousness of the Wise Man, the Sage.

Nothing suggests that the Sartrean consciousness, which in the second volume will set the universals into motion in order to follow the class struggle, takes itself to be that of a Wise Man. Moreover, assuming that it understands the human adventure as it understands individual existence, it will not differ very radically, if at all, from a primitive understanding, the understanding of a consciousness that projects itself towards the future and determines its situation by doing so. Such a model seems to follow from the Sartrean analysis of perception (his obsession with the look of the *Other*). A consciousness does not *perceive* a socio-economic regime by totalizing it, but by taking a partial perspective of it, which is also a general one, in the vague sense that it retains certain traits judged to be dominant and essential. *A fortiori*, no consciousness can totalize human history, even if, to use Dilthey's expression, it is compared to the biography of humanity, save by choosing the aspects of this adventure that confer a meaning upon the ensemble. Such a totalization, whether it is a matter of a life, a regime, or the whole of history, demands a certain amount of cutting apart, of analyses and comparisons, in other words, of analytical Reason. This is true even if understanding, the supreme reward for one's efforts, gives itself the more or less well-founded illusion of reliving what others have lived.

Strictly speaking, in the existential psychoanalysis of a person, understanding attains a kind of unity within totalization only because Sartre postulates, in *Being and Nothingness*, a unifying choice on the basis of which the diverse episodes of a destiny are clarified. *L'Idiot de la Famille*[5] illustrates the properly indefinite nature of this totalization, even when it is privileged by having recourse to an original and determinative decision. But where would the equivalent of this decision be in the biography of Humanity?

Scarcity gives a kind of answer to the question, which is a philosophical rather than a rhetorical question. Scarcity is itself contingent but it makes the class struggle necessary: having been internalized by consciousness, it makes each the enemy of the other and of everyone the enemy of each. *Deus ex machina*, it puts history in motion. It precipitates a consciousness immediately conscious of itself, a translucid, fatally free consciousness, into this human and inhuman world where it is alienated by a contingent necessity and at each instant retains its freedom to recover itself. However imprecise it remains, the idea of a victory over scarcity suggests, in the end, a transformation of history, a transformation that would not determine but would favour the radical modification of the economic milieu. Whatever function Sartre has set aside to impute, in the second volume of the *Critique*, to the hypothesis or the utopia of a victory over scarcity, the end of prehistory can only result in an authentic Revolution or, in other words, in a Revolution that would not begin once more the cycle of decline and degradation—alienation from common *praxis* to the sovereign group. One could say that the end of prehistory is a Revolution that does not devour its own children.

The *Critique* lends itself to a pessimistic reading; it presents us with a new version of the myth of Sisyphus. Just as, according

[5] Sartre's study of Flaubert [Tr. note].

to Rousseau, laws must permanently resist the weight of circumstances in order to preserve equality, rebellion, according to Sartre, would at every propitious occasion, send humanity forth again in struggle against alienation by matter, the malignity of men, and the exigencies of organization or institution. Against this pessimistic and leftist interpretation, a more optimistic one, more compatible with Marxism–Leninism, would take over the achievements of Soviet socialism (the collective ownership of the means of production) and place some hope in democratization (even though the procedures of formal democracy, according to the *Critique,* belong to the serial order and to extero-conditioning).

In any case, retrospective totalization, in the light of the class struggle and ending in a conversion, would not fill in the gulf between ontological individualism (and, moreover, methodological individualism) and a philosophy of history that is Marxist at the same time as it is Sartrean. Such a totalization cannot accomplish the project outlined by Sartre in his lecture given at UNESCO,[6] on the occasion of meetings devoted to Kierkegaard. The retrospective understanding of the historical ensemble must neglect neither events nor the unique quality of lived experiences. In short, it would realize the synthesis of the particular and the universal, of *existentialism,* which knows only individual realities, and *Marxism,* which takes account of the capitalist system as it is actually operating and is condemned to death by its own contradictions.

In the last analysis, such a synthesis is impossible. A totalization of history is not a perception or a vision, but a conceptual narrative. It clearly comes from an inspiration, from a fundamental choice. Perhaps it gives the reader the feeling of a general understanding. Its procedure is nothing less than selection and reconstruction, its instrument is language and conceptualization, and its objective is the truth of the narrative. If the truth of the narrative depends upon the Truth having come to pass, such Truth also requires selection and reconstruction, or in other words, it determines what of the past will escape being forgotten. Not much would be left of the past if only the modal-

---

[6] 'L'universel singulier,' in *Kierkegaard vivant* (Paris: Gallimard, 1966), pp. 20–63 [Tr. note].

ities of the class struggle inspired totalization on the basis of a Truth reduced to the utopia of a non-antagonistic reciprocity.

3. The defenders of methodological individualism are probably wrong to believe that methodological collectivism more or less necessarily leads to the philosophies of history that they detest–those of Hegel, Marx, or Toynbee. But are they right to believe that methodological individualism prevents one from succumbing to the temptations of such philosophies? Sartre's ontological individualism adds the implications of a philosophy of empty freedom, a freedom without bounds or criteria, to the possible implications of an historicist philosophy inspired by totalitarian claims.

Between historical thought and knowledge of society, on the one hand, and political decisions and actions, on the other, a connection is inevitably established. Sometimes it is evident and necessary but, in different circumstances, it may be subtle and devious. Sir Karl Popper's critique of historicism has, *inter alia,* the objective of refuting what I once called a politics of Reason [7] (in opposition to a politics of compromise). We do only know and can only know but fragments of the milieu in which we live; it is for us to criticize institutions received from the past that have become contrary to our idea of what is rational or just. The engineer constructs, controls, and repairs machines but does not transform the laws of the universe. Likewise, the historical actor observes, judges, and reforms but converts neither men nor societies. This reformist attitude does not, under certain circumstances, exclude the revolutionary choice: if a ruling class is shown to be incapable of assuring order or progress, to use the concepts of August Comte, the choice of revolution does not contradict the politics of understanding. Moreover, neither does revolt against intolerable injustice: *Hier stehe ich; ich kann nicht anders.*

The slide from Marxist millennialism and proletarian messianism to politics of the Party-Prince or the cult of personality is familar, and requires but this brief reminder. The slide from dialectical Reason or ontological individualism to a philosophy of violence, a typical movement of Sartre's thought, but one

[7] *Introduction to the Philosophy of History,* p. 328.

that is half hidden beneath the abundance of his analyses, deserves a more detailed commentary.

The *oath*, as we have said, plays a role in Sartre's political philosophy, including the *Critique*, comparable to that of the *contract* in Rousseau's philosophy. Both Sartre and Rousseau, as well as Lévi-Strauss, set off from the idea that the legitimacy of power, in the last analysis, derives from an act of unanimity. The unanimous act by which the city, with its assembled citizens, declares itself one, and the unanimous, common *praxis*, wherein each one becomes in turn the third-man mediator and is united by the oath of all consciousnesses, which are separated but tending towards the same objective, mark off the simultaneous birth of rebellion and humanity.

Rousseau based his unanimity upon the law of the majority. But he did not deduce the imperatives of action, and even less of rebellion, from the ultimate conditions of legitimacy, at least not without supplying any transition. He was conscious of the radical heterogeneity between the ultimate problem posed in the *Social Contract* and the sociological problems of Montesquieu's *The Spirit of the Laws*. What Rousseau advises doing, *hic et nunc*, derives much more from the wisdom accumulated by Montesquieu and from historical experience than from the pure theory of legitimacy, even when the pure theory alone clarifies the meaning of the whole of human history.

Everything in the *Critique* takes place as if Sartre passed directly from the pure theory of legitimacy to the imperative of action, which, from this fact, becomes a revolutionary imperative. Freedom implies terror by reason of its very structure: it can be guaranteed against itself only by granting in advance the right of others to punish betrayal, which is the equivalent to Rousseau's famous formula, to force men to be free. The immediate transfiguration of the oath into terror (a philosophical version of the practise of members of the Resistance and partisans) provides the first justification for the Sartrean obsession with violence.

Sartre's refusal of all secondary or derived legitimacy comparable to Rousseau's majoritarian law brings with it a second justification: states, sovereign groups, and representative democracies are neither legitimate nor illegitimate. They are given as facts to individuals who support them or submit to them. From a refusal to submit follows the primacy not of progress over order, but of violence over law. Unless law is linked to the original oath and is constitutive of a common *praxis*, violence that is destructive of order runs the risk of attaining a sort of moral privilege and greater value than violence stabilized in the law. (In the Sartrean, and equally in the vulgar sense, there is always an element of violence in the established law.) The revolutionary party bears the violence of fraternity within itself along with the hope of humanity, since without it, men would be resigned to their servitude.

Very much *en passant*, Sartre can admit that socialism in its first phase inflicts more constraints or restrictions upon individuals than do bourgeois democracies once they are stabilized. It makes little difference to him. It leads to no conclusion. He describes neither the institutions of capitalism nor those of the regime that will succeed it. Violence becomes the recourse, the only recourse, against violence crystallized in a class society, as if reasonable deliberation over the respective promises of reform and revolution and the respective merits of various regimes did not deserve the philosopher's interest.

Since violence means the domination of some men over others or over the vast majority, and since it is constitutive of any political or economic regime known to man, the negation of the existing regime amounts to revolutionary violence against institutionalized violence. By Sartre's postulate, revolutionary violence projects a non-violent future, in the absence of which nothing allows us to confer any plausibility whatever upon it. Fascism also starts off from the ubiquity of violence in order to exhort the masters, who are identified either by history or by themselves, to victorious violence. Sartrism starts off from the ubiquity of violence and dreams of radically eliminating it in favour of a non-antagonistic reciprocity. The will to universalism does not exclude the possibility that revolutionary *praxis* is finally incarnated in the will of a single man. Despite its inspiration, the Sartrean philosophy of violence risks teaching, the same lessons as do the philosophies that Sartre, the man detests.

The Preface to Fanon's book perhaps suggests that Sartre

believes in the cathartic virtues of violence. Those who have been crushed manage to regain their self-esteem only by violence against him who has, so to speak, deprived them of their being. Otherwise, they will turn their violence against themselves and will hate themselves by hating others. Let us leave to specialists the task of commenting upon the psychological theory of violence and how it accords with the violence of Sartre the man, the verbal violence that takes place in the quiet of his study, and how that violence fits in with his refusal of face-to-face dialogue.

Reason and Violence is the title given by two English writers to a summary of the *Critique* and Sartre's book on Jean Genet.[8] Is there an accidental or a necessary link between these two terms? We have just recalled the philosophical motifs whereby the *Critique* lays the foundation for a politics of violence. But is it a politics of Reason? Yes. But only to the extent that dialectical Reason is mixed with *praxis* and *freedom* or, in other words, with the negation of the given and the project of an undetermined future. Such a conception of freedom condemns every condemnation of utopia. The *praxis* of dialectical Reason is creative: no thing and no one would be able to restrict, either in thought or in action, its power of creation. This power, by an undefined assumption, is transferred to human history.

Is the transfer legitimate? Must one bring the innovative capacity of history into agreement with that of writers who, with a limited stock of words and syntactical rules, compose an indefinite number of statements and works? Or must one make it agree with the diversity of kinship relations in primitive society, by reducing them to a small number of types made up from a few elements? Morals and manners in their inexhaustible richness suggest the indefinite diversity of works; economic and political regimes suggest a typology by their structure.

Until that day, until such an argument is made, it is the artist and he alone who unfailingly creates forms that ever are new. As for the Prince, whether individual or collective, perhaps he acts out each moment in its unique configuration of

[8] R. D. Laing and D. G. Cooper, *Reason and Violence* (London: Tavistock, 1964).

circumstance, but, in the last analysis, he does not escape the historical condition of man: he creates cities, but he does not know the cities he creates. His children or his children's children recognize in them the familiar traits of the domination of man by man.

Appendix

Two passages in the *Critique*, one at the beginning, where a
definition of the critical experience is made, and the other
regarding Lévi-Strauss, include the terms *evidence, necessity,* and
apodicticity. Two notes, on pages 150 and 159, try to analyse
the relations between evidence and necessity or, in other words,
the synthetic movement of which we have a complete intuition
and its material trace. The note on page 150 distinguishes 'intuitive evidence (and dialectic)', on the one hand, and 'geometrical demonstration' on the other. 'Nothing is to be understood here if not the generative act, the synthesis that brings
all the bits and pieces together or that holds the abstract elements of space in an ensemble. What is *new* is the trace left by a
totalizing temporalization upon the absolute inert dispersion
that represents space. It is intelligible *in so far as* the dispersed
inertia that it brings together *adds nothing to the ensemble by itself,*
and is nothing but the set reproduction of the generative act.'
The intuitive and dialectical evidence is grasped by the synthesizing act, the creative *praxis* of innovation. The unifying or
synthesizing act is of a consciousness or *praxis* that is externalized
in space and leaves a trace of itself there. The simple example
chosen was of a straight line that, if it crossed a circle at one
point would *necessarily* meet another point of the circle in order
to pass through it. 'The geometer understands his partial operation on the basis of a double and total *praxis* (drawing the
straight line, closing the circle) . . . The geometer is not interested in acts but in their traces.' Geometrical demonstration 'has

destroyed the qualitative and sensed unity of the *circle-Gestalt* in favour of the inert divisibility of "geometrical lines".' 'What interests [the geometer] is to rediscover the relation of radical externality beneath the seal of internality that is imposed upon the figures by drawing them. But suddenly the intelligibility disappears.' Intelligibility disappears at the same time as movement, synthesis and novelty. But the separation of evidence and demonstrated necessity remains no less paradoxical: it may be dialectically evident that *praxis* is externalized, but how can it be evident in advance that a *free praxis* is externalized (would act) in such a specific way? It could be that alienation is apodictically necessary (necessary not in a causal sense but in the sense of a dialectical necessity): but then, could not the History of alienation have been other than it has been, if it has been an adventure?

A second difficulty is involved with the usage sometimes of the term necessity and sometimes of the term apodicticity, and in particular, his usage in the note on page 159. 'Evidence tends to reject apodicticity to the same extent that necessity tends to repel evidence.' In the Kantian table of categories, apodicticity is derived from apodictic judgements within the rubric of *modality*. The category comes after the problematic judgements (possibility–impossibility) and judgements of assertion (being-non-being). Besides, the Kantian categories that correspond to apodictic judgements are those of *necessity* and *chance*. The Sartrean distinction between apodicticity and necessity remains equivocal. He wants to exclude, it seems to me, logical necessity as well as causal necessity: y and z being given, it cannot be that x is not produced—thought as well as evidence would disappear. All that is left is necessity, causal necessity in this instance, geometrical or mathematical necessity in another, and eventually, logical necessity. There must be novelty, movement, and synthesis in order for there to have been thought.

Sartre again employs these terms when he comes to comment upon *The Elementary Structures of Kinship* and tries to inject the method and the results of Lévi-Strauss into dialectical rationality. He admits *en passant* that: 'In fact there is no doubt that reciprocal relations are susceptible to being studied by the "exact sciences"' (p. 487). He then comes to the problem of structures, 'synthetic products of a practical totalization and the always possible objects of an analytical and rigorous study.' Analysis of the rules of marriage in terms of reciprocity allows Sartre to insert the theory of structures into the theory of organizations as a particular modality of organizations, abstract rules, or as a system of relations in a sense external to *praxeis* but actualized only by the *praxeis* in whom the inertia of these rules or systems has been injected.

On this occasion Sartre twice employs the term apodicticity. The first time, he indicates that the rules of marriage lend themselves to a deduction in the style of mathematics, to a kind of apodictic evidence that belongs to mathematics. This time evidence and apodicticity go together and are opposed to dialectical evidence. On the previous page, Sartre said that we would find in the organization an apodictic experience of the agent that would on first sight present analogies with that of alienation. This time what is involved is the necessity with which freedom is externalized or alienated, an externalization that cannot avoid happening even though this necessity has nothing in common with causal necessity since it emanates from freedom within the material milieu.

NOTE B

On many occasions Sartre qualifies individual *praxis* as *transparent* or *translucid*. One may wonder what the meaning that he gives to these adjectives may be. In fact, consciousness of something is always non-thetic self-consciousness. But even so, it does not know itself in the way that the other knows it. Flaubert did not know himself to be *l'idiot de la famille*, at least not according to the interpretation that Sartre himself gives to the existence of the author of *The Sentimental Education*. Translucidity or transparency thus does not designate an integral consciousness or knowledge by *praxis* of itself. On page 149, we read that 'transparence has its origin in the inseparable connexion of negation and project', a negation that 'totalizes *in situ* what it negates' and a project that is defined in comparison to the abstract *whole*, 'which the practical agent projects into the future and which appears as unity reorganized from the negated situation'. *Praxis* is therefore translucid *qua* totalization by means of the negation of the given and the reorganizing project. Just as, according to *Being and Nothingness*, we live in bad faith, the transparency of *praxis* only appears to me to designate the coincidence of the act and the actor, of the action and the acting subject. Man is indistinguishable from his action. He is his action and his action, *qua* dialectic, requires the totalization and the project that is itself the totalizer. Why does Sartre insist upon transparency and translucidity, while in *Being and Nothingness* he never stopped drawing attention to the interval between individual selves (we are dealing with the mode of being-what-one-is-not)? The reason appears to me to be the following. In the *Critique*, Sartre has set himself the task of finding the same intelligibility (teleological explanation, negation, and totalization) in universal history as in individual *praxis*. He says and repeats that 'the sole practical and dialectical reality, the motor of everything, *is individual action*' (p. 361). Thus it is a matter of showing that the practico-inert, the social field, and universal history, are ultimately accorded the same intelligibility as individual action, that in the final analysis they are susceptible to the same transparency as individual *praxis*. From which comes the metaphysical hypothesis (p. 145) that we should know everything. Thus, transparency does not mean that the actor should know everything about his own action (which, wedged into the practico-inert or into the group, is mediated by things and actions) but that action, as totalization and negation, should be the model of intelligibility in the ideal instance of understandability.

Let us again read the lines on page 279 that open the section, 'On Necessity as a New Structure of the Dialectical Experience'. 'At its most immediate level, the dialectical experience is revealed as being *praxis* itself producing its own information in order to control its own development. The evidence of this first experience, where the *deed* itself lays the basis for its own self-consciousness, tells us one thing for certain: it is reality itself that is discovered as self-presence. The sole concrete foundation of the historical dialectic is the dialectical structure of individual action.' The *deed*, *praxis*, makes self-consciousness evident:

one knows what one does at the very moment it is done, not because the actor integrally knows himself but because, within the historical field, he is blended with his doings, or rather because, at this level, project and motivation are not differentiated.

NOTE C

Is scarcity authentically contingent, a pure and simple fact, given to men upon the earth not according to some logical necessity or according to the determinism of living beings? I think that it is *necessary* in the sense that every living species, in a natural milieu from which it borrows what it needs in order to live, comes up against certain limits. A species that must labour to survive—to hunt, cook, cultivate the soil, or raise animals— is under the sway of the law of scarcity, scarcity of time and space or even of non-renewable resources. It is possible to conceive of a society that may have triumphed over scarcity at the point when the historically given aspects of human existence should radically have been transformed. But even then, it is only upon one condition: the voluntary, conscious, and rationally organized restriction of population size. It is not absurd to suggest, as Sartre does, that the aggression man has for man in part comes from the fact that individuals cannot all obtain goods that are, in essence, scarce. The diverse forms of scarcity, the relations between scarcity and surplus, scarcity and relative overproduction, scarcity and aggression call for precise and detailed analyses rather than a metaphysical decree by which an apparently inevitable characteristic of the biological condition of man serves (on the basis of contingency) to mark the violent nature of man and his history with the stamp of necessity.

NOTE D

Does the intelligibility of the practico-inert result from the constituting dialectic? Is the practico-inert intelligible or understandable? How can it be known? On all these points, Sartre's thought is not without certain ambiguities. Without claiming to dissolve all the obscurities, here are the points I would deem to be essential.

1. The critical experience, itself a reflection of the dialectical movement, alone discovers the authentic sense of the practico-inert, of exigency, of interest, of class-being, etc. Ontologically, transcendentally, it is on the basis of the dialectic that the anti-dialectic is understood. If one does not start off from the constituting dialectic or individual *praxis*, inevitably the reified world, the man with an interest, and classes are assimilated into objective, given, normal reality. In other words, the world of the liberal economy, the world of capitalism and the economists, can be *understood* only as anti-dialectical and then only on condition that the critical experience, the reflection of the dialectic, takes individual *praxis*, freedom, as its starting point.

2. This alienation is no less necessary in the determinist sense, namely, that which signifies that *praxis*, mixed with an organic being and acting in a natural milieu, cannot avoid being made into matter in order to act upon matter and, consequently, it confronts, within worked-upon matter, the action of others, which has become passive. In abstract terms, materiality or alterity (or plurality of *praxeis*) necessarily determines (and not, therefore, by accident) the alienation of *praxeis*.

3. The *praxis* of such an individual remains free in the sense that each one freely takes upon himself the condition that he finds himself in within the practico-inert. In *Being and Nothingness*, Sartre took the example of the Jew facing the notice on the door of a restaurant that read 'No Jews Allowed'. The Jew can submit to this prohibition or violate it. Likewise the worker can go on strike or, like a scab, put himself at the service of the employer. The power of *praxis* is *limited* by given conditions, but freedom remains *unlimited* since it retains the choice of death, from which comes the exemplary value of torture and the reaction to it, silence or betrayal.

4. Understanding grasps individual *praxeis* within the practico-inert. Does it also give an adequate account of the passage from dialectic to anti-dialectic, from *praxis* into the practico-inert? Yes and no. What is involved is a critical experience, not a transcendental deduction. Sartre therefore must observe

totalities, follow out the dialectic of needs as it applies to them, and, in any case, put *praxeis* in a milieu of materiality so that alienation becomes intelligible for dialectical Reason. Let us repeat that the fall into the practico-inert becomes intelligible (not understandable) when *praxis* is put back into a milieu of materiality and alterity (plurality).

5. Scarcity is given as a *fact*, a contingency. To the extent that alienation results from scarcity, it too becomes contingent rather than necessary. Thus, it is appropriate to distinguish the alienation that necessarily results from materiality and alterity outside of any scarcity, from History such as it has unfolded, which is necessary on the basis of the contingent fact of scarcity. Without scarcity, human History would not have been ordered by the struggle of man against man, by the class struggle. History, which is essentially class struggle, is intelligible as being necessary on the basis of a contingency.

6. Is the practico-inert, as an alienated world, understandable, intelligible, or knowable by analytical Reason alone? As each consciousness freely assumes its own condition, the alienated world is understandable. In theory, if we had all necessary knowledge at our disposal, we would be able to understand how each *praxis* assumes its own identity. If we consider the ensemble of the practico-inert world, it remains intelligible: it is not answerable generally or in each sector to an individual intentionality, but remains wholly articulated in each of its aspects by means of the dialectical structure, or in other words, by the synthesizing nature of the links among its elements, the externality of collectives returning to the internality of consciousnesses.

7. In spite of everything, can there not be an objective knowledge, objectifications, and thus a knowledge by analytical Reason of the externality within which the internality of *praxis* is dispersed? Sartre must answer *yes* since, after all, analytical Reason and natural sciences are applied to the world of machines, which comes from human *praxis*. Why would an analytical knowledge of the human world not be possible when the world, which is externalized, loses the characteristics closest to those of the world created by *praxis*? Sartre hesitates to answer affirmatively because he fears returning to the position

of those he calls 'our eclectics' (as far as I know,[1] I am among them), namely, those who 'envisage some cultural sectors that are conditioned from within, others that remain products, and finally others that (according to the knowledge involved) possess both characteristics. One could just as well define the sectors by their internal conditioning, which would be dialectical, and deny that their relations are different than pure contiguity (or are different than certain *external* ties)' (p. 144). Sartre refuses this solution, at least in principle. He wants a totalization of total History to be possible, which is just what the concept of a totalization defined on the basis of individual *praxis* seems to exclude.

NOTE E

Why, a reader objects, write this paragraph? Why reproduce quotations, unworthy of Sartre, that are self-contradictory or play too much the game of adversary? I do not intend in the least to score points by provoking smiles to the detriment of a philosopher capable of enormous things (in more than one sense of the term).

In spite of everything, three ideas emerge from the preceding paragraph that are indispensable for the interpretation of the *Critique*. By insisting upon the *plurality* of significations, the *irreducibility* of systems, and the necessity of *mediations*, Sartre returns to the phenomenology of historical reality that he was able to borrow from Dilthey, Max Weber or from my *Introduction to the Philosophy of History*. He presents a theory of existence and understanding in the form of a critique of Marxism–Leninism, a critique that, at the level of epistemology, is derived from German historicism and is opposed to Marxism–Leninism, and perhaps even to the Marx of *Capital*.

The formulae concerning the 'unsurpassable philosophy' of our epoch, which is simultaneously afflicted with a total sterility, appear at first to take us back to Zhdanov himself. But Sartre writes them seriously and consciously, not inadvertently.

---

[1] *As far as I know*, from what students have told me after a lecture, I am included among 'our eclectics' just as I am among the 'tender souls' of the liberals.

The primacy of dialectical Reason, and thus of the particular adventure of Humanity of which dilectical Reason is at once the motor and the knowledge, leads to a version of *historicism* in the sense of both the Germans (Dilthey, Troeltsch) and Sir Karl Popper. Analytical Reason is distinguished from dialectical Reason to the extent that the latter makes itself into matter in order to act upon materiality. The result is that every synthesis of our present culture is either based upon the exact sciences and analytical Reason or it lays claim to Marxism (not Marxism–Leninism, but to dialectical Marxism). The choice of the first alternative implies the elimination of *praxis* and historical creativity; what is left in existence is but a world of facts and laws into which scientists would attempt vainly to inject values when it was too late. Moreover, they would do so without even being conscious that their values were no less determined than the rest of the world. As for the second choice, it leads to a broadly understood Marxism according to the interpretation that Sartre gives to it, which is to say, to a philosophy of the self-creation of man by himself through the becoming of societies.

Of course, Sartre expresses these ideas in a simplified form. The synthesis of knowledge, of our awareness or of our culture, in the strict sense of synthesis, represents even more a regulative idea at the horizon of thought. But once again, Sartre is fully aware that he evokes it in order to avoid dispersion, the heterogeneity of the historical totality that he imputes to the 'eclectics' (*Critique*, p. 144) whom he reproaches for doing the same thing. Let us no longer forget that Dilthey, responsible for the concept of a *Critique of Historical Reason*, was in search of an answer to Marx and Nietzsche, of the foundation of a philosophy to serve as a prolegomena to all the social sciences and the principle of an historical politics (or ethics). Sartre believes, not out of vanity but from metaphysical pride, that he has completed the project that so disturbed philosophers (of a specific school, the phenomenologico-Hegelian) for nearly a century.

This achievement does not only imply the primacy of the historical adventure and dialectical Reason but also the Truth of this particular adventure and a Reason capable of reconciling the particularity of events with the universality of concepts. The Truth of this adventure implies, in turn, a certain kind of necessity or apodicticity: how could Truth have been other than it is, even though it starts out from free *praxis*? Thus, the particular adventure must be free in its movement and necessary in its realization. This is a simple reconciliation, if the future is not necessary (or is not known to be) and if, on the other hand, the past can no longer change (or is recognized as no longer being able to be other than what it has been). But even so, the contradiction continues to exist, seeing that Sartre endeavours to stamp a particular adventure (the liquidation of the French Revolution by the Emperor) with the seal of necessity.

In the *Critique*, he tries to get over this contradiction (the preceding example is taken from *A question of Method*) by raising *understanding* to *dialectical Reason*, by moving from the epistemological to the ontological level. It is dialectical Reason that brings to light the necessity of alienation on the basis of a contingent fact (scarcity), the freedom of *praxis* within alienation, the contingence of necessity, and the necessity of contingence. We still must know if and in what sense necessity and contingence can be reconciled within the particular event, and if and in what sense Truth can 'happen' when organic being seems condemned to alienation by a milieu of materiality and plurality, an abstraction made from scarcity. Can *praxis*-consciousness await Truth in the fashion of the contemplation-consciousness of a Wise Man?

NOTE F

The dialectic of *praxeis* in the *Critique* differs from that of *Being and Nothingness*. The look made an object for the Other of each for-itself. No consciousness can make itself master of an other consciousness since the other consciousness is only a subject for itself and, once possessed by the other, by his look, by his will, it is no more than an object and, as such, escapes his possession.

Consciousness becomes *praxis*, labour, doing, and is perhaps recognized as such. In this sense, labouring *praxis* no longer wills the death of the other. But are the four conditions of reciprocal recognition realizable? Are they the definition of an authentic intersubjectivity, to use an expression of Merleau-Ponty? Curiously, Sartre confines himself to indicating the conditions without giving them any specific weight. His reason for this quasi-indifference seems to me to be the following. Within the practico-inert and within the class society, each individual finds himself imprisoned by practice-oriented ensembles that imply conflict relationships among individuals. The *Critique* deals only marginally, if at all, with private life. It does deal with social or political life. Now, social and political life, as they remain dominated by class conflicts, cannot include the equivalent of this authentic intersubjectivity.

NOTE G

'It is not necessary to hope for a moment when analytical Reason could provide an account of the transformations of Spanish gold precisely, as we have seen, because the quantitative ties of externality without disappearing have returned or have been caused to swerve by ties of internality. Or, if you prefer, because each gold coin is both a unit within a sum and, by means of its reference to all the others, is a part within a whole. In contrast, dialectical intelligibility is entirely preserved, since it is what allows the kind of negative unity that represents materiality to be grasped from the swarm of acts. No doubt we do not find the transparency of *praxis* at this level. But it is necessary to understand that there is a dialectic within the dialectic. That is to say, that within the perspective of a realist materialism, the dialectic as totalization produces its own negation as absolute dispersion' (p. 281). In fact, we can easily understand the relations of each *praxis* to gold and also the non-willed or negative unity that creates the swarm of individual actions. But, without considering that the 'transparency' of *praxis* is an obscure notion (*praxis* is transparent to *consciousness*, which is another word for a non-thetic self-consciousness), knowledge has no need to follow the infinite dispersion of individual acts in all their details. Whether or not it is a matter of Gresham's Law, bad money driving out good, or, in this instance, the more or less subtle formulae of the quantitative theory of money or of the effects of Spanish gold, analytical Reason explains what has happened at the macroscopic level and is content with a general understanding of the most frequent kinds of behaviour that are typical of individuals concerning money.

NOTE H

Sartre writes that nothing prevents him, philosophically, from writing the second volume of the *Critique*. Just as nothing in the future prevents him from writing an ethics. *Being and Nothingness* announced an ethics; the *Critique* shows the necessary priority of a politics by following our dialectical experience— the experience that consciousness acquires by reflecting upon its social destiny, upon its inevitable alienation by means of the fact of materiality and alterity, upon the free assumption of its own social being, and, finally, upon its own free commitment, within the class struggle. How should each individual live his social being, his alienation, and his commitment? It is not inconceivable that Sartre answers this question, even though the transition from the freedom from which no one can escape, the inevitable responsibility for one's self, to duty-freedom or obligation does not appear, to me, to be easy. Besides, it may be that Sartre's ethics does not admit of obligations even though it requires sanctions.

On the other hand, the second volume of the *Critique*, whatever Sartre may say, appears to me to present some intrinsic difficulties. Of course, we know that all the modalities of social *exis* and social *praxis*, set forth conceptually in the first volume, are to be set into motion in the second, with the class struggle constituting the directing thread. Once more he must add to the class struggle, the struggle of colonialists and colonized and, with this second form of struggle, all the other kinds of discrimination and non-recognition of man by man, whether real or possible. Even though intelligibility does not demand that totalization had been the work of an individual consciousness, the retrospective totalization of History, assimilated to an individual existence with no totalizer other than the historian-philosopher, seems to be a project that is by nature contradictory.

Let us take as a starting point a favourite example of the neo-Kantians, that of an event that includes an innumerable multiplicity of individual *praxeis* divided into two institution-alized groups (the army of each side is an institution) thrown one against the other, each according to a totalizing project, the battle plan of the Sovereign. Fabrice and Napoleon lived the battle, each in his own way. Nobody totalized it. Did the historian totalize it? In fact, the totalization of the historian differs in nature from the lived experience of the ac-tors: he is constrained to tell the story, to formulate true judgements on what has happened. He can only do this by putting himself successively at the point of view of first one side and then the other; in this sense, he sees the battle neither as Blücher nor as Wellington nor as Napoleon. In fact, he does not *see* the battle; he reconstructs it and thinks it through. The historian writes fiction, Tolstoy said, because, in the final analysis, the projects of leaders do not determine the event, because the event issues from individual *praxeis* into a setting that is no more than a confused mêlée. Let us say no more. It may be that under certain circumstances it is this way, and that under different ones it may be otherwise. Assuming that the outcome did not depend upon the *praxeis* of sovereigns, intelligibility continues to exist since the dialectic produces the anti-dialectic. Putting the worst possible interpretation to events, the victory of one camp would be a fact to verify, not the equivalent to a decision taken by one consciousness as a result of a practical syllogism. In this example, even though the his-torian was far from being committed to one or another of the camps and, moreover, had no duty to be committed, yet he plays the role of *third-man mediator*, for it is he who creates the unity of the army coming to grips with the enemy. Can one think of the philosopher of history as one who understands the Truth of History or the advent of Truth in history in the same way as the historian of the battle, the third-man mediator between Kutusoff and Napoleon, who, moreover, dismisses both leaders in order to follow the chaos of dispersed actions and to discover the ungraspable secret of victory and defeat?

With this hypothesis there is a totalizer, namely, the historian, and it may be asked why there should have to be a totalization without a totalizer. The first reason I see is that the third-man mediator in the example chosen differs essentially from the historical actor. Naturally, he also includes in his conscious act a plurality that is less given than constructed by the very act of understanding. But the historian who is not actively committed does not project himself towards the future; he does not will a future, but wishes to understand what has happened in the past. If he can understand without willing anything at all, the assimilation of understanding with the unique objective of knowledge and the understanding of a *praxis* falls apart. The historian understands actors on the basis of their project: he does not necessarily have a project of his own other than that of Truth. In this sense, the totalization without a totalizer that Sartre is looking for in the second volume is not necessary at all: it would be enough to accept a totalizer who is not actively committed. At least at the level of understanding the battle, such a totalizer presents no problem. Why does he do so at a higher level?

The difficulty, it seems to me, results first of all from the Sartrean refusal of neutrality, and then from the exigency of the advent of Truth, the condition for the unity of a *single* History. Sartre does not wish to be neutral himself—and he does not want the historian to be neutral either—between proletarians and bourgeois, colonizers and colonized, masters and slaves. He no longer admits of a dialectic of master and slave nor, it seems to me, of the cunning of Reason. The history of the class struggle must become the advent of Truth and History. It must become *one*, not in an integral discourse, but at the level of the lived, at the level of *praxis*. From this notion come the vague indications concerning the conditions under which consciousnesses would genuinely treat each other reciprocally. Beyond that, a philosophy of freedom remains radically inconceivable in advance.

The totalization without a totalizer thus would be the totalization of history as a function of and on the basis of the end of the class struggle, which would mark the victory of the proletarians and the colonized peoples. At the same time, victory would mark the end of their proletarian and colonized being, as it would eliminate the bourgeoisie and the colonizers.

In what sense would such a history be comparable to that of a *single* person? If the biography of Flaubert requires thousands of pages, how many would be required for the biography of Humanity? At times (such as in his speech at UNESCO on Kierkegaard) Sartre projects a synthesis of Hegel and Kierkegaard, *one* History and *one* advent of Truth that would allow nothing of what men have lived, whether glorious or obscure, to be forgotten. Now, whether it be written by the victors or the vanquished, such a history drives back into nothingness what has been for millions and millions of men and their unique reason for living.

NOTE I

Existential choice is not the non-temporal choice of intelligible character in Kant's sense.[2] But there is a relation between these two conceptions. I once wrote a dissertation on *The Non-temporal in Kant's Philosophy*. Sartre had read this text during the year when he was preparing for the second time, for his *agrégation* in philosophy. We discussed together the non-temporal choice of intelligible character as a means of reconciling the absolute of freedom, which was necessary for responsibility, and phenomenal determinism. In *Being and Nothingness* (p. 480), Sartre rejects, *en passant*, the Kantian conception, just as he rejects the reconciliation between the oath and the contract. Quite often, when he does this, he shows the origin of his own thought or its affinity with the thought of another. The fundamental project, according to Sartre, 'concerning not my relations with this or that particular object in the world, but my total being-in-the-world . . . This project posits for its end a certain type of relation to being, which the for-itself wills to adopt . . .' He adds that this project is neither instantaneous (since it is not 'in' time) nor 'non-temporal' so as to be able to 'give time to itself' later on. And he adds, 'that is why we reject the "choice of intelligible character" of Kant'. It is not certain that Kantian non-temporality is the equivalent to the temporalization of the fundamental choice through the succession of acts within

[2] Cf. Kant, *Critique of Pure Reason*, A539, B567; (Book II, Ch. 2, Sec. 9, para 3.2) [Tr. note].

the totality of behaviour. On the other hand, the Sartrean project, like the Kantian choice, retains the notion of 'liberating instants', conversions. This is less because the Sartrean project is in the world and related to the world than that it differs from the Kantian choice. The Kantian choice is defined by a relation not to being but to the alternatives of good and evil, or disinterestedness and self-interest. In spite of all this, however, kinship does exist between the Kantian choice and Sartre's original project regarding Being or ethics. A project that creates the totality of existence does not exclude conversion, and is expressed only through innumerable decisions, which are also choices, (*Being and Nothingness*, pp. 480–1), and which weave together an existence.

NOTE J

There is no trace in *Being and Nothingness* of any theory of the group-in-fusion and revolutionary freedom. In this sense, there is no doubt that the *Critique*, whose ties with *Being and Nothingness* we have found after the fact, represents neither a conclusion nor a simple expansion of the first book. What is involved is a development, if you like, but an innovative and creative one that was not forseeable in advance any more than Bergson's *Matter and Memory* was foreseeable from *Time and Free Will*. To make the *Critique* emerge from *Being and Nothingness* would be to commit the error that both Sartre and Bergson denounce, the retrospective illusion of fatality.

The contrast between the phenomenological description of the we-subject in *Being and Nothingness* (pp. 423 ff), and the group in the *Critique* illustrates the innovation. To be sure, some of the ideas or experiences of the *Critique* are already expressed in *Being and Nothingness*. The concept of worked-upon matter can be found in it: 'the worker, whoever he may be, experiences in work his being-an-instrument for the other. Work, when it is not strictly destined for the ends of the worker himself, is a mode of alienation. The alienating transcendence here is the consumer, that is, the "One" whose project the worker is limited to anticipating' (*Being and Nothingness*, p. 423).

The example chosen to illustrate the we-subject is the crowd in the subway corridor. 'In this corridor, there is but a single and same project, inscribed a long time ago in matter, where a living and undifferentiated transcendence comes to be absorbed . . . I have the experience of a common transcendence directed toward a unique end of which I am only an ephemeral particularization. I insert myself into the great human stream that from the time the subway has first existed has flowed incessantly into the corridors of the station "La Motte–Piquet-Grenelle"' (*Being and Nothingness*, p. 424). Sartre adds that what is involved is a psychological not an ontological experience. The reader will immediately notice that the common project resembles that of people wishing to catch the bus, not the common project of those wishing to storm the Bastille. Accepting the common goals means rejecting personal ones: my transcendence becomes undifferentiated, indistinguishable, one among others. Of course, at a given moment, Sartre feels the temptation to fall back into the crowd. Would not the we-subject be the symbol of an absolute and metaphysical unity of all the transcendences? 'It seems, in fact, that it overcomes the original conflict of transcendences by making them converge in the direction of the world. In this sense, the ideal We-subject would be the "we" of a humanity that would make itself master of the earth. But the experience of the "we" remains on the ground of individual psychology and remains a simple symbol of the longed-for unity of transcendences . . . the subjectivities remain out of reach and radically separated' (*Being and Nothingness*, p. 425). As for the manufactured object, it only appears to me if the other be first of all given to me in some way or other. Ultimately 'the experience of the We-subject has no value as a metaphysical revelation; it depends strictly on the various forms of the for-another, and is only an empirical enrichment of certain of these forms' (*Being and Nothingness*, p. 428).

Closer to *Being and Nothingness* is the passage in the *Critique* where Sartre contrasts two experiences of the We-subject, the experience of the oppressed class and that of the oppressing class. The oppressed class experiences itself as an Us-object confronting an indistinguishable 'one' who is a third party, or the oppressing class; on the other hand, the oppressed class does not experience itself as a We-subject opposed to the oppressed class. The bourgeois denies the existence of classes. Classes exist for the bourgeois only when, by its rebellion or the abrupt increase of its power, the oppressed class is established clearly opposite the members of the oppressing class as an 'anonymous look'. It is only then that the oppressors feel as an Us. But that will be in fear and shame, as an Us-object.

The conclusion leaves no opening towards an optimistic philosophy of history or a completion of History. 'Is it really a question of an Us-object? That depends directly in the *third-party*, which is to say, upon my being-for-the-other. And it is constituted on the foundation of my being-outside-for-the-other. As for the We-subject, this is a psychological experience that supposes in one way or another that the existence of the Other as such has been already revealed to us. It is therefore useless for human-reality to seek to get out of this dilemma: to transcend the Other or to allow oneself to be transcended by him. The essence of the relations between consciousnesses is not the *Mitsein*. It is conflict' (*Being and Nothingness*, p. 429).

Even more, when he was writing *Being and Nothingness* Sartre condemned Marx at the same time as Marxism. 'Marx proposed the original dogma of the serious when he asserted the priority of the object over the subject. Man is serious when he takes himself to be an object' (*Being and Nothingness*, p. 580).

NOTE K

The opposition between Lévi-Strauss and Sartre, or rather the rejoinder Lévi-Strauss made to the *Critique*, has already given rise to so much commentary that I have hesitated to take part and add my bit to this great debate, a debate that has not been without its misunderstandings on both sides. It is a debate that contains both obscurity and ambiguity because the participants use the same words without necessarily giving them the same meaning. The difficulty stems from the fact that the debate, presents simultaneously ontological, epistemological, and political dimensions (tied to a philosophy of history) and these diverse dimensions are sometimes not separated and are sometimes separated according to one side but not to the other. For example, structuralism, at any rate the structuralism of Lévi-Strauss's disciples, if not of him himself, to the extent that it misunderstands *praxis*, the action of overcoming the given towards a new future, becomes, *volens nolens*, in Sartre's view, an instrument of conservatism in the service of the bourgeoisie.

On the other hand, points of convergence between Lévi-Strauss and Sartre are not lacking: both admit, it would seem, the link between the structure of the object and the method (or nature) of knowledge. Consciousness, according to Sartre, includes *praxis* because the object presents the same dialectical structure as the subject. The dialectic of reality cannot be understood except on condition that reality is itself dialectical. The structures of wife-exchanges or the binary oppositions of myths, according to Lévi-Strauss, reproduce the structure of social reality or the human spirit. In the same way, one can find in both of them the search for totality or totalization: totality of the system of oppositions for Lévi-Strauss, totalization by *praxis* of an individual lived experience or perhaps of the lived experience of a general society for Sartre.

In addition, if one recalls that every social rule, every social phenomenon is arbitrary, as Marcel Mauss has put it, or in other words, that it could not be, or that it could be other than it is, and if by dialectic one means consciousness itself in its creative activity, nothing prevents one from putting the constituting dialectic as the starting point of social systems that analytical Reason can subsequently study or explain. Sartre, as Pouillon[3] remarked, discovered in the very course of the dialectical experience the structures that give rise to analytical Reason: '. . . the work of Lévi-Strauss provides an important contribution to the study of these strange internal realities, which are at the same time both organized and organizations, synthesized products of a practical totalization and ever-possible objects of an analytical and strict study' (*Critique*, p. 487). What Sartre maintains is that structures are not organic totalities and that they exist only by means of the decisions and the action of free *praxeis*—*praxeis* that bear within them the inertia or the constraint of kinship rules or rules of language,

[3] Jean Pouillon, 'Sartre et Lévi-Strauss', *L'Arc*, 26 (1965), pp. 55–60.

but that also safeguard their freedom by detaching themselves from these rules and moving beyond them. Lévi-Strauss has no reason either to deny the distinction between structures and the lived experience of structures nor to exclude the concrete understanding of a social group. Sartre's dialectical Reason, thus, can use structural analysis in terms of a tool for grasping inert objects or systems that issue from dialectical reality. That Lévi-Strauss may see an ethnographic document in the *Critique* is not yet sufficient to condemn the book, since the mode of primitive thought and that of our own are not fundamentally heterogeneous. Then where is the irreducible opposition to be found?

1. *Ontologically*, Sartre takes the constituting dialectic, that is to say *praxis* or individual consciousness, to be the primary and essential reality; all understanding returns to this lived experience and this constituting Reason. Lévi-Strauss holds structural analysis to be the mode of scientific knowledge *par excellence*, since he is convinced of the primacy of binary systems of opposition, the rules according to which language, wife-exchanges, and myths all function.

2. *Epistemologically:* structural analysis, even if it has lived totalization as its starting point, only attains scientific truth by being detached from the lived, by escaping from subjectivity, by looking from a distance at the obviousness of our own society. Sartrean understanding, as Lévi-Strauss interprets it, never leaves the Sartrean ego, which is to say, at the same time, that it never leaves the western, civilized ego for which primitive people constitute but a stage of the historical dialectic.

Between structural analysis and totalizing understanding, there would not have been the radical incompatibility that exists up to the present, if Sartre drew out the consequences of the affinity between the structures of inertia and analytical Reason, or if Lévi-Strauss explicitly recognized (which it must be said, he does from time to time) the role of understanding lived experiences both before and after structural analysis. To be sure, an opposition would continue to exist between the analysis of systems and the understanding of totalizations. But Sartrean ontology fears systems. He grants that dialectical

Reason is alienated into structures, not that thought or society functions according to inflexible rules even though these rules do not prohibit a plurality of combinations of arrangements and rearrangements. The structures of language, of social institutions and, in the last analysis, of thought itself are incompatible with the absolute of Sartrean freedom, with the unlimited nature of possibilities towards which Sartrean freedom can be projected. To save freedom within the historical world, where the for-itself appears always to be alienated and oath-bound, which is to say, socialized, Sartre must reject a philosophy that claims to find invariables, the rules according to which all thought functions and, in the final analysis, all society also functions.

3. *Existential:* Sartre's dialectic becomes dialectical Reason only on condition that it leads to a totalizing Truth, or in other words, to a philosophy of history in the tradition of Hegel and Marx. It may be, as Jean Pouillon writes, that the two interlocutors begin from the same existential experience, namely the establishment of communication among all societies, in particular between those that we call primitive and our own developed and industrialized society. From this common experience, Lévi-Strauss thinks of the diversity of societies, all of which are placed on an equal level as so many varieties of the same species, or as diverse combinations of the same elements, while Sartre thinks of the becoming of Humanity being made through the mutual grasping of social totalities by each group until a totalizing Truth is attained.

Nothing, however, proves that it is necessary to choose between these two radical and extreme positions. Each society incarnates meaning for itself; for the society that is situated at the moment when the totalizing Truth has arrived, be it only in the imagination, all societies lose their own being and their own meaning and become means or, if you prefer, food, for the Sartrean or Marxist Reason that swallows up varied meanings within a meaning claiming to be all-encompassing.

4. *Political:* The structural analysis of language does not prevent the composition of original poems nor the analysis of the social systems the dreaming of unknown societies. Even more, if these rules or structures are unconscious or non-conscious, they limit the freedom of *praxis* without *praxis* being

conscious of it. But the accent placed upon structures or systems, the non-reference to *praxis* as the source of all structures and all totalizations, appears in Sartre's eyes as a choice of conservatism, the primacy of the given over consciousness, of nature (even if what is involved is the nature of a constituted culture) over freedom, and thus, *par excellence* the sin against man. If one does not start from man and his freedom, one chooses the inhuman, the anti-man.

Passionately involved in his youth in politics, Lévi-Strauss subsequently gave it up for a career devoted entirely to science. He is hardly fond of the industrial society we live in. Outside the comparative analysis of social systems, he has suggested two perhaps converging perspectives: one beyond society of perpetual changes, the other beyond oppression and classes, which arose at the same time as handwriting. Would such a society arise thanks to a complete fulfilment of technology? Or by a conversion to the wisdom of relatively immobile societies? Sartre has followed the opposite course. He has passed from the philosophy of the for-itself to the revolutionary dialectic. But if alienated *praxis* remains ontologically free, we cannot even conceive of what a philosophy, and therefore a practice of freedom would be. Then, does nothing remain of the freedom of *Being and Nothingness* in the *Critique*? What remains, I think, is the essential: we choose our way of being a worker or a bourgeois, we choose to speak or to hold our tongue under torture, we choose the party of the oppressors or that of the oppressed, we choose to resign ourselves or to fight, we choose to remain loyal or to betray, to obey the laws or break them. But we never discover anything but the constituted dialectic, the oath others have taken for us and before us. By violating it, we make the instant of conversion loom up: betrayal or liberation? The essence of freedom has been destroyed neither by need, scarcity, nor classes. What remains is that we exercise our freedom only within alienation and that the alternative 'totally free or totally alienated' apparently condemns us to chains: 'man is born free and everywhere he is in chains'. The free society presupposes a unanimous will, whether of the original contract or the oath. But if the anti-dialectic is necessary, how could the oath be perpetuated within unanimity?

NOTE L

Sartre refers a number of times to Descartes' conception of freedom. Sartrean freedom, in fact, does not admit of a norm, any more than does Descartes' God submit himself to a truth. Exigency, value, self-interest, and class-being mark the successive stages of the socialization of consciousness and of the filling-in of an empty freedom, which is obedient to the exigencies of worked-upon matter only in the mode of alienation. In the *Critique*, the analysis or phenomenological description tends to save the absolute of freedom in spite of alienation. In *Being and Nothingness*, the same analysis tends to save this same absolute in spite of time and without 'returning to the instantaneous conception of consciousness from which Husserl was never able to free himself' (*Being and Nothingness*, p. 465). 'To choose ourselves is to nihilate ourselves, that is, to make a future come to make known to us what we are by conferring a meaning on our past. Thus, there is not a succession of instants separated by nothingness—as with Descartes—such that my choice at instant *t* cannot act on my choice at instant *t'*. To choose is to effect the upsurge along with my commitment of a certain finite extension of concrete and continuous duration, which is precisely that which separates us from the realization of my original possibilities' (*Being and Nothingness*, p. 465). 'But in the very development of our temporalization, we can produce instants if certain processes arise on the collapse of prior processes' (*Being and Nothingness*, p. 466). 'A beginning that is given as the end of a prior project—such must be the instant' (*Being and Nothingness*, p. 466). One could say, in a free translation of Sartre's meaning, that the instant arises with conversion, with the objectification of the former project, whether it be finished or rejected, and, at the same time, that it arises with a new project. But as this rupture never ceases to be possible, the instant can arise at any time, just as a Kantian conversion (in Kant's *Religion within the Limits of Reason Alone*). 'At each moment I grasp this initial choice as contingent and unjustifiable; at each moment I am thus at the very beginning, so as to consider it suddenly, *objectively*, and consequently to surpass it and to make-it-past by causing the liberating *instant* to arise . . .

One may recall the *instant* when Raskolnikoff decides to give himself up. These extraordinary and marvellous instants when the prior project collapses into the past in light of a new project, which arises on its ruins and which yet exists only in outline, in which humiliation, anguish, joy, and hope are delicately blended, in which we let go in order to grasp, and grasp in order to let go—these have often appeared to furnish the clearest and most moving image of our freedom' (*Being and Nothingness*, p. 476). Sartre adds that such moments are but one manifestation among others, which is true enough, but it is an essential and symbolic manifestation, since Sartrean freedom must not be a prisoner even of its own choice and since this freedom with regard to its temporalizing choice can only be shown and demonstrated in and by instants of conversion.

NOTE M

That Sartre does not wish himself bound by his own past does not, in some circumstances, prevent everything happening as if he had forgotten it or as if he reconstructed it in a way that was less embarrassing as regards his present. Thus he writes: 'we were against the capitulation of Munich, we other "Munichers", of '48.' Now, Sartre was not at all against Munich in 1938. I remember perfectly a lengthy conversation, in October, 1938 with Sartre who, anti-fascist and anti-Hitlerian as he was (and on this point there was never any difference between us, even of degree), did not accept the diplomacy of those who were against Munich to the extent that their diplomacy led or could lead to war, that is, to the death of others. He declined to decide upon the lives of others. What is surprising is that the postponement of war did not bring forward any pro-Munich politicians as a 'positive hero', no one who had been in favour of the Munich agreement for morally or politically valid reasons. In 1948 Sartre had already chosen the Manicheeism that transforms each difference of *opinion* with one of his friends into a violent conflict, into a rupture accompanied by polemics typical of 'antagonistic reciprocity' (each wishes the death of the other). The reader is referred to Contat and Rybalka, *Les Écrits de Sartre*, p. 419, where Simone de Beauvoir is quoted: 'Sartre refuses to admit he has any identity whatsoever with his own past.' Or to page 691 of the same book: 'We were against the capitulation of Munich, we "Munichers" of '48.' Do I have to say that Sartre's pacifism in 1938 seemed to me perfectly honourable?